Reproducing families

Reviewing the course of English population history from 1066 to the present, this book challenges current orthodoxies about the evolution of English family forms, and offers a bold new interpretation of the inter-connections between social, economic, demographic and family history.

Taking as the point of departure the well-known observations that England was the first industrial society, that it was the first society to have its peasantry replaced by proletarians and that it was a society that was always dominated by nuclear family households, the main question David Levine asks is how these elements were connected in time and space. In answering this, he looks to contemporaneous changes in the labour process, and, in particular, to the disposition of labour within the family. His central theme is the impact of proletarianization on family formation. He argues that the explosive transformations of family and demography that occurred between 1780 and 1815 were the culmination of a protracted transition from a feudal to a capitalist social structure; and that the post-1870 decline in marital fertility took place within a context of demographic, familial, social and political adjustments which were themselves a response to the earlier population explosion. David Levine also offers a radical new interpretation of the statistics provided in Wrigley and Schofield's classic work, *The Population History of England*. His book is nonetheless not a work of quantitative analysis, but rather an explication of statistical meaning.

This innovative study will appeal widely to readers interested in the social, economic, demographic and family history of England.

Themes in the Social Sciences

Editors: John Dunn, Jack Goody, Eugene A. Hammel, Geoffrey Hawthorn, Charles Tilly

Reproducing families

The political economy of English population history

DAVID LEVINE

Department of History and Philosophy,
The Ontario Institute for Studies in Education, Toronto

The right of the
University of Cambridge
to print and sell
all manner of books
was granted by
Henry VIII in 1534.
The University has printed
and published continuously
since 1584.

CAMBRIDGE UNIVERSITY PRESS

Cambridge

New York   New Rochelle   Melbourne   Sydney

CAMBRIDGE UNIVERSITY PRESS
Cambridge, New York, Melbourne, Madrid, Cape Town, Singapore,
São Paulo, Delhi, Dubai, Tokyo

Cambridge University Press
The Edinburgh Building, Cambridge CB2 8RU, UK

Published in the United States of America by Cambridge University Press, New York

www.cambridge.org
Information on this title: www.cambridge.org/9780521337854

First published 1987
Re-issued in this digitally printed version 2009

A catalogue record for this publication is available from the British Library

Library of Congress Cataloguing in Publication data
Levine, David, 1946–
Reproducing families.
Bibliography.
Includes index.
1. England – Population – History.
2. Fertility, Human – England – History.
3. Demographic transition – England.
4. England – Economic conditions.
5. England – Social conditions. I. Title.
HB3585.L48 1987   304.6′0942   86-26372

ISBN 978-0-521-33256-9 Hardback
ISBN 978-0-521-33785-4 Paperback

For Ruby

Contents

Preface

Far from INDUSTRY'S pride in apogee
I've still not gained the grace of exodus –
Engels renews its stark obscenity
In profit lettings of laudable pus –
Serried pigpens house seething pullulations
Of declassed proletariats' novel
Irruptions of national populations
To swarm labyrinths of fetid hovel
Destined offal of a system dispensed
To an imperial glory past belief:
A world renewed the old emoluments
To robber baron, entrepreneur, thief,
As exploitation rioted on flesh
Of carrion its process must enmesh.

In his *Seventh Thesis on the Philosophy of History* Walter Benjamin writes that the "historical materialist . . . regards it as his task to brush history against the grain". Even before my academic interest in the history of the family developed, my parents introduced me to this practice. From a very early age my mind was suffused by their stories of social life in and about Manchester. Their conversations took me back a generation or two, halfway around the globe, to a world as remote in space as it seemed in time. My parents belonged to a transitional generation, in every sense of the word. Their parents had been driven out of the *stetls* and ghettos of eastern Europe and found themselves, around 1900, foreigners in England. These grandparents of mine – I only ever knew my maternal grandmother – had four and seven children; each couple lost one babe in infancy. Of the nine survivors, only my father went to school past the minimum leaving age, and he stayed on because he was one of only twelve scholarship boys who were elevated to the Grammar School in Manchester. At a stroke, his world changed; or at least part of it did, since he was tied to his family by bonds far stronger than those inculcated by the imperialist pedagogy of his Edwardian schoolmasters. He graduated from that school winning an open scholarship and keenly wanting to go up to Oxford and to read classics. But a classical education could not be pursued free of cost; he had to re-pay his family for the expenses they had incurred in foregoing his wages. So much for the vaunted individualism fostered by "modernization"! He therefore used his scholarship at Manchester University and became a doctor practising in Denton, a district of town dominated by three huge factories. I was born there in 1946, the Jewish doctor's baby in a completely proletarian world. My parents' experience brushed them against the grain of that social life – insiders as outsiders. Social ambivalence is an exacting teacher and I was privileged to learn about it second-hand in their recuperations within the discourse of my own daily life. They have been insightful and gentle instructors. Around our table, oral tradition was history so that by the time I went to university the familiar brush against the grain had penetrated into the core of my consciousness.

This inheritance has informed my academic studies by encouraging me to reflect upon other realities "shot through with chips of Messianic time", as Benjamin writes in another place. In precisely this regard my second family has contributed immensely – their lives, too, have forced upon them alternatives to that middle-classness which the later twentieth-century machinery of cultural homogenization demands. Or, rather, they have been caught up in that machinery and have taught me to appreciate its costs and to be wary of its benefits and, above all, "that the magnitude of lives is not as to their external displacements, but as to their subjective experiences".

Books are written by individuals, yet they are almost always a product of that individual's social experience. This essay is no exception. In writing it I have accumulated many intellectual debts and not a few social ones. And although *Reproducing Families* was written in an exuberant period of five months, it is the culmination of some twenty years of study and teaching. At the University of British Columbia, Murray Tolmie, Jean Elder, John Norris, Jim Winter and, above all, Ed Hundert were inspiring teachers. Later, I was fortunate to work with Peter Laslett, Tony Wrigley and, especially, Roger Schofield at the Cambridge Group for the History of Population and Social Structure. Then, in 1975, I was doubly lucky – first, to land a job at O.I.S.E. and, second, because to live in Toronto is to be placed at a point of intersection between the Third World and the First. Living here has helped me put my own experience as a triple immigrant – coming direct from Cambridge and, before that, Manchester via Vancouver – into another context. It has been a place to learn and to grow, both inside and outside the walls of the academy as I have learned from the patient tutelage of the one-and-only Hesh Troper. My students at

O.I.S.E. have had to listen to the formation of this argument. In response, they have questioned, prodded and probed – from such exchanges ideas were born and, hopefully, refined. In particular, I should like to thank Wally Seccombe for his unrelenting challenge to my supposed authority. I have also bounced my half-baked ideas off a diffuse network of colleagues and am especially grateful for the support and encouragement which Stan Engerman, John Gillis, Hans Medick, Louise Tilly, Susan Watkins and Keith Wrightson have continued to provide; I am deeply saddened that neither Allan Sharlin nor Andy Appleby are able to continue arguments so unfairly cut off in mid-stream, with so much left unsaid. Finally, there is a group of scholars with whom I have been in a perpetual dialogue, a relationship which has been largely unknown to them but very real and important to me: J. C. Caldwell, Christopher Hill, Eric Hobsbawm, E. P. Thompson and Charles Tilly have been my contemporary mentors; behind them stand two haunting spectres, Karl Marx and Thomas Malthus, whose ghostly influences pervade the discourse of this essay.

Introduction:
production and reproduction

We live today in a world dominated by the twin processes of exploding population and proletarianization. It is also apparent that the one engenders the other in a sort of vicious circle of desperation and, all too often, death. Yet, parts of our world have broken this Gordian Knot and now experience social reality in ways which are at several removes from the primal struggle against nature. At the centre of this revolution in social organization, one finds the revolution in family life: the transition from a regime of high fertility to another in which human reproduction is controlled. This demographic transition is a "great divide" in human history: when it occurs the compass swings around 180 degrees and the configuration of social experience is radically transformed.[1] Strategies of family formation thus provide the wider context in which this essay is situated: what were the mechanisms and social relationships which led men and women to disregard the traditional wisdom of their families, stretching back "time out of mind", and set out on a radically new course of their own? The specific context of this study is England. Because the social compass has swung in history, and because English historical time has had its own counterweight, this epochal transformation of family life is explained *within the context* of English social and economic history.

The feed-back mechanism between production and reproduction had different results in historical time precisely because of the specificity of context in which it operated. It is my belief that one can only begin to recuperate the dimensions of family life by focussing on its interaction with time and place. There is, however, a problem here: one which I like to think of as "historical nominalism", by which I mean that tendency in recent scholarship which only allows for the specificity of events, the specificity of time and the specificity of place, therefore denying the efficacy of overarching paradigms with which we might attempt to situate specific experiences within a broader continuum. One thinks here of so many recent squabbles among academic historians deriving from the "revisionist" perspective which only sees events as meaningful *in and of*

1

themselves thereby questioning useful historical constructions by nibbling at their edges, putting nothing in its place except that form of "historical nominalism" which masquerades in the camouflage of FACT – as if objective facts exist, independent of the historian. The historian's explanatory framework should give us an idea that there is something which needs explaining. Indeed, as E. H. Carr has written on this very point, the historian has "the dual task of discovering the few significant facts and turning them into *facts of history*, and of discarding the many insignificant facts as unhistorical".[2] I start from this position. My own operating principle belies a statistical and social-scientific bent – I am interested in the *regularities* of experience while trying to remain cognizant of the distribution around whatever measure of central tendency is used to describe average behaviour. In a certain sense, of course, nothing is average or normal – or, indeed, representative of anything except our own perceptions – so that all points in our field of view are slightly out of focus; yet, it seems to me that if we are to resist the siren's voice of "historical nominalism" then we must attempt to find the best fit with the available evidence. To use an analogy from optics – it should be possible to fit both the general and the particular within a depth of focus without being lost in the image's circle of confusion.

While it is no doubt true that history has usually been experienced as being both variable and unpredictable, my concern in this essay is rather more with structural relationships than the crazy-quilt of individual experience. No attempt is made to account for or to describe aberrant behaviour nor is a concerted attempt made to put a "human face" on tendencies to which the group conformed; rather, the experience of family life is viewed through the prism of historical contingency. For most people, who saw through that prism darkly if at all, reproductive strategies were employed to balance individual demands with the force of circumstance. Therefore, the approach followed in this essay is to focus attention on *representative* behaviours by considering "central tendencies" at the expense of "standard deviations". In a sense such an approach abstracts individuals and thereby, some might argue, desiccates their humanity. That is true; specific examples do tell us quite a bit about individual experience but they inevitably tend to be idiosyncratic and therefore unreliable in the sense that other, contrary examples can almost always be found.[3] There is much to complain about in any historical recuperation since it cannot, necessarily, comprehend the complexity of experience nor the multi-faceted character of history itself. In seeking to comprehend, we inevitably simplify. If that is the historian's dilemma then it seems to me that the best response is to face up to it by adopting a critical stance towards the past and interrogating it in the manner that seeks dialogue, not answers. If we cannot capture its totality in our lens' field of view then, surely, we must focus selectively by highlighting those forces and factors which provide perspective to our image of the past.

My emphasis largely dwells upon hegemonic modes and historical periods at the expense of individuality, local variations and alternatives because social history necessarily concerns itself with *representative* experience. My reason for choosing this approach is largely heuristic: I want to propose a series of structured family formations, in which production and reproduction were conjoined, in order to put forward an integrated explanation of why most English men and women behaved as they did. I am proposing my explication of English family history in the absolute and certain knowledge that it will not please most of the people, at least some of the time. This argumentative position is taken for argument's sake. It is well to keep in mind that "traditional wisdom is always refractory ... [so that] one is forced to oppose it polemically, [and] to phrase the necessary revisions dialectically".[4] In so doing we learn from the past not just to comprehend its totality but also to heighten our appreciation of both human behaviour and our own social experience.

"Wild genes", social mutation and English history

Humankind lives according to biological imperatives, human beings are social animals. In essence, this is the framework within which Malthusian concerns regarding human reproduction and Marxian ones about the social organization of production must be balanced. We might therefore think of English society as a kind of "wild gene" whose unpredictable evolution was almost wholly at variance with the processes scholars have described in other places and at other times. To carry on with the analogy, once the genetic code has been reformulated in English, other species were endangered and have since had the choice between evolution and extinction.

Peasant societies are inherently conservative, they usually conceive of economic life as a "limited good" in which horizons are limited. In explaining the growth and decline of the medieval peasantry and the extinction of its early modern successor, one comes face-to-face with the central characteristic of England's novel historical experience. Of course, this kind of revolutionary end was not what most peasants had in mind when they assembled in 1381 to demand more equitable taxation, when they rebelled in the sixteenth and seventeenth centuries to protest against depopulating enclosures, or when they rioted in the expectation that the royal government would re-assert its patriarchal control over the moral economy in foodstuffs; yet, the tensions inherent in their social system impelled it in a direction which did not finally result in a zero-sum-game. The history of England is therefore of interest to comparativists for whom it represents the prime-mover in the development of the modern world. They have seen England as an exemplar of other, broader trends and so have been less impressed by the exceptionalism of its history or the individualism of its people. They have been in sympathy with those who have argued against the "little England" perspective. This second point is important because from the middle ages until the day before yesterday this so-called "little England" has been a hungry, expansionist power: a seemingly insatiable appetite has led it to cast its gaze across the Atlantic strand, first, to the Americas and soon enough to compass the whole world in a *pax Britannica* ruling both the waves and the counting houses of the modern world. It is in this sense that English history and world history can only be disentangled by sacrificing one of the twins in a Solomonic choice. And because a prime-mover in this imperialism has been, first, the growth of the feudal economy based on peasant cultivation and then, after the transition, the mushrooming capitalist political-economy which was itself based upon the expropriation of these same peasants and their replacement with new productive arrangements using the labour power of their proletarian descendants, one returns to the "peasant question". More specifically, one returns to the reproduction of bearers of this labour power and their connection to the changing configuration in the social relations of production.

In my reading, the family represents that intersection of individual motivations and social forces. The family is thus, to a certain extent, transparent. It seems to me that what we would like to think of as "the family" was the product of strategies of production and reproduction. That *inter-connectedness* between the repetitive reproduction of daily life and the ceaseless movement of history impinged itself upon the contingency of the historical present. Such an insistence on the *inter-connectedness* of production and reproduction – and their existence within a specific field of historical forces – is the real point of departure at which this study of English family history begins.

In the light of this point my essay has two thrusts: the first delineates the relationship between political change and social structures with special emphasis on the character of English rural society as a cause of, and also a result of, the transition; the second investigates the inner workings of the plebeian family and its reproduction as a biological and social unit. I have thus tried to draw attention towards the family as an independent variable of real importance. In so doing the debate about the dynamism of social change has been shifted away from the consideration of "vanguards and followers" and towards a reconceptualized framework in which the micro-level decisions of individual social units are seen to be both a condition of, and be conditioned by, macro-level changes in production. In forcing a revision in which production and reproduction are accorded equal (or, at the very least, near-equal) weight, the argument concerning the demise of the peasantry and the emergence of the proletariat gains a measure of reciprocity lacking in earlier explanations. In addition, this revisionist viewpoint makes it possible to force a Marxist concern with the social relations of production against a Malthusian emphasis on the cumulative characteristics of population growth, extending far beyond the historical moment during which such growth occurred. Moreover, much insight can be gained by forcing these arguments against each other. Such a process of threshing and winnowing is greatly needed in any attempt to distinguish necessary from sufficient causes. Indeed, it is probably the case that the notion of a single sufficient cause is hopelessly simple-minded and that one might reconceptualize the problematic by suggesting that the point at issue is the concatenation of a series of necessary causes and that, furthermore, one can only locate the sufficiency of an explanation in its specific historical nexus. Once the transition had taken place in England then every other social formation was reconfigured by its place in relation to the over-determination of history itself. That is to say, we have no photo-finish but rather a quite distinct ordering between social formations which was set in motion by the successful transition in the English one. There was no need to re-invent the wheel; once the breakthrough occurred in England, others had no real alternative but to accommodate themselves to this new reality. The novelty of the English experience with industrialization at the end of the eighteenth century was very quickly followed by a series of imitations as others followed. The peculiarity of the English experience was rapidly submerged in the nineteenth-century convergence. What was left for the English was their experience of historical *forwardness* and the imprint it left on social relations of production and reproduction in the birthplace of modern industrial society. As we shall see, this was an ambivalent inheritance and one whose impact cannot be underestimated in assessing the contingency of the modern revolution in the family in England.

The reproduction of the social formation has been situated at the heart of my argument so as to capture one of the most revolutionary features of English history: the silent, cumulative pressure exerted by peasants living on the edge of subsistence, with just a toe-hold on their ancient rights and liberties. It created a reservoir of labour which was exploited by colonizers and industrializers alike. By focussing on the mentalities and survival strategies which motivated peasant producers (and, of course, reproducers), afflicted as much by social contradictions as their own fertility, we can see a micro-motor powering English expansion: first, within the British Isles; next, across the Atlantic; and, third, around the whole globe. For the erstwhile peasants, colonization and industrialization offered something into the bargain – they could maintain some vestigial control over their own lives in the face of enormous odds. To be sure, this was a losing battle but we are well advised to avoid an unduly teleological perspective since that was clearly not the point of view of those who lived and died in this unredeemed time. The very protracted nature of the transition from peasant to proletarian – a process at the centre of the social history of the mass of the English population for almost the whole of the period in question – provides a context in which we can suggest some answers to Bertholdt Brecht's worker's questions.

> Who built Thebes of the seven gates?
> In the books you will find the names of kings.
> Did the kings haul up the lumps of rock?
> And Babylon, many times demolished
> Who raised it up so many times? In what houses
> Of gold-glittering Lima did the builders live?
> Where, the evening that the Wall of China was finished
> Did the masons go? Great Rome
> Is full of triumphal arches. Who erected them? Over whom
> Did the Caesars triumph? Had Byzantium, much praised in song
> Only palaces for its inhabitants? Even in fabled Atlantis
> The night the ocean engulfed it
> The drowning still bawled for their slaves
>
> The young Alexander conquered India.
> Was he alone?
> Caesar beat the Gauls.
> Did he not have even a cook with him?
>
> Philip of Spain wept when his armada
> Went down. Was he the only one to weep?
> Frederick the Second won the Seven Years' War. Who
> Else won it?
>
> Every page a victory.
> Who cooked the feast for the victors?
> Every ten years a great man.
> Who paid the bill?
>
> So many reports.
> So many questions.[5]

The agenda of this essay is, therefore, a large one: I will first consider how the dissolution of the feudal social formation promoted novel relations of social life, the emergence of both capitalist agriculture and an industrial economy; second, I will argue how these novel productive relationships were filtered through the familial grid of reproduction and family formation; and, third, the modern "revolution in the family", the compass-swing of biological reproduction, is explained within the specificity of its timing and its local variations. We have here an inter-related knot of demo-economic problems, whose resolution can only be resolved with reference to the contingency of historical context. It should be clearly stated at this point that my essay is primarily concerned with the socially constructed reality experienced by the vast majority of the population whose labour produced the "surplus value", the foundation upon which structures of political and social domination were erected. The reproduction of their labour provided a motor-force of its own which is too frequently forgotten in accounts of historical change or, if included, is usually considered outside of its historically contingent context.

This essay begins from the premise that the plebeian family was not simply the object of change but that its demographic response to economic forces created conditions which profoundly influenced subsequent historical developments. At the heart of the phenomenon there is a feed-back mechanism through which modes of production responded to forms of social reproduction, the foremost being the labour supply (i.e. the number of available proletarian hands) which was itself developed in the context of pre-existent arrangements. The demographic side of the argument relates to the persistence of comparatively low rates of population growth for almost all of the period in question, in spite of the fact that the transition from feudalism to capitalism *should* have created a tendency to faster growth rates. In crude economic terms, it is clear that the issue is not only the demand for these new forms of labour but also the *stickiness* of their supply and I have therefore accorded at least as much attention to the supply of labour, especially proletarian labour, as its demand. Additionally, prominence has been given to the characteristics of that labour supply; not least to its reproduction. Here, then, the peculiarity of the English, with their nuclear family households and their relatively late age at first marriage for women, has been subjected to considerable comment. It is simply not possible to see these cultural characteristics outside the nexus of material forces in which they breathed life.

It is the historians' credo that the past weighs heavily on the present while that present is contingent, in the sense of being unpredictable. Historians seem to be inherently wary of theory which, so they seem to feel, forces the contingent particularity of the past into determined and thus predictable routes. There is something of an evasion in this position – one can readily accept its historicity without necessarily agreeing that there is nothing to explain but, rather, a lot of things to describe. This essay is written from the position that historians of England, especially social historians, have a lot to explain. It is my belief that while "theory" may inform the questions I ask that theory must be subject to revision in the light of the available evidence. The answers I propose are proposed in an attempt to interrogate that evidence and to situate those answers in a specific context. Historical events cannot be "structured", and only for heuristic purposes can they be modelled. It is a self-evident fact that historical events occurred; we need to explain their particular occurrence. Yet, we also want to understand not only how things fell out in the way that they did but also why they did so. And it is this form of interrogation which inevitably leads us to consider the exigencies of the past. Things did not simply happen; forces – social, economic, demographic, political and cultural – provided a momentum which caught up individuals. Caught up in the flow, individuals' choices of action were limited and defined by the context in which they acted, the context in which they thought, the context in which they planned and the context in which they made their choices. It is in this sense that individuals faced a determinate set of choices, not of their own choosing. It is in this sense that history impinged itself on individual decision-making. And because history presented itself to individuals as a set of determinate forces, one cannot understand the organization of personal life outside that set of historical forces which defined the specific character of the moment. My account is therefore as much about English economic and social history as the family formations which gave shape and meaning to personal life.

By relating the transition from peasant to proletarian in England to its specific historical context we must pay heed to the complementarity of production and reproduction within the plebeian family. It is my firm belief that there was an underlying rationality in family formation strategies, informed by the persistent need to balance hands and mouths in the daily reproduction of family life. For this reason I am concerned with the interaction between historical contingency and the material necessities imposed by the fetters of production and reproduction. Demographic events are thus assumed to have been responsive to *contemporaneous* changes in the material world. My political economy of English population history attempts to make these connections without recourse to ahistorical, neo-classical theorizing. Nor, I should add, will I have much time for social-scientific research into the minutiae of historical demography. Readers for whom the study of historical populations is incomplete without a battery of tables and graphs can look elsewhere.[6] *Reproducing Families* is about the political economy of population history; it is only secondarily concerned with nitty-gritty mechanisms of demographic change. Finally, I have located these material imperatives within a distinctively English familial milieu – and vice versa. My account is about the feedbacks between the changing social relations of production and reproduction – both between classes and between men and women, parents and children – during the protracted metamorphosis of the

English political economy. I have argued that it was in this way that the mass of the population made their history – indeed, they made themselves – and in so doing they imprinted their impressions on the world of their children and their children's children.

1

Feudalism and the peasant family

In the year 1000 England was one of the most thickly wooded parts of Europe; perhaps four-fifths of the land was forest, waste and marsh. By the time of the Black Death, in 1348, most of this primeval ground-cover was gone.[1] In the three centuries after the Norman Conquest these uncultivated lands had been colonized as the primitive economic life of the Dark Ages was transformed. Across the length and breadth of western Europe, the 350 years after the year 1000 witnessed enormous colonizing efforts in order to accommodate rising levels of population. Populations grew because the weather was then warmer and drier that it was before or would be subsequently; but, primarily, populations grew because between the Justinian pandemic (541–c. 750 A.D.) and the Black Death the plague had relaxed its grip on Europeans. English population growth in the high middle ages was thus part of a far larger phenomenon of demographic and economic expansion. But by the end of the thirteenth century, as the climate became colder and wetter, the ratio between humans and natural resources worsened. Thus, even before the Black Death of 1348 (and its successive visitations during the next 150 years) created a human wasteland, the long cycle of the climate had turned the tables against an over-extended rural population. From the late thirteenth century rural England, like the rest of rural Europe, was the site of recurrent and horrific famines. If the "Malthusian" nightmare of population pressing against resources and tipping the balance against life itself ever had any actual relevance in the day-to-day reality of English history then that time was most assuredly between the closing of the thirteenth century and the Black Death.

1066 and all that

The primeval economy of the peasantry was a long time dying – as J. H. Plumb has written, "the death rattle of the English peasantry lasted for generations".[2] Until the end of the early modern era a very large part of the population still lived within the confines of a social system of production for use, subsumed within various forms of predatory extraction. We should not therefore be surprised that as late as the eighteenth century the commoners could still vigorously object to a social economy whose laws required that "Property must be made palpable, loosed for the market from its uses and from its social situation, made capable of being hedged and fenced, of being owned quite indepedently of any grid of custom or inheritance." Because the law was designed to protect property, not natural rights, early modern radicals "reversed the values of their betters. The law became the enemy, the symbol of Normanism."[3] These developments took a long time to work themselves out; resistance to them was based on both popular memory and the myth of earlier, better times.

The Norman Conquest was accompanied by the creation of a legal system in which existent common rights were incorporated into the juridical conception of property. The retention of common rights in property limited the scope for the exercise of private rights in property by forcing the owners of private rights to act in conformance with legal nostrums. In this way the inheritance of the conquerors, just as much as that of the conquered, was caught up in the politics of property as defined by the feudal law set in place by the Normans. The English political economy was thus set in motion by the dictates of a great pacemaker, overseeing all and giving it an inner coherence which distinguished England from its continental neighbours in which royal law was hedged by particularism, prerogatives and countless dispensations. The great medievalist Marc Bloch recognized this uniqueness and commented that "England was a truly unified state much earlier than any continental kingdom."[4] It is in this sense that the Norman Conquest was, quite probably, the single most important event in English social history. Because the Normans conquered all of England, the English were effectively subject to one legal system; because the Norman king gave out title to his followers in a moment of reciprocity – in return for their loyal service – all his followers remained in a dependent status of fealty to the Crown and hence subordinate to the Crown's law; and because the early medieval English warrior class was so remarkably successful in more or less continuously expanding its horizons for depredation, subordinates were kept at heel. A *quid pro quo* developed. The king and his close comrades-in-arms – "the political nation" – carved up control over the land and people of England and draped their compromise within that legal framework which they entrenched along with Norman feudal relations.

The Normans were the latest in a long line of sea-borne invaders who had crossed the emerald seas and plucked the jewelled crown from its erstwhile owners. The Normans' arrival must have been greeted with not much more than a cursory, acquiescent nod by the subservient peasantry. The Normans were conquerors – they exacted some booty, installed a system of tribute and then went back to the demands of their station: fighting and hunting. Having come into a monopolistic control over the land they needed labour power to work it so, in effect, they traded privileged access to their land for privileged rights to the peasants' labour. A social contract was instituted, without the knowledge or assent of one of the parties. It was a lasting bargain and an unequal one. Most of the peasantry was enserfed. Allowing for some temporal and geographical variations, two-thirds of the land in medieval England was subject to the feudal system: about half of this feudal land was demesne (the landlord's private farm) and the other half was subject to feudal tenure and worked by *villeins*. The essential characteristic of feudal society was that the mass of the population were subject to the political, economic and legal subjugation of the ruling elites – the fighters and the churchmen. Because they lost their rights to the land at the time of the Conquest, they had little option but to give up control over a large portion of their labour power in exchange for regaining access to the land. Such, in a nutshell, was the political economy of the Conquest. The law legitimated this state of affairs.

Faced with an enserfed population working a fifth of the land, the nobility turned the screw of oppression by tying the peasantry to their land. Four-fifths of their resources stood idle. For a gang of pillaging warriors this state of affairs was not so troubling. They simply demarcated large chunks of the greensward for private hunting grounds and, following the lead of the chief comrade-in-arms, they did so with great abandon. The Norman Conquest had systematically designated vast tracts of woodland to be royal forests governed by the hated forest laws. By the reign of Henry II (1154–89) the privatized greensward may have covered a third of the whole country. Frank Barlow has written that "the strength of a medieval king can be gauged by his success in defending his forests against the general opposition".[5] The forest laws were enacted to maintain privileged access to the products of these woodlands. They also limited the common rights of the peasantry for whom the produce of the forest had constituted an essential supplement to their agrarian incomes. In effect and almost at a stroke, the forest laws minified the land mass of England by designating no-go zones for the peasantry. One might even argue that given the very longest perspective, a most important theme in the history of the rural population is the one which focusses upon its separation from the natural economy of the forests, fens, marshes and wastes. Correlatively, when these lands were domesticated within the orbit of the Norman political economy, they were thereby removed from the domain of custom. The economy of use was thus subordinated to the rule of law, with its sanctification of private property and exchange relationships.

History does not, however, stand still. While the landed peasantry was firmly attached to the soil by a newly installed legal system, this system had its limits. Perhaps the most important was administrative in the sense that a man could only be considered to be a serf to his own lord; such a condition was usually enforced by the granting of privileged access to the man over some of the lord's land. If the population remained stationary – in both senses: that is both immobile and unchanging in size – such a state of affairs could be consolidated and kept working. But if the population was destabilized then a more complex set of relationships would prevail. And, indeed, it was this complexity which came to characterize the social, economic and juridical relations in the countryside.

The colonization of the greensward

The English have been a colonizing people; even before they cast their eyes beyond their borders they had had to colonize their own land. Under the Norman conquerors, and their successors, the incipient anarchy of the Dark Ages was kept at bay and the necessary social conditions for internal colonization – reasonably peaceful social relations, freedom from invasion, and population growth – were met. Let us turn our attention to the last of these three forces since it bears most strongly on the subject of this essay. The English population had grown three-fold after the Conquest and, by the end of the thirteenth century, a demo-economic crisis of harrowing magnitude had replaced the earlier conditions of colonizing the greensward's frontier.

It is evident that populations do not inevitably grow. And when they do grow we need to explain this growth not only in terms of the biological imperatives of reproduction but also in the social context of time and place. We need, therefore, to incorporate some sort of feed-back mechanism with which to accommodate the social system's ability to export its surplus and so to avoid something akin to *involutionary entropy* – in which population and resources face off against each other in a deadly zero-sum-game – seemingly so characteristic a feature of almost all other peasant societies. The medieval English peasantry did not entirely avoid this characteristic social stance although they were caught up in it for an abbreviated period, cut short by the exogenous force – the Black Death. The disintegration of feudal relations introduced a new dynamic into the double helix of family life– production and reproduction.

In this next section I want to dwell upon the implications of a brilliant piece of historical reconstruction by the Israeli medievalist Zvi Razi. His work is of fundamental importance since it provides us with a fairly firm grasp on the micro-structure of population processes. Razi has used the methods of modern historical demography, those of family reconstitution pioneered by Louis Henry, to disentangle the interplay of economy and population on the manor of Halesowen, a few miles from the modern city of Birmingham.[6] The core of Razi's analysis is provided by the manorial court record in which transactions between the lord and his tenants were enrolled. Because the court record was concerned with the extraction of income for the lord, from the peasants, the relationship of the peasants to the lord's property was of the most eminent concern to the record-keepers. The lord's income could be enhanced by charging the customary tenant with countless small exactions bearing on his/her servile status. For Razi's purposes the importance of this relationship was that he had an almost-yearly check-list with which to keep track of the tenants-in-chief and the changing configuration of their families. These personal characteristics were, of course, of monetary interest to their lord, the Abbot of Halesowen, who could extract tidy sums from the birth of a child, its passage into adulthood, and so on. The best-documented individuals appear under Razi's microscope hundreds of times during the course of their lives. By *reconstituting* all the linkages between the tenants mentioned in the documentary record between 1280 and 1400, Razi has painstakingly built up a series of profiles enabling him to probe statistically such topics as life expectation, average family size and age at first marriage. In addition, and most importantly, he has cross-tabulated these demographic indices with measurements of landed wealth.

The starting point for Razi's analysis is the fact that men were recognized as adults in the court record at twenty years of age. Thus Razi has an essential point of reference from which he is able to follow villagers across time. Having recourse to model population tables, he has constructed a series of probabilistic measurements pointing towards the highly stratified life-chances of the villagers. It would seem that two factors distinguished one villager from another: first, the landed wealth of one's father; and, second, the size of one's sibling-group which would determine if all or only a part of the family wealth was inherited. Finally, Razi has been very attentive to those socially specific dynamics which set the life-chances of individuals into relation with one another, albeit in an orbit described and controlled by their feudal masters.

The world Razi has recovered was beset with difficulties for the smallholder. Statistics describing mortality and nuptiality seem to point to a socially specific demographic regime in which the poor married late and died with alarming frequency. In contrast, the wealthiest villagers seemed to have married at a surprisingly early age – around twenty, on average – and enjoyed very substantially better health. Razi seems to have also uncovered a recycling mechanism, built into this system of production and reproduction, which resolved the centrifugal forces inherent in these two divergent regimes. This social formation was thus characterized by an essential element of restraint – practised by both the individual and the group – which kept the poor from multiplying out of control. The landed wealth accumulated in the course of a lifetime by individual, rich peasants was redistributed at their death among their children. The process of generational recycling prevented the village social structure from polarizing between a wealthy minority surrounded by a teeming mass of smallholders and landless labourers. In short, the poor seem to have died out and the rich seem to have over-burdened their family resources so that the next generation was kept orbiting within the gravitational field of force of peasant society. In this way the rich peasants were unable to break free of the fetters of production and reproduction imposed by feudalism.

There is an elegant functional symmetry to this picture of social life in a feudal community; it is especially satisfying in that it allows for loco-motion to develop within peasant society itself. Yet I remain unconvinced by its demographic analysis which seems to me to be improbable – the rates of reproduction among the rich peasants seem to be well beyond anything ever uncovered for any other European population. The dispari-ties in demographic behaviour between the top and the bottom elements in Halesowen seem to have been so marked that we are presented with two divergent cultural worlds, not two variants on the same theme. And this in spite of the fact that the socio-economic differences between top and the bottom strata were not particularly great – rich peasants had 25-acre holdings while smallholders usually had less than 5 acres but were able to supplement their income through additional resources, so vital to the perpetuation of the *cottage economy*. The rich peasants were not differentiated from the dwarf-holders by a completely disparate style of life so much as by the fact that they simply had more of the basic necessities. This distinction may have been important in crisis years but even Razi does not claim that in the period of *involutionary entropy*, after c. 1275, all years were crisis years. The opposition between the top and the bottom of peasant society in Halesowen is thus drawn too starkly and one cannot help wondering if the fact that the poorer elements in the manorial society were more mobile (and thus less recognizable in the documentary record) might have served to introduce an important bias in the results. I remain unconvinced that Razi's appropriation of family reconstitution techniques has been as completely successful as he would have us believe. The medieval record is apparently bedevilled by the complexity of separating individuals of the same name from one another as well as the fluidity of surnames. These factors have probably meant that "observa-tional limits" are extraordinarily hard to describe for the village elite which was densely inter-named, both between and across generations. Thus differences between the rich and the poor peasants may be biased by a series of technical elisions which have conjoined two generations within the top stratum far more frequently than among the near-landless.

Razi's model is well-regulated but the resulting interaction is far too stable when put against the perspective of two centuries of internal colonization prompted by peasant population growth. But rather than worrying overmuch about the difficulties of Razi's input–output demography, I should like to consider its implications for the earlier period during which the political economy of colonization created novel social relations in which some peasants were freed from some of the burden of their feudal obligations. In fact, Razi's analysis of peasant reproduction provides a wedge with which to prise open the puzzle of colonization – the provenance of the colonizers. Let us allow his analysis the benefit of the methodological doubt and begin this following discussion from the point for which he has argued so vigorously – the fertility of the richer peasants.

In an age of surplus land, such as that prevailing before the Norman Conquest and for several generations thereafter, the frontier would have been a natural outlet for their sons and daughters who were produced in excess of simple replacement. In an age of surplus land there was no need to recycle village resources within the family, rather the "excess" people colonized the woodlands. They might have been accompanied by the children of poorer peasants who were either unwilling or unable to wait for their inheritance or, indeed, for whom no inheritance was likely to be forthcoming. The forest fastness provided an irresistible lure to the indigent and the resourceful alike. Moreover, from the landlords' perspective the possibility of gaining some additional rental income from their greensward must have been inviting. Indeed, the eagerness with which landlords seemed to have granted dispensations to colonizers – particularly, freedom from servile status – makes it seem likely that they actively encouraged some of their villeins to colonize the waste. The supply of this land could only be met by the demand from the peasantry so that we come back to the question of surplus fertility.

Now we have a set of chronological points with which to hedge in Razi's analysis: colonization was more or less completed by the last part of the thirteenth century, at the very point in time when his stream of manorial court records commences. One is therefore led to ask if the differential demographic regime he describes for the 1280–1340 period – a time of land-hunger and declining living standards, *involutionary entropy* according to the usual chronology of medieval economic and social history – was the product of an historical conjuncture brought on by the end of colonization or was a deeper characteristic of peasant society, a crisis in the feudal mode of production. My own preference is to view this conjuncture within the framework of the former explanation. That is to say, the peasant family had had generations of experience with a high-pressure demographic regime and had had the ability and resources to put off the day of reckoning, as it were. However, in the later thirteenth century the limits of growth were broached. A crisis developed when the frontier closed at the same time that a fast-expanding population, dependent upon the crops from marginal farmlands, faced an inhospitable material world in a period of worsening climate. A series of contradictions ensued which played themselves out during the two generations before the Black Death. What one needs to keep in mind is the contingency of that extended moment – nothing was ordained and the Black Death introduced a new and completely unexpected mutation into the genealogy of social relations.

With the expiry of the external frontier English peasants were forced to have recourse to internal colonization – more intensive forms of agriculture – and some form of prudential reproduction. There is abundant evidence for this conclusion. M. M. Postan, the great medievalist of the last generation, has written on this very point emphasizing how English agricultural practices in the high middle ages reflected the press of numbers. Around 1200 there was already a shortage of pasture in most regions of mixed husbandry so that available grazing-land was at a premium. In conditions of high land demand, extensive pastoral husbandry was traded off against the higher rents which could be gained from intensive peasant farming. It was in this context that "The medieval Englishman's propensity to concentrate on corn-growing at the expense of sheep-farming or cattle-grazing [became] one of the hallmarks of the economic geography of the thirteenth century."[7] Postan's thesis regarding declining productivity has not been without its critics but the balance of opinion seems to hold that while he may have overstated the case there can hardly have been any significant *gains*. The very best that the lesser peasants could have achieved was an intensification of their cereal diets, supplemented by second-class leguminous proteins. It has further been argued, against Postan, that this kind of intensive agriculture would necessarily keep the land in "good heart" because of the nitrogen-fixing qualities of the legumes. In essence, the force of this argument advanced by Edward Britton and H. C. Hallam is that the poorest elements among the medieval peasantry ate coarse maislin bread and pease porridge in much the same way that Irish peasants ate potatoes – all the time.[8]

Because the nuclear family household seemed to be the basic unit of both production and reproduction which accompanied English feudalism, the means for achieving demo-economic retrenchment were at hand. By simply throttling back the advent of demographic independence, tying it to the achievement of economic independence *via* inherit-

17

ance, the inherent logic of prolific reproduction could be halted. Moreover, it would seem that the process of restraint would bear more forcefully on the poor than the rich, as Razi would have it. The colonization of so much marginal land and its incorporation into the national stock of arable land speaks directly to the fact that population pressure had led to land-hunger and methods of alleviating it which had all the earmarks of *involutionary entropy*. Thus, in the early middle ages the demographic growth of the peasantry is a factor of some importance both in its own right and insofar as it created conditions which led to the crisis of feudalism.

In England there were, as we shall discuss, a large number of peasants who were "free" of feudal exactions. While they were important in some areas, and may even have been a majority in some places, it would be mistaken to suggest that their presence constituted anything more than a deviation to the central tendency of the period. The common people (known as serfs or villeins) owed services – at first in labour-time but later in money-equivalents – to their overlord. This social group, "the customary population of arable England", was *"roughly representative* of English rural society viewed as a whole".[9] They were the ones who paid "feudal rents" which were heavy and varied; these exactions were tangible expressions of the lord's ability to tap the peasants' production for his own private benefit.

To begin with, nearly all customary holdings in the thirteenth century were burdened with money rent, supplemented by other rent-like charges like churchscot or various 'pennies' representing some very ancient commutations of still more ancient labour services. Then there were various 'farms' for additional pieces of land, payments of pannage of pigs, the agistment of animals and the use of the lord's pastures. These were from time to time augmented by various 'once-for-all', or 'capital' payments, such as heriots from deceased men's property or entry fines from new tenants. There were also personal payments characteristic of a villein status such as 'chevages' or 'recognitions' levied on various pretexts, as well as marriage fines and, above all, amercements imposed in manorial courts for transgressions of every kind. The latter were punitive in theory, but were in fact so regular and apparently unavoidable as to constitute a regular imposition. On many estates, however, the miscellaneous fines were overshadowed by tallage which was frequently a heavy annual tax, almost as heavy as the rent itself . . . *the average was very frequently near or above the 50 per cent mark [of the villein gross output].*[10]

In theory the villein's labour-services were to have been spent working on the lord's demesne (i.e. his private lands) but historical evolution meant that by the later thirteenth century, when English feudalism was in its prime, the neat boundaries of demesne, villein lands and common lands were blurred at the edges.

Once the manorial land had been divided among the villein population, its possession (and the obligations attached to it) became the subject of historical evolution. Within the unfree population, owing services to their lords, there was thus a distinct gradation of wealth. Some peasants controlled nothing at all but others worked very much more than they could farm with just their own family's labour. What seemed to be an ideal arrangement for generational production became, in the event, rather more complicated. Most families had irregular holdings and they further complicated the real-world situation by adding bits and pieces when they were able to do so. By the time the medieval rural economy comes into sharp focus, in the middle of the thirteenth century with the advent of manorial court rolls, there was no symmetry in landholding patterns even though lists of tenants might give that superficial impression.[11] Social differentiation was the product of historical evolution since in the lottery of demography and economy some did better than others: whether because they were not over-burdened with too many heirs (and heiresses) and could therefore amass resources over a couple of generations or simply because they had more strength, skill and initiative. A small group of prosperous peasants benefited from the conditions of the day although it would seem that on most thirteenth-century estates very nearly half of the tenants held under ten acres. In conditions of long-term population growth, which obtained in the several generations after the Norman Conquest when the population trebled, "the workings of the land market served only to heighten, not to lessen, the inequalities of distribution, since its most common feature everywhere was the emergence of a class of wealthy peasants holding more than a virgate and the multiplication of small holdings and sub-tenancies".[12] Such "wealthy peasants", however, had a fragile grip on their wealth so that prolific or (more appropriately, perhaps) profligate parents could see the material index of their wealth disintegrate into a series of smallholdings. Evidence from the court rolls of 104 manors suggests that 45 per cent of the tenants were smallholders whose landed resources were most likely insufficient to maintain entire families in the bare minimum of subsistence.[13]

The *cottage economy* and the peasant family

We should note that Postan's discussion relates to agricultural incomes, *not* to total family incomes. These smallholders supplemented their agricultural earnings from a variety of sources: wage-labour, crafts and trades, as well as by-employments which supplied "consumer goods" and services to the rural population. This kind of rural economy, immortalized as the *cottage economy* by William Cobbett as late as the nineteenth century, was an enduring element in the English countryside. "The essence of this economy was *thrift*, and the barter of goods and services rather than a money economy, which played a small part in their lives; the careful use of all the natural resources of their parish, even the humblest; [and] an unyielding meanness."[14] The salient point is that this was a *catch-as-catch-can family economy* which, to a greater or lesser extent, availed itself to wage-labour to make up the difference between its agricultural income and its subsistence needs. The strategy of wage-labouring was "situational" depending on the actual size of the landholding and relative population pressure, family size and life-cycle stage, geographical location and access to common rights, as well as a host of other factors.

While it is true that "development" and "evolution" might be strangers to this world, only the teleologist should be unduly frightened by their absence. What we see here, therefore, is a *permeable* family economy. Allied to this permeability was a deep-rooted resistance to the imperatives of capitalist society which would wreak havoc on the ability of these people to deploy their labour according to their own requirements. To understand their "own requirements" we have to set aside our own cultural expectations of what constitutes "self-evident laws of Nature" – themselves the product of the last 300 years – and adopt an Aristotelian posture focussing on the mode of economic life. To do so we need to contrast an economy based on use-values with one based on profit derived from exchange. Immediately, then, we can gain a sense of perspective – an anthropological overview – in which to set the revolutionary economic system within which we live and also to pit our ingrained expectations against the more usual system of production and reproduction which characterized the pre-capitalist world. In seeing the refractory nature of our own traditional wisdom we can not only oppose it polemically we can also learn from that opposition in a dialectical fashion. Thus, it was simply not the case that labour was performed as "an absolute end in itself, a calling". Indeed, as Max Weber realized, "such an attitude is by no means a product of nature . . . but can only be the product of a long and arduous process of education. Today, capitalism once in the saddle, can recruit its laboring force in all industrial countries with comparative ease. In the past this was in every case an extremely difficult problem." Culture resisted this so-called "rationalization" of economic life. In fact, economics was only a part-time activity of pre-capitalist society so that its pattern of work was accordingly unintensive, intermittent and susceptible to interruption for "cultural alternatives and impediments ranging from heavy ritual to light rainfall". Marshall Sahlins suggests that the domestic mode of production entertains limited economic goals, defined in the terms of a way of life rather than being abstracted into wealth. Sahlins would have us understand that there is "an enduring quality of traditional domestic production, that is production of use values, definite in its aim, so discontinuous in its activity".[15] For all these reasons it is obligatory for us to understand that the *cottage economy* was a social formation which was grudging in its supply of labour and usually only did so when forced by circumstances out of its control. It was therefore characterized by its "backwards bending supply curve of labour" which means that people worked enough to attain their targeted income and then simply quit. The supply of such rural labour most likely exceeded demand for it so that there was a significant level of underemployment in the thirteenth-century countryside.[16]

A zero-sum-game

If we were to have a "snapshot" of the farming arrangements on a typical thirteenth-century manor we would find peasants with large holdings who employed the labour of some of their fellows, others who were by-and-large self-sufficient, and a large mass who did not have enough land to support themselves and had to make ends meet through a combination of wage-work and by-employments. The relationship between the distribution of working holdings and the distribution of rental property is an exceedingly vexed one. The evidence which survives detailing sub-tenanting arrangements would seem to vitiate most attempts to delineate social structure from the juridical designations which were usually attached to land itself rather than its occupiers' actual holdings. As we have seen, Postan has argued that behind the stable and symmetrical surveys and extents "the actual occupation of the land by families may have been both unstable and unsymmetrical".[17] Such a "snapshot" taken two generations later might reveal much the same structural characteristics but the personnel would find themselves occupying different niches from their grandparents. Because the "rules of the game" in the high middle ages remained essentially the same, there was little room for the villeinage (as a group) to improve or even change their position *vis-à-vis* their lords; the most they could hope for was to make gains at the expense of their neighbours. In fact, there is abundant evidence to suggest that the villeinage saw its social and economic position decline during the high middle ages. There is no doubt that their bargaining position *vis-à-vis* their lords had deteriorated. By 1300, then, vigorous population growth had wiped out the benefits of colonization.

We might therefore consider serfdom to have been a "zero-sum-game" in which gains more or less cancelled out losses and the villeinage remained in much the same place. But to adopt this perspective is to stand outside the experience of the villeinage for whom the prospect of gain or loss was the object of their economic lives. "There is a good deal of evidence of a highly stratified manorial society, and of a determination on the part of the prosperous 'better sort' to manipulate affairs in their own interest individually and as a 'ruling class' just as far as they were able."[18] For this reason, and more particularly because a series of losses would most probably mean starvation, the game was played out in deadly earnest. The medieval village was thus no bucolic frolic; all the evidence from court rolls points to a rough-and-tumble existence in which assaults and trickery were in the nature of things. Social life did not, however, approximate the hopeless anarchy of a Hobbesian war of all-against-all; rather, it seems to have been the case that a working compromise was worked out between the forces of social solidarity and the "moral economy" of the peasants on the one hand and the forces of competition and *ressentimente* on the other. Furthermore, the weight of the whole system was in the former direction since most of the land was worked in common fields which required considerable discussion, planning and co-ordinated work. Medieval peasants were members of a co-operative enterprise, not agricultural proletarians under constant supervision, nor were they made to work at a dictated pace; their communal life stressed mutuality.[19] R. H. Hilton has argued that the peasantry's domestic economy was inpenetrable in the sense that feudal lords could demand labour-services and/or money-payments but they could not and did not attempt to regulate the peasantry's disposition of its labour or its husbandry practices.[20]

The feudal lord not only controlled some of his villeins' labour, external to the domestic economy of the peasant household, but he was empowered to maintain the peace amongst them. Sometimes this only meant settling squabbles; at other time his jurisdiction was exercised at the expense of the individual peasant or even the whole peasant community. While the lord was the arbiter of the local peace it would be absurd to suggest that he was an impartial one. It is well to remember that, as Rosamond Faith has written, "the unfree tenants were the human stock of the manor. The 'villeinage' were regarded as part of the demesne; villeins' goods were the lord's goods, and peasant income, extracted through rent, labour tallage and fines, a major source of seigneurial income [which meant that] . . . as far as the lord was concerned, villeins *were* property."[21]

Rising prices for agricultural products and the increased cost of maintaining their lifestyles led the great landlords to tighten the screw of feudal exaction during the later years of Henry II's reign when "The common law doctrine of villeinage was created . . . on the premise that a lord's relations with his servile tenantry were his private business."[22] The "private business" of the local court went hand-in-hand with the lord's need to extract labour-time or money-equivalents as well as other kinds of payments in cash and in kind from his villeins. The timing of the seigneurial offensive, in the later twelfth century, is significant because it coincided with the intensification of demesne farming and, therefore, the need for "the reimposition or redefinition of labour services to provide the large labour force necessary for intensive arable farming".[23] For this reason it is wrong-headed to separate feudalism from manorialism; they were two aspects of the same set of power relationships. Legal inequality stood the heart of the daily process of "extra-economic compulsion".[24]

Along with the servile farmers existed a body of wage-labourers who laboured next to the customary tenants. Postan has argued that feudal labour-services and wage-work were "alternative" but that it was the landlord who had the discretion to choose which would be employed. Seasonal, discontinuous operations requiring the simultaneous deployment of a large labour force were usually performed by the labour dues of customary tenants but those operations which demanded either specialized skills or continuous application were the province of wage-labour since it was impossible to depend upon the intermittent services of the villeinage to carry them out.[25] While he never exactly specifies the numerical proportion of the labour force who were "wage-earning pro-letarians",[26] Postan notes that the "the estimates [relating to the total valuation of services] invariably bear out the general impression that the labour of *famuli* and hired labourers formed a high proportion of the labour force". On the Crowland manor of Cottenham the total wage bill, including food, was more than twice the value of customary services performed by villeins. On other manors which demanded more in the way of customary labour-services, the ratio was rather lower but Postan is quite emphatic that the Crowland figures were neither exceptional nor unrepresentative.[27] In this example he is, of course, only considering labour on the lord's demesne; later, in a most interesting aside, Postan writes that "it was in peasant households [by which he seems to mean family farms] that labour freely hired was most generally employed".[28] This point will come up again and is a crucially integrated part of the way in which *family farmers* co-ordinated their own *family economies*.

Postan describes a chronology of wage-work which was tightly bound up with the economic development in the middle ages. By freeing Saxon slaves and transforming them into Norman villeins, the landlords solved two problems at once: first, they provided a mechanism for colonization and, second, they retained discretionary control over some (but not all) of the labour power of the subordinate classes.[29] Over the next two centuries the imperatives which lay behind this policy changed. As we have seen, the later twelfth century marked the apex of the colonization period and the emergence of a new one dominated by population pressure on increasingly scarce resources. In these circumstances the supply of able-bodied men owing labour-services rose dramatically while the pressure of numbers – and their own needs for ready money – made it advantageous for lords to intensify demesne production for the nascent market in foodstuffs. Around 1300 the customary tenant's feudal services were at their peak, whether paid for in labour-time or commuted into money-equivalents. The pressure on the villein's holding was gravely affected by his servile legal status, his deteriorating economic position and the general pressure of population on resources.[30] All historians seem to agree that living standards at this time were at a low ebb – they seem to have deteriorated and were continuing to deteriorate.

Not all medieval peasants were servile, however. Substantial numbers held their land in free tenure. In part this juridical status can be related to the conditions of peasant assarting because there was a strong correlation between the encouragement of colonization and increase of free tenure. It would seem that in return for the peasants' labour in clearing the land some lords offered strictly market-rents, free from feudal services, as a *quid pro quo*. Indeed, the areas of freedom were most likely to have been those forests, marshes and wastes which were brought into cultivation after the Norman Conquest had declared the whole body of customary tenants unfree. The areas of large manorial estates usually had a high proportion of bondsmen who were obliged to forward both market-rents and feudal services to their lords. Not infrequently these two types of political economy were situated cheek-by-jowl and the "juxtaposition of tenants of very different juridical status and economic position would add considerably to the tensions of the countryside".[31]

In the first stage of the English middle ages – from the Norman Conquest through to the thirteenth century – the number of smallholders, both free and servile, proliferated. While there is no certain knowledge about aggregate population levels, historians have delineated the trend and it seems to be agreed that "there was a threefold rise at the least between 1086 and 1300".[32] Two centuries of vigorous population growth had meant that the pattern of landholding became polarized. The morcell-ized holdings of younger brothers and the growing numbers of poor spinsters without dowries were part of the process whereby the poor accumulated at the bottom of the social pyramid which grew most rapidly at its base.[33] The sheer press of numbers increased the demand for food precipitously while the primitive agrarian techniques of the time meant that the supply of food could not keep pace. The bottom of the social pyramid became "harvest-sensitive"; their poverty engendered "slow, long-term starvation".[34] Without supplementary wage-work a small-holder could not subsist but even this stop-gap was not enough. Ghastly agrarian crises, provoked by the familiar wage-price scissors, cut into lives of the working people.[35] On the Bishop of Winchester's estates it would appear that adult mortality levels during the crisis years were close to 100 per 1,000, something like five times that of normal years.[36] These deaths appear to have been disproportionately concentrated among the very poorest tenants; but because the manor court rolls usually did not cover the heriots (feudal death duties) of landless labourers or even "dwarf-holders", mortality rates derived from these documents have most probably underestimated the horrific suffering they experienced during crisis periods.

Family formation and social formation

The family formations of those at the bottom of this society can only be understood within the wider set of relationships in which they were enmeshed. In the feudal period, as in all others, men and women living in society had discrete boundaries placed on their behaviour by a combin-ation of forces – political, economic, social and cultural. In this sense, we all live in history. When we consider the family formation strategies of the medieval peasantry we must of course pay due attention to the social constraints on their range of action; but we must pay at least as much heed to their own decision-making acts. This means that we must get at the logic of their family formation strategies within the framework of the social/productive world they inhabited. The magnetic power of the land, its occupation and production, was the lodestar by which the peasantry oriented itself. Their family strategies were geared to maintaining, and if possible improving upon, its subsistence income.[37] By understanding why they acted in the ways they did it is possible to reconstruct how they made their own histories.

There appears to have been a widely held sentiment towards keeping landholdings of a size that would be viable for the maintenance of a family unit; this sentiment is crucial towards understanding the peasant's land-hunger.[38] But sentiment was confronted by hard demographic facts during the high middle ages when population growth was placing enormous pressure on this most crucial resource. As we have already discussed, it seems that holdings were broken up and the village commu-nity was polarized. Nevertheless, as Hilton has written, "poor small-holders and richer peasants were, in spite of the differences in their incomes, still part of the same social group, with a similar style of life, and differed from one to the other in the abundance rather than the quality of their possessions".[39] Those without land, the agricultural proletariat, do not seem to have been sufficiently numerous to have created an oppo-sitional culture, different from that of the peasantry. Indeed, the bound-ary separating the completely landless from the smallholders was indis-tinct; both groups were part of the *cottage economy* and not infrequently members of the same family, at different stages in their life-cycles. Moreover, landholdings only tell us part of the story regarding the subsistence strategies of the poorest medieval villagers since the availability of commons and tenement gardens were sometimes of more value than a scrap of customary land.[40] Thus, we have identified the peasant family's changing relationship with the land and the owners of that property in order to discover the fields of force within the material environment.

Medieval society, then, was built upon the foundation of household economies each of which was, to a certain extent, hermetically sealed from the outside. Nevertheless, the feudalist's demands for payments, the need to purchase consumer goods and the transformations imposed by the historical process in general and the local landholding pattern in particular all served to puncture this inwardness. Furthermore, the human need to reproduce meant that separate household units came together to transfer land, labour and personnel every generation. For all these reasons, then, it would be mistaken to overestimate the isolation of the household which is why all historians of the medieval peasantry devote considerable attention to the peasant family's relationship with the wider community. If we took another "snapshot" of the peasant family we might discover that, frozen in time, it was largely self-sufficient; yet, if we were to have a time-lapse photograph of the peasant family's activities, this second diachronic "snapshot" would reveal a web of connections and relationships all of which acted in a dialectical fashion to intrude upon the isolation of the private sphere. Although the sentimental world-view of the peasant would have emphasized the self-sufficiency of the family/ household unit, economic and demographic forces operated to break down this independence. Thus, production and reproduction were set in historical time.

As we have seen, the medieval village was both variegated and stratified. Thus, it is quite likely that the motivations and behaviour of the "peasant aristocrat" and the cottager or rural industrialist were different. Unfortunately, our knowledge largely relates to "the solid central core of landholding families . . . [which] constituted the social centre of gravity of the peasant class". In addition, because of its illiteracy and inarticu-lateness we must piece "together the fundamentals of peasant ideology from fragmentary expressions of opinion, or from demands made from time to time, or from formulations of accepted custom".[41] Most of what we know is for this reason based on prescription rather than description.[42] This account is mainly focussed upon the central tendency, Hilton's "social center of gravity"; the family formations of proleterianized vil-lagers can only be considered within the imperatives of the field of force to which they were subjected. Its rhythms dictated the organization and self-image of the *cottage economy* to which they belonged.

Within the orbits of economic and juridical restrictions – that is, landholding distribution and feudal control – the peasant family was able to act in such a way as to control its destiny. It would quite be wrong to consider the manorial authorities akin to commissars, regulating every aspect of thought and behaviour. In fact, it would appear that as long as business went along as usual there was a kind of repressive tolerance which allowed the villeins to sort out among themselves the precise ways they met their obligations. The feudal governing class simply did not have the resources to invigilate their subordinates; indeed, it would probably have been counter-productive for them to have tried to do so. Even the Church adopted a grudgingly tolerant attitude. Compared to the social discipline of the Reformation the medieval Church was latitudinarian, practically an accomplice in the pantheistic beliefs of the common people.[43] Thus the private lives and thoughts of the common people were rarely the subject of concern to their rulers. Only to the extent that villein marriage involved complicated or unusual property transactions did the manorial court interest itself in the proceedings. The lord's property in his serfs' labour power was so important to the feudalists that there was a fear marriage outside seigneurial control might mean the loss "without hope of recall, [of] the breeders plus all cultivators and other revenue-producers the couple would produce".[44] This point, however, speaks more to juridical control over the villein's body than to social control over his/her behaviour.

To the extent that its interests in the villeins' obligations were threatened the courts might intervene, but in all other aspects the common people were free to act as they saw fit. "The question of marriage upon the manor presents small difficulty. The serfs, in general, found themselves subjected to little control. Unlike other people – the nobles, the great landholders, the wards of the rich merchants – no one had much interest in their marriages among themselves and upon the same manor."[45] In practical terms this meant that the age at marriage and the choice of partner was essentially a private affair. Moreover, the strength of the common law meant that a couple could be legally married simply by the exchange of vows, without formalization in a Church wedding. In the middle ages there was, therefore, considerable scope for individuals to construct their own relationships and in this way to make their own history. They did so within the parameters which were "given" by the social formation.

Given the centrality of land to the peasant's domestic economy, its transmission between generations was a major event. Of course, the peasant did not have full property rights in the land because he could only dispose of it according to the custom of the manor which varied from place to place. Customary peasants *occupied* the land; landlords *owned* it. Most of England, especially those areas of open-field farming, was governed by systems of *impartible inheritance* so that the land was transmitted to one heir, the eldest son. There were, of course, other parts of England in which the patrimony was divided at the death of the head of the household. Such areas were often wood-pasture districts. But, whatever the mode of farming or the method of inter-generational transmission, its connection to the land was the central economic relationship for the peasant family and its *cottage economy*.

While the precise mechanism for inheritance varied widely, marriage was closely connected with the assumption of the family holding by the heir of the younger generation. Homans, whose classic study of the thirteenth-century peasantry is based on a close reading of numerous court rolls, wrote that "in many places, the man who was to inherit the tenement did not marry until its last holder was ready to turn it over to him".[46] Marriage was in every sense a *rite de passage* marking the transition from youth to fully-fledged adulthood for the younger generation and from adulthood to semi-retirement for the older one. As Homans' quotation makes clear, the element of discretion on the part of the older generation was substantial; it was only mitigated by the fact that in many places the custom of the manor dictated the ultimate heir. On the other hand, there seems to be no evidence indicating that a specific moment for transmission – except early death of the parent – was customary.

If we make the assumption that life expectation at thirty, the mid-point in an adult's childbearing life, was about twenty-five years then fully a half of the peasant families would have been broken by death before the question of inter-generational transmission would have been broached.[47] It appears that the customs of most manors were quite clear that a widow enjoyed "Freebench" (lifetime privileges) as long as she remained unmarried and chaste. On this point Homans remarks that widows' "interests in the tenement were only life-interests: after their death their shares reverted to the heir of the blood".[48] Among the surviving peasants we might assume that the strength of a man in his mid-fifties would have been diminishing so that the tensions inherent in retirement would have thereby been modified. Homans quotes a number of examples of *pre-mortem* inheritance in which "the father stipulated that he and his wife should be cared for in their old age, and the details of the treatment they were to receive [which] were carefully recorded".[49]

The well-regulated flow of family property between generations suggested to Homans that household structure could be characterized by the "stem-family system".[50] Homans' argument in favour of a family system in which some households were extended across three generations has not been without challenge, however. H. E. Hallam, basing his arguments on serf lists from the Spalding district of Lincolnshire, has suggested that nuclearity was the predominant organizing principle of the peasant household.[51] Hallam's evidence, too, is not without its problems; it comes from an area of the country with an exceptionally high percentage of freemen for whom the connection between impartible inheritance and stem-family structures may not have been so common. In a more apposite comparison, Britton's study of the manor of Broughton, an open-field community in Huntingdonshire, suggests that "maintenance agreements" probably led to extended families. He is careful to note that, rather than being an iterated system, the household structure of the peasants on this Ramsey Abbey manor was "situational".[52] Commenting on this squabble concerning medieval household structure, Bolton writes: "The best solution to the problem is probably a compromise that the family moved naturally from one state to another. Aged parents and others would live with the family for a time. Then, by a process of death or migration, it would revert to the nuclear condition, until the children took over from their parents."[53]

Because some sort of dowry on the part of the woman and "property" on the part of the man was expected before a marriage could be contemplated, it would seem that for the smallholders, and even more especially for the landless, marriage would have been rather more difficult to finance than for the comparatively well-off peasants who had inherited the economic mainsprings for their household's subsistence. Among non-inheriting sons and daughters there was an entitlement to a portion of their father's movable goods and chattels; they would probably have needed further accumulation to put together the necessary competence, however. Having to seek their fortune alone, away from the home and hearth, must have made for longer, if freer, courtships. It would thus appear that the "asymmetrical" pattern of land usage underwrote the ability of almost everyone to gain a foothold as fully fledged adult members of the *cottage economy*. Because the land was divided and subdivided into many plots there was an opportunity for men and women who were smallholders or even proletarians to create the ingredients for a subsistence income which was necessary to establish their own family. Clearly, many of these people lived precipitously, yet in marrying they, too, were in an orbit described by the gravitational fields of force of their social formation.

Marriage was an act of material necessity for peasants, especially for peasant men. Their wives were partners in a co-operative venture and without their help it would have been impossible to look after the stock and make the butter and cheese. But, in fact, there seems to be little evidence of the gender-specific tasks which came to characterize the more specialized capitalist agrarian economy. The sexual division of labour was "generally flexible" and "non-exclusive". Women, according to surviving evidence, "were engaged in most male tasks – such as reaping, binding, mowing, carrying corn, shearing sheep, thatching, and breaking stones for road maintenance". Women were carrying out almost every role which would later be identified as "male work". It can be further argued that "the housewife role was but weakly developed in the poorest strata" which, as the evidence makes abundantly clear, comprised the plurality in most village populations. During the harvest and other times of high labour requirements, women provided a hand in the fields. Indeed, bye-laws from the high middle ages *required* all villagers – both men and women – to participate in that most crucial event in the agrarian calendar.[54] It is probably true to say that a peasant household could survive the loss of the husband far more easily than that of the wife. The husband's labour could be replaced but the innumerable tasks which a wife fulfilled were not usually available for purchase. For this reason remarriage among widowers has always been far swifter than among widows.[55]

Marriage was also an act of social solidarity joining together two families. It was therefore the subject of intense negotiations and often protracted discussions. "Among peasant families, fathers and mothers, or uncles and elder brothers, or a semi-professional village match-maker, were required to initiate courtships."[56] Once the prospective bride's and groom's family interests had agreed on the financial side of the undertaking, their children were given the opportunity to consent to the bargain. The prescribed sequences of the marriage process have been neatly summarized in the great vernacular poem of the later middle ages: "thus marriage was made – first by the consent of the father and the advice of friends, and then by the mutual agreement of the two partners".[57]

The couple's wedding was a communal act, publicizing the alliance between village families. The wedding feast and the attendant partying were enjoyed for themselves but were undertaken to validate the contract. In fact, clandestine marriages were sanctioned by Church law but, in reality, they created very messy situations for both the Church and the feudalists. Furthermore, if a clandestine marriage was later renounced by one of the parties what would be the status of children born to a later, adulterous union? Illegitimate children were an affront in the eyes of God and the feudalist; illegitimate children were free of villein status because their fathers were unknown and therefore they could not inherit their condition.[58] Whether the marriage was celebrated publicly or privately, the contract between the partners was the critical moment about which everything else revolved. Homans reports an Oxfordshire case in which a Church wedding was required "not because it was a religious ceremony but because it gave publicity to the endowment. A clandestine marriage did not."[59] In this publicity and contractualism we see the fusion of several aspects of the marriage process: the legal, economic, social and inter-personal. Homans suggests that among the English villagers of the thirteenth century something like the later ceremony of hand-fasting "may well have marked the making of the marriage covenant. After the trothplight the couple were bedded, and only certain weeks later were they married at the church."[60]

The crisis of feudalism

The fourteenth century was a period of extraordinary turmoil and upheaval. It began in the wake of a century of intensified feudal exactions, but by its end villeinage was in the process of withering away. The population of England appears to have been halved in this century – it was first attacked by horrific famines and then by recurrent plagues. The fourteenth century thus marked the crisis of feudal society; it never recovered. In discussing the transition from feudalism to capitalist relations of production it is necessary to distinguish necessary from sufficient causes of the change. In particular, was the plummeting population in itself sufficient to have provoked the collapse of the old order or was it a necessary pre-condition to other, even more important considerations? The answer to the foregoing question is that population changes by themselves were insufficient; changes in the level of population or the supply of land could alter the supply and/or demand axes but the power of the lords was not *essentially* concerned with economistic measures.[61] Their customary powers were economic as well as social, political and juridical. These powers were backed up by their monopoly on military force.

Seigneurial coercion was abetted, right after the Black Death, by the legal tactic of fixing wages for labourers. The 1349 Ordinance of Labourers and the more famous, supplemental 1351 Statute of Labourers were made the law of the land because "a great part of the people, and especially of workmen and servants, lately died of the pestilence, many – seeing the necessity of masters and great scarcity of servants – will not serve unless they may receive excessive wages, and some rather willing to beg in idleness than by labour to get their living".[62] The first response of employers – landlords and the wealthier peasants – to the crisis of diminishing population (which was from their point of view, of course, a crisis of diminishing income and rising wages) was the repressive exertion of political control over the labour market. Feudal rents and the other incidental payments demanded from villeins did not immediately spiral downwards as might be expected in a situation in which labour became scarce literally overnight. Hilton suggests that "there was a general seigneurial reaction between the first plague [1348] and the 1370s, showing itself in the successful depression of wages below their natural level and in a relative increase in revenues from land".[63] There was a two-pronged, popular response to this seigneurial offensive: first, many simply walked away from their obligations and negotiated new contracts

31

as free men; and, second, there were continuous uprisings and revolts, the most famous of which occurred in 1381. The first tactic proved to be the more successful because it probed the upper class at its weakest point and set its members against each other whereas armed resistance provoked draconian measures of repression.

Set against the perspective of their longstanding experience of feudal exactions and their newly acquired knowledge regarding the economic benefits of freedom, the competition for labour gave the unfree population an unparalleled opportunity to seek out a new life elsewhere. Because villagers in the thirteenth century had, in effect, been punished by manorial lords for their freedom it is not surprising that they had attached surprisingly little value to it. In the high middle ages labour was plentiful and land was scarce so that villeins had been rewarded by manorial lords for their servility; they, not freemen, had access to manorial land because they, not freemen, could be subject to feudal exactions.[64] In the later fourteenth century the changing terms of trade between now-scarce labour and now-plentiful land made a mockery of the earlier state of affairs so that the cost, as it were, of villeinage would have become painfully obvious. Moreover, it should not be forgotten that the manorial lords' immediate response to their declining incomes was to turn the feudal screw even tighter. In these new circumstances the indignity of villeinage would have been exacerbated by the increasingly heavy economic penalties attached to it. One hardly needs to imagine why villeins would have struck out against their servitude and resisted feudal exactions. The *quantitative* extent of such flight is not really germane because if some fled then the others bargained from a much stronger position. The real point is not why the peasantry resisted feudalism but why the landlords were unable to maintain it.[65] The English landlord class itself was in a state of flux. It had been successful in the early middle ages because of its "extraordinary intra-class cohesiveness ... manifested simultaneously in its formidable military strength, in its ability to regulate intra-lord conflict, and in its capacity to dominate the peasantry".[66] Now, pressed hard by rising expenditures and driven to the wall by declining manorial revenues resulting from their inability to dominate the peasantry, the feudal lords resorted to simple plunder in which it was each man for himself while the devil took the hindmost. Many individual members of the feudal nobility were immensely enriched by the wars with France.[67] Seeing this lucrative source of revenue collapse, the greater aristocrats attacked the architect of war-time failure. For, as A. R. Bridbury has written, "Civil war was the retribution visited upon the medieval king whose foreign policy did not fix the gaze of his aristocratic feudal host on objectives which discharged the frictions generated by life and politics elsewhere than at home."[68] Thus, the monarchy's inability to maintain the feudal system by failing to lead its barons in war created dissension among the great magnates. In the middle of the fifteenth century we see the disintegration of the feudal kingdom as it first lost its foreign territories in France and then settled into its long winter of discontent during the internecine Wars of the Roses. By focussing its energy on prizes and looting – the spoils of warfare in the middle ages – the nobility evaded the implications of their loss of power over their English tenants. Of course, it is equally true to say that by choosing warfare over estate administration the English ruling class was simply showing its true colours: they were caught up in the contradiction of their social situation. Indeed, one and the same man might have been pursuing both strategies – estate administration and warfare – at the same time. Furthermore, and crucially, it is most probably the case that if the later medieval feudalists had prosecuted the social war against their tenants with the vigour, energy and ruthlessness of their French campaigns then villeinage might not have simply withered away.

The disintegration of feudal political power

In addition to promoting social instability at the top, the Hundred Years War must also have had very significant destabilizing effects among the popular classes by raising the demand for manufactured goods – uniforms, armour, weapons and ships – and, hence, non-agricultural labour; it also provided an "escape hatch" for an unknown number of able-bodied men who were either dragooned into their lords' bands or else simply pressed into service. In either case, these hands too were lost to the manorial economy. Postan suggests that perhaps 10 per cent of all adult males were diverted to war-related employment.[69] It is not clear from his account if this figure represents a high-water mark or an average of war-related non-manorial employment. In fact the 32,000 men brought together by Edward III for the siege of Calais, in 1346–7, was the largest English army assembled in France during the Hundred Years War.[70] Given the relatively small size of the fighting forces in the feudal armies it would seem that the main impact of the hostilities was in their stimulus to supplying equipment and provisions. The vigorous demand for labour in these enterprises during the period when the feudalists were desperately trying to keep their villeins down on the farm must have exacerbated the tensions within the ruling class as they competed with one another for an increasingly scarce resource. The war-related demands for labour must have given both peasants and proletarians an added dimension of leverage in dealing with their masters. In these circumstances the threat of expulsion from manorial land must have been increasingly hollow. And we should not forget that the land – and its occupation – had been the feudalists' stick and the feudalists' carrot in their dealings with the peasantry for the whole period of the high middle ages, since the Conquest in 1066. Gradually, not overnight, landlords had to adjust to the new reality in which they could no longer control their villeins through feudal methods of extra-economic compulsion. They lost control because their land, access to which was their ultimate economic sanction against the peasants, lost its value in a dramatic fashion and the villein could, as it were, substitute one lord for another at far better terms – "a villein was no villein save to his own lord".[71]

On the Bishop of Worcester's estates studied by Christopher Dyer we can see the way this later medieval resistance undermined the feudal system of "extra-economic compulsion". The Bishop was a feudal land-owner and "the threat of a mass exodus" sufficiently frightened him (because of its danger to his estate) that his recourse to "unpopular exactions" (i.e. feudal rents) was curtailed. He had to be content with a "depleted tenant population paying part of their rents, than to have no tenants at all".[72] In a very real sense, then, the fourteenth century had seen a radical reversal in the terms of trade between labour and capital of such a magnitude that the whip-hand of the feudal lord was restrained and he could only get a market-rent for his property. Dyer's research on the fifteenth-century "rent strikes" on the Bishop of Worcester's estates is very important because it makes precisely this point: "Collective refusals of recognitions, tallage, commuted labour services and similar dues, together with individual denials of servility and a general lack of respect for the demands of the manor court are valuable pointers towards peasant attitudes to [feudal elements in] rent." Interestingly and of the very greatest importance, resistance to feudal elements in rent was co-ordinated while resistance to "economic" rent on the land itself tended to be individual and sporadic.[73] The lord's ability to demand "non-economic" exactions from his tenants became a dead letter. The *political* ineffectiveness of the Bishop of Worcester's relations with his tenants thus points to the sufficient pre-condition for ending feudal landholding practices: the decline in population obscures the main point that if the seigneurial offensive had been successful – and it was in many other countries at this time – then feudalism would have persisted. The struggle against feudal exactions was enormously facilitated by the circumstances in which land became plentiful and labour scarce. But it only confuses the issue to insist that demographic decline undermined the feudal mode of extraction: falling population set the stage for this struggle but it was not in itself sufficient to determine the outcome. Of course, the old regime did not simply evaporate; rather, "Villeinage was never abolished; it withered away."[74] It withered away because the nature of the *political* struggle was its diffuseness as a result of the need for the same battle to be fought over and over again, in different localities and against different landlords. For this reason the withering of feudal exactions was a process, not an event. One finds them, manifesting themselves vestigially, throughout the early modern period. Nevertheless, the significant fact is that they no longer controlled the respiration of the social structure. Rather, they were like foggy breath on a frosty morning – they proved that it still breathed life.

It would appear that landlords and their administrators were very well aware of the fact that commutation of services for money-payments gave the customary tenant a new kind of bargaining chip. It was thus crucial for landowners to distinguish freeholders' rights from those of copyholders who held their land as a disintegrating form of villein tenure. Estate administrators in the later middle ages were concerned to verify title to land, much of which had lost its characteristic "feudal tenure". They were concerned to verify title so as to distinguish occupation from ownership, even if the customary occupant had substantial security in the land during his lifetime and that of his children.[75] The land which was not simply transformed into leasehold but remained copyhold was kept from full peasant control because most of it was subject to discretionary entry fines. These "often appear to have provided the landlords with the lever they needed to dispose of customary peasant tenants, for in the long run fines could be substituted for competitive commercial rents".[76] Brenner goes on to argue that the upshot of this late medieval struggle paved the way to the future:

With the peasants' failure to establish essentially freehold control over the land, the landlords were able to engross, consolidate and enclose, to create large farms and to lease them to capitalist tenants who could afford to make capitalist investments. This was the indispensable pre-condition for significant agrarian advance, since agricultural development was predicated upon significant inputs of capital, involving the introduction of new technologies and a larger scale of operation.[77]

The feudal regime broke down over its inability to control the persons of the villeins. Yet, the landowners maintained discretionary control over their property which was, in the final analysis, of even greater importance to their survival, albeit in a metamorphosed condition.

The Indian summer of peasant society

The peasants who survived the devastation of the fourteenth century appear to have had material lives which were dramatically more secure than their predecessors. The marginally propertied elements in the village seemed to have come out best in relative terms, if not absolutely. Their ranks were decimated to a far greater extent than those above them because the rising mortality rate broke the older system of social recycling in which downward mobility was the first stage in the extinction of the cadet line.[78] As a result of their diminishing numbers "the purchasing power of wages in terms of wheat rose between 1300 and 1480 by 220 per cent".[79] The fifteenth century is still very much the "dark age" of English social history although recent studies of manorial court rolls are beginning to illuminate some of its murky depths.[80] Nowhere, perhaps, is our ignorance greater than in the history of the lesser peasants, wage-labourers and their families. Almost all of what we know is derived by inference from the economic history of the period. To be sure, most of the population remained firmly attached to the *cottage economy* but their successful struggle against feudalism meant that their struggle for subsistence was far easier than it had been. It seems neither far-fetched nor implausible to suggest that the later medieval economic retrenchment was accompanied by a cultural retrenchment.[81] The embryonic economy of production for exchange was still largely submerged in the preponderant economy of production for use. This emphasis on the peasant family's independence was found in the poetry of the time which stressed the peasant's labour:

> Our host him axed, 'What man art thou?'
> 'Sir,' quod he, 'I am an hyne;
> For I am wont to go to the plow,
> And erne my mete yer that I dyne.
> To swete and swink I make a vow,
> My wyf and children therwith to fynd . . .'.[82]

It would not be altogether surprising if those elements in the peasantry's consciousness which stressed the independent egalitarianism of a community of primary producers were given an added resonance because they were especially likely to be realized in these economic circumstances of the later middle ages.

The substance of the medieval peasantry's world-view seems to have revolved around a family-centred production unit. For this reason labour-services were deeply resented, the more particularly because they defined the forced labourers as serfs. In addition, family farmers disliked the surplus extraction inherent in rental arrangements and their landlords' practice of skimming off the product of their labour even before the family's subsistence needs were met.[83] To the peasant land was something more than a "factor of production"; "it was worth possessing for its own sake, and enjoyed as a measure of social status, a foundation of family fortunes, and a fulfilment and extension of the owner's personality".[84] The value placed on "land" did not mean that it was only some "land" which was valued; rather than mystifying this resource it would appear that medieval villagers had a straightforward understanding of its elemental material value. This familial strategy would have been far harder to achieve in the high middle ages when the terms of trade were stacked against the cottager. In this sense, then, the demographic caesura of the later middle ages would appear to have been even more significant for the familial organization of the peasantry than for its relationship with its feudal lords. The social result may very well have been the consolidation of the English family system with its tripartite emphasis on late ages at first marriage and the establishment of nuclear family households through the achievement of economic independence before marriage. As we have seen, the existence of this family system in the middle ages is a matter of some debate among historians who have identified its lineaments but seem reluctant to allow more. Thus Bolton's survey of the literature led him to an even-handed compromise which stressed the *situational* character of medieval peasants' family structures as opposed to the iteration of a nuclear (or stem-) family system.[85] Moreover, we know almost nothing about (properly defined) demographic statistics before the advent of vital registration. In contrast, the existence of an iterated "English family system" in the sixteenth century is not now regarded as a subject for controversy among historians who have been able to use parish registers, local censuses and autobiographical material to flesh out its distinguishing characteristics. We will briefly touch upon the relationship between the English peasant family and feudalism at a later point in the argument when we can usefully compare it with the proletarian families which succeeded it. Using this kind of comparative strategy should allow us to fill some of the remaining blanks in the preceding discussion of economy and demography in the feudal period.

2

Agrarian capitalism and rural proletarianization

The human impact on the English landscape

Villages in medieval England were quite literally carved from the forest. By the end of the thirteenth century much of the available land had been settled and turned into arable farms to feed the growing numbers.[1] Much of this early medieval colonization was focussed on marginal land; the fact that it was cultivated speaks to the very fact that population pressure had led to land-hunger.[2] English agricultural practices in the high middle ages thus reflected the press of numbers. Around 1200 there was already a shortage of pasture in most regions of mixed husbandry so that available grazing-land was at a premium. In conditions of high land demand, extensive pastoral husbandry was traded off against the higher rents which could be gained from intensive peasant farming. It was in this context that "The medieval Englishman's propensity to concentrate on corn-growing at the expense of sheep-farming or cattle-grazing [became] one of the hallmarks of the economic geography of the thirteenth century."[3] The fifteenth century witnessed a remarkable reversal in agrarian priorities as vast amounts of land were shifted to pasture and villages were "lost". In the classic account of this later medieval reorganization of the human and geographical landscape M. W. Beresford has written

Such a transformation of cornfields into pastures was more than a transformation of scenery. It took away the need for the services of most of the villagers – all, perhaps, except the shepherd and his family who turn up so often in contemporary documents. The [other] villagers left or were evicted. The pastures would be watched over by the shepherd, and his cottage was the only house in the parish; or from the profits of wool the lord of the manor might build himself a new manor house on the site or enlarge his old house. Around it would stretch the parkland that was both attractive to the eye and useful to the pocket: in it roamed the deer for ornament and the sheep for income. Many a lost village stands in the shadow of the Great House.[4]

The main part of the damage caused by depopulating enclosure and the conversion to pasture, which led to the phenomenon of "lost villages", appears to have been caused before 1485 although the political controversy reached its height some decades later, after the fact as it were.[5]

The declining population of the later fourteenth and fifteenth centuries demanded fewer cereals, thereby prompting the switchover to pasture. The legendary Sir John Fastolf's profits from the Hundred Years War were recycled thereby enabling him to become a rich grazier; his manors in East Anglia carried some 7,800 sheep in 1446.[6] Other great landowners also had enormous flocks. The Townsends of Norfolk had 8,000 or 9,000 in the 1480s, Sir Robert Southwell had 13,000 sheep on fourteen different fold-courses. Such men were not unusual although the scale of their enterprise was extraordinary.[7] The England which later struck Daniel Defoe as "a vast magazine of wool" had its origins in this period.[8] W. G. Hoskins has written that there were "far more sheep than human beings in early sixteenth-century England".[9]

Depopulating enclosure in the pastoral regions was one response to the agrarian crisis engendered by falling numbers in the fifteenth century; the concentration of landholdings in the arable regions was another. In a word, the English yeoman appeared on the scene. These men held double-yardlands, and more, by any one of a number of different tenurial systems – freehold, leasehold, year-by-year and even copyhold in all its bewildering varieties. Their farms seem to have been limited only by the capital and especially the labour at their disposal.[10] In the first half of the early modern period "there is every reason to believe that yeomen were advancing as a class both absolutely and relatively more than any other landed group of the time".[11] Capitalist farmers and rich graziers signalled a definitive break with the past. Their emergence marked a radical discontinuity with the *agricultural involution* of medieval peasant society in which there was a "marked tendency (and ability) to respond to a rising population through intensification; that is, through absorbing increased numbers of cultivators on a unit of cultivated land".[12] In contrast to the replication of subsistence-level, peasant households, the emergence of the yeomanry suggested a quite different economic organization in which specialization of function, oriented towards production for exchange, replaced the older world in which undifferentiated production was geared to use.[13] At the end of the middle ages the issue was still very much in doubt and, indeed, the balance could have swung against an economic order in which the land – and everything else – was turned into a commodity and priced at a market value. It could have but it did not.

The yeomanry accumulated capital through their frugality, industry and care for detail.[14] The accretion of wealth in small increments meant that the process of differentiation traversed several generations. If the yeomen were the winners in the social struggle to separate themselves from the mass of the villagers then the lesser peasantry were the losers. The decline in their economic and social status was evident to contemporaries like the Elizabethan William Harrison who lumped these husbandmen together with day-labourers since both had "neither voice nor authoritie in the common wealthe, but are to be ruled and not to rule other".[15] The growth of the yeomanry and the proletarianization of the rest of the peasantry are but two sides of the same coin.

The metamorphosis of the English peasantry: a quantitative discursus

It is now appropriate to describe the changing social composition of rural England and, in particular, the relative importance of employers (i.e. agricultural capitalists) and employees (i.e. wage-labourers). Having done this, we will gain a valuable perspective within which to frame our discussion of material structures and family formations in rural England between the final disintegration of the feudal economy and the heyday of its capitalist successor. In absolute terms the numbers of adult male wage-labourers seem to have grown from 125,000 in 1524–5, to 204,000 in 1688, to 902,447 in 1851; peasants and farmers, conversely, declined from about 375,000 to 223,318 in the same time-period. Let us discuss the provenance of these statistics, their shortcomings and then, finally, their meaning.

The survival of the subsidy assessments from 1524–5 provides us with a marvellous documentary record specifying the size of the wage-earning component of the population. There was considerable variation both between counties – about 20 per cent of the adult males in Leicestershire were assessed on wages in contrast to over a third in Devonshire – and within counties – in Kent, for example, over one adult male in two was a wage-earner in the arable hundred of Downhamford whereas in the thinly settled sheep pastures of Romney Marsh only one man in six was so described.[16] One might settle for a compromise figure of 25 per cent although it is more likely the case that many of these wage-workers were single, boarding-in servants-in-husbandry and that labouring was, for many of them, merely a life-cycle phase before they assumed their adult positions as husbandmen, on the fringe of landed society.[17] Moreover, few adult males assessed on wages would have been completely landless and therefore wholly dependent upon wages for their subsistence because wage-work was often supplementary. Most early sixteenth-century proletarians would have had a small tenement garden, perhaps an acre or two, and also common rights to pasturage, forage and a host of other usages. "England still remained an overwhelmingly peasant community:

a land of small family farms where outside labour was only occasionally employed at peak periods."[18] If 25 per cent of all adult males were labourers, assessed on wages, it would not be far short of the mark to suggest that for our purposes almost all of the remaining 75 per cent of the population were peasants. Of course, there were some aristocrats, gentlemen, clerics and urban dwellers but they cannot have accounted for as much as 10 per cent of the total in the 1520s and so it is not necessary to consider them at this point. For the schematic purposes of our analysis we might consider 375,000 adult males to have been peasants and the remaining 125,000 labourers. The next set of statistics for us to place alongside the graduated wealth-tax assessments of the Henrician subsidy are Peter Lindert's findings which have been derived from occupational information in tax and burial registers of the later seventeenth century.[19] Lindert calculates that in 1688 there were 241,373 adult male "agricultural-ists" (both freeholders and tenants, capitalists and peasants) and 206,933 adult male labourers. Our final information comes from the published 1851 census returns in which it was reported that there were 902,447 adult male agricultural labourers and 223,318 farmers and graziers in England and Wales.[20]

In terms of the dynamic relationship between wage-labourers and the employers of wage-labour there were 33 proletarians for every 100 employers at the start of the early modern era and more than twelve times as many, 405:100, at the end.[21] Now, of course, this kind of exercise is rough at its edges – that is to be expected – but it does give us a very clear picture of the quantitative dimensions of social change in the countryside. The rest of this chapter is concerned with the historical meaning of these statistics.

The "Tudor Revolution in Government"

Feudalism did not simply end overnight; it disintegrated. Its demise was protracted; so, too, was the stillbirth of Absolutism in England. On the ruins of the feudal kingdom they inherited, the Tudors and Stuarts attempted to erect a "New Monarchy" in which bureaucratically organized personal administration replaced the ramshackle household government of their predecessors. Henry VII secured the Crown's hold over the country by reducing "overmighty subjects" to his control. The feudal nobility were ruthlessly cut down. A new class of royal appointees was elevated in its place. Uneasy lay the head of those annointed by the favour of a Tudor monarch. Until the reign of James I (1603–25) there was *never* a majority of nobles who had inherited their titles.[22]

Rather more than his father, Henry VIII was the model Renaissance Prince. His reign was characterized by the ruthless deployment of absolute power which was made possible by the centralization of authority resulting from the "Tudor Revolution in Government". Reflecting from his prison cell on the awesome coercion, wide-ranging dominion and sheer caprice which marked Henry VIII's reign Sir Walter Raleigh wrote:

> If all the pictures and patterns of a merciless prince were lost in the world, they might all again be painted to the life, out of the story of this King. For how many servants did he advance in haste (but for what vertue no man could suspect) and with the change of his fancy ruined again, no man knowing for what offence? To how many others of more desert gave he abundant flowers, from whence to gather Hony, and in the end of Harvest burnt them in the Hive.[23]

Having destroyed the feudal contenders and monopolized the means of warfare, Henry VIII set about using the violence of the state to promote his own power and his own glory. To pay for his foreign adventures he plundered the Church with a ruthlessness born of desperation. It is estimated that Church properties were worth ten times as much as Crown lands but in a whirlwind of expropriation and an orgy of graft and self-promotion, the single greatest land-transfer in English history since 1066, this property passed through the sausage-fingers of Henry VIII and into the hands "more or less rapidly, to the nobility and the gentry, mostly the latter. The new men were lawyers, government officials and merchants, and some of these, as in Devon, were younger sons of old families who had been trained in the law in default of inheriting the parental estate."[24]

Breaking the power of the medieval Church was an act of immense significance: it signalled the end of the middle ages. Not only did it subjugate the only credible moral opposition to royal patronage but it also released immense amounts of property on to the market thereby providing the new class of *parvenu* aristocrats with a material basis for their position. In so doing it made their dependence upon Royal whim absolutely transparent. The Tudors were able to supplant a class of feudal warriors with a court of preening peacocks, all of whom danced the Royal jig. To pay off these Royal "favourites" who in turn kept a menagerie of their own "creatures" (i.e. clients), they plundered the Church. An outstanding example of the politics of Tudor Absolutism took place in the County Palatine of Durham during the reign of Elizabeth. There, ecclesiastical depredation and the world of clientage advantaged the coterie surrounding the monarchy at the expense of the "commonwealth". Indeed, the rights and justice of the commonalty seem to have been the furthest thing from Elizabeth's mind as she pillaged the once-independent Bishopric of Durham to keep her greedy courtiers and their retainers at heel.[25]

The "Tudor Revolution in Government" restructured the English political universe by creating a new form of government in which the Crown's power and prestige were considerably enhanced at the expense of the aristocracy who were reduced to dependence upon the centralized authority. But because there was no provision for financing the administration of government apart from the discretionary income of the monarch, the Crown became increasingly dependent upon taxation granted by the representatives of the politically enfranchised, common taxpayers in Parliament. The failure of the Tudors and Stuarts to secure sources of revenue independent of parliamentary approval severely limited their freedom of movement. This financial straightjacket put the forces of Absolutism and those of representative democracy on to a collision course. Political competition is largely concerned with reflecting the division of wealth and influence in society. Power, then, is the ability to co-ordinate social behaviour in such a way as to maximize one's property and wealth at the expense of other claimants. Groups ally with each other for the protection and furtherance of common interests but such coalitions are inherently unstable because, and this is really the most important fact, the mainsprings of wealth are themselves unstable. Technical invention, geographical discovery and the increased efficiencies of co-operative labour all had a continuous effect upon production and so continuously transformed the firmament of political power by shifting polarities and fields of force. Elizabeth I and James Stuart were clever, astute and dextrous enough to put off the day of reckoning; Charles Stuart was not – he paid for his maladroit regality with his head.

Rural proletarianization: the first phase

The proletarian component was very small in the Henrician period; 150 years later it had grown immensely. We shall look more closely at the quantitative dimensions of this issue in the later part of this chapter but, for now, let us focus our attention on its historical development. There are two different aspects of this mushroom growth: first, impartible inheritance practices among the landed population in conditions of rapid demographic growth effectively proletarianized extra men and women, over and above replacement levels, just as had been the case in the high middle ages; and, second, the original landed population was differentiated. Some peasants amassed sufficient resources to become yeoman farmers while others were, in one way or the other, expropriated and proletarianized. For the mass of the population these national trends provided the essential context within which their intensely local, deeply provincial lives were led. For them, being always perched more or less close to the *cottage economy*'s subsistence imperatives, the transformation from medieval to modern times pivoted on sanctioning a new moral economy in which production for exchange came to be preferred over production for use. In the early modern period we do not see the clear-cut emergence of "free labour" but rather the transmutation of medieval notions of lordship into the patriarchal ideal of household government in which the "better sort" directed the minds and bodies of the "poorer sort". Such changes did not occur overnight and, to be sure, they were almost always mitigated by the prevailing ideology of patri-archalism. Nevertheless, the material and cultural distancing of patrician and plebeian had its roots in the lineages of the stillborn Absolutist state and the social gospel of the Reformation.

The changing orbit of patriarchal politics was reinforced by structural shifts in the rural economy which brought about significant changes in village society. Let us next consider the changing organization of agri-cultural production and then look at the ways that social relations in the countryside reflected these adjustments. It will be useful to consider these early modern agrarian developments in an historical perspective in order to draw attention to their departure from the peasant farming techniques of the middle ages. The emergence of rural proletarianization and agri-cultural capitalism in the sixteenth century signalled the end of the solidarity of the village community based on the replication of family-based units of production. In so doing it signalled the advent of a new mode of production based on the systematic employment of wage-labour and a market-orientation, predicated on the accumulation of capital.

At the beginning of the sixteenth century England was again a country in which tracts of land were given over to forests and commons. The English landscape was markedly different from contemporary France as is made clear in a 1549 document called "The Debate of the Heralds" in which it is claimed that "a great part of it [England] is waste, desert, and salvaige [i.e. savage] ground, not inhabited nor th'erth tylled, but consys-teth in forestes, chases, parks, and enclosures".[26] To a significant extent this plenitude of woodland represented the process of re-afforestation which had taken place in the wake of the immense decline of population levels from their apex c. 1300. There was not one but a great many rural economies: wood-pasture and open-field represented two polarities, most villages were distributed somewhere along the continuum stretching between them. Over and above the perduring influence of geographical location, one must also allow for another series of permutations which resulted from villages' prior histories. The feudalists' ability to subjugate some villagers in the early middle ages still reverberated in the lives of their descendents several hundred years later, not least in regard to the conditions under which they had access to the land. This medieval inheritance was revealed in the extraordinarily intricate local patterns of landownership which, in turn, profoundly influenced the social fabric of village life, as did the local residence (or absence) of a noble or gentleman.[27] Just as there was no "typical" medieval village – some were free, others were manorialized – so there was no such thing as a "typical" sixteenth-century rural economy. Rural England was a crazy-quilt, patterned from the intense locality of geographical and historical factors which were themselves transmuted over time to shape the political economy of rural social formations. Social structures in the countryside revealed the imprint of earlier forces so that the most striking characteristic of these local social ecologies was their high degree of variation, within even small regions. Generalizations, therefore, must necessarily be couched in terms which allow for variation from central tendencies.

There was nothing inevitable, inescapable or pre-ordained about the way villages developed; they evolved within an historical crucible and the fields of force in one community were quite frequently unlike those of its neighbours. The social history of rural England in the early modern period pivots on the struggle to turn the land into a commodity, its exploitation into a source of capital accumulation, and its tillers into mere units of labour power. From our vantage point we can find evidence making it clear that farms did become bigger, that land utilization did become more sophisticated, that the scope of the food market did grow by leaps and bounds, that rent-rolls did fatten, that rural housing was improved, that there were massive improvements in the elementary material comforts of daily life and that labour power was becoming proletarianized. It is well and good to identify these indicators which seem to point in the direction of triumphant agrarian capitalism but it is also necessary to look at the underside of this equation to comprehend how the success story of the new social order occurred at the expense of its predecessor. For every yeoman farmer, there were a great many cottagers who were inexorably losing control over their land and entitlement to commons. When the losers lost their land they lost their birthright and had to sell their labour in order to make ends meet. The success of the few was necessarily predicated upon the failure of the many. By seeing the successes and failures within a single field of view we can appreciate the political dimension of this struggle. Just as the decline of feudalism did not occur without a social struggle, the attack on the peasant society based on the *cottage economy* cannot be understood in solely economic terms.

What was at issue in the early modern countryside was not the ups and downs of individual familes – or even the success of particular communities – but rather the wholesale supersession of a way of life. One can hardly emphasize this point strongly enough because it distinguished the stakes at issue in the social centrifuge of the early modern village from its medieval predecessor which, as we have seen, was founded on a system of social/familial recycling.

Common fields and pastures kept alive a vigorous co-operative spirit in the community; enclosures starved it. In champion country [i.e. Midland England] people had to work together amicably, to agree upon crop rotations, stints of common pasture, the upkeep and improvement of their grazings and meadows, the clearing of ditches, the fencing of fields. They toiled side by side in the fields, and they walked together from field to village, from farm to heath, morning, afternoon, and evening. They all depended on common resources for their fuel, for bedding, and fodder for their stock, and by pooling many of the necessities of livelihood they were disciplined from early youth to submit to the rules and customs of their community. After enclosure, when every man could fence his own piece of territory and warn his neighbours off, the discipline of sharing things with one's neighbours was relaxed, and every household became an island unto itself. This was the great revolution in men's lives, greater than all the economic changes following enclosure. Yet few people living in this world bequeathed to us by the enclosing and improving farmer are capable of gauging the full significance of a way of life that is now lost.[28]

In these circumstances it must have been the case that individual children from large families had very different experiences: the essentially human dimension of this struggle is all the more significant when we realize that, inevitably, the winners and losers in the rural economy's capitalist recomposition were brother and brother, sister and sister.[29] Demographic growth added a profoundly decisive twist to the proletarianization of the losers but it did not, in and of itself, set these events in train. The transformation of village social structures occurred within a national framework and was in a very real sense conditioned by forces outside local control. Just as the local history of village communities displayed enormous variation, so too would the history of peasant families during the transition from feudalism to agrarian capitalism. One cannot simply trace out currents and streams without being cognizant of backwaters and eddies in which the flow was slower and sometimes even reversed.

The people caught up in this historical rip-tide struggled desperately to retain their hold on the land. Enclosures were frequently pulled down, food riots were common, sectional grievances against political centralization sparked rebellions, and nostalgia for "neighbourliness" spoke volumes about the breakdown of communal solidarity and the commercialization of inter-personal relationships. For all intents and purposes, the ideology of the dispossessed was a sentimental yearning for the world they were losing. Their demands were framed by the moral economy of patriarchalism and it is interesting to note that the emigrants to New England quite consciously set up communities in which moral sentiments and social solidarities were given pride of place. In fleeing across the Atlantic many were decisively rejecting their society's commercialized social relations just as much as its religious apostacy. But whether they stayed in England and slid down the social scale or ventured to try their luck in the New World, the force of authority ran against them.

Early modern English history was violent and bloody; English justice was frequently vindictive and almost always concerned with the material rights of property at the expense of the natural rights of people. The Tudors' amazing success in de-militarizing English society riveted aristocratic attention on the pursuit of status and position – an expensive activity in any society. When the upper classes lost their ability and even their resolve to fight they became a new breed of men: courtiers. In the "new monarchies" of Henry VIII, Elizabeth and the first two Stuarts, it became increasingly important to preen like a peacock in full sight of the monarch. To pay for social climbing, courtliness and other forms of non-violent aggression, money was squeezed out of tenants, particularly from the 1590s when rent-rolls first caught up with and then surpassed the rising cost of living. The disintegration of feudal tenures demanding military obligations created a vacuum in the relationship between lord and tenant; the cash-nexus filled it. From the last years of Henry VIII to the first years of the American Revolution, from the 1540s to the 1770s, landowners enjoyed a vast profit inflation in which wages rose three and a half times, whereas rental values increased twenty-fold.[30] Successful tenants, like the remora fish which swim alongside sharks, also enjoyed the gains registered by their landlords. The massive redistribution of income towards those with capital – whether working or rental – was achieved at the expense of social structural reorganization and the incipient proletarianization of a huge portion of the lesser tenants and cottagers.

Rural capitalism: the first phase

The complexion of the landscape changed as the smaller peasants were expropriated and the common fields were enclosed. The English countryside began to assume its distinctly modern colouration of individually operated farms, with separate fields, under private management. Some locales held out, although the course of events and, particularly after the 1650s, the weight of the political authorities were on the side of the encloser and engrosser.[31] Common lands – heaths, woodlands, meadows and fens – were reclaimed from their natural state and incorporated into the national stock of farmland. The reorganization of field systems was at the heart of the agricultural revolution of this period; its main consideration was commercial gain, not popular usage. Arable systems were themselves being transformed as convertible husbandry superseded the traditional three-field rotation that had been geared to subsistence farming and was maintained by the persistent undercapitalization of farmers. The new techniques were predicated on private enterprise, commercial cropping and large inputs of labour and capital. Nitrogen-fixing legumes and vast increases in the animal population contributed to the fertility of the soil and consequent increases in yield. East Worcestershire after 1540 provides a model of this process of comparative advantage. There, as J. A. Yelling has discovered, field systems and cropping patterns were completely reorganized as the light, sandy soils became the centre of convertible husbandry and arable farming, whereas the heavier clays were relegated to pasturage.[32]

Specialization and an agricultural redivision of labour led to a dramatic reordering of the local agrarian economies across the length and breadth of the country.

The more intensive use of the land in the seventeenth and eighteenth centuries did not bring the plough back to the sheep-walks. Men turned to the remaining open-fields of their villages, seeking to use them more economically; seeking to enclose them by agreement where they could; others turned to the still plentiful areas of forest, heath and fen. In general this new war against the natural landscape was conducted from old and existing bases, and (the Fens apart) there are not many records of new settlements being founded or deserted ones refounded. Although the total population c. 1750 was no greater than that of the early fourteenth century it was centred in fewer settlements. To add the villages of the fourteenth century on to the maps of the mid-eighteenth-century county cartographers is to see how far – in terms of the number of village units – the retreat of settlement has been carried, and how much of the ground won for grass by the mid-sixteenth century was never recaptured.[33]

One might also add that the fact that the eighteenth-century population was well-fed compared to its medieval ancestors further emphasizes the enormous improvements in agricultural productivity occurring in the early modern period. Furthermore, the eighteenth-century rural economy was able to produce a surplus to feed both an expanding urban sector and a mushrooming rural industrial population and it frequently had enough left over to export cereals overseas. This massive increase in grain production was accomplished, as the quotation from Beresford underscores, by farming a smaller area of land.

Successful entrepreneurs behaved in ways that were completely dissimilar to the traditional subsistence peasant; the huge inflationary spiral enabled them to reap enormous profits from the reorganization of agricultural production. A significant amount of this profit-taking was re-invested and provided the accumulations which underwrote the expansion of capitalist agriculture. In order to cope with the increased commercial activity a national transportation infrastructure developed so that local isolation was broken down. Roads and navigable rivers crisscrossed the land and by the first decades of the eighteenth century a truly national food market had been established. The triumph of capitalist agriculture in England meant that famine was expunged from the lives of the meanest and poorest a century or more before it was banished from the lives of their French counterparts.[34]

The first phase of capitalism in rural England did not, therefore, bring massive immiseration in its train although it is quite clear that if their bellies were more or less filled it was achieved at the expense of their independence and self-sufficiency. Evidence drawn from post-mortem inventories gives proof that the later seventeenth-century labourer probably lived at a higher level of material comfort than did the early sixteenth-century cottager or husbandman. It was, therefore, a hard bargain in which even the losers gained something palpable; but in relative terms the gains of the winners were enormously greater than the security of a "mess of pottage". Surely, the point of the social struggles of the early modern period was not just the redivision of the economic pie but also the reconfiguration of the rural economy. Indeed, the two factors were complementary aspects of the same process. A way of life, conveniently encapsulated within the paradigm of the *cottage economy*, became the subject of cost-accounting. The losers in this bargain were under no illusions regarding the "benefits" devolving upon them even if later historians have obfuscated the political struggle over their relative shares of material resources by employing a massive cost-benefit analysis to price their way of life in terms of bread alone.[35]

The "Tudor Revolution" and the village community

Members of the *cottage economy* seemed to work for wages only in order to supplement the production for use derived from their holdings. When their own resources proved inadequate they made themselves available for hire to furnish themselves with the difference; when they had reached their targeted income, they quit. This form of behaviour was integrally related to the "underdeveloped" character of the English economy and its "backwards bending supply curve of labour".[36] What seemed to particularly infuriate the governors, and none more so than the jumped-up village puritans, was any display of self-sufficiency or independence on the part of the "lower sort". The reason is, of course, clear: labour was coming to be regarded as a commodity in much the same way that villeins had been regarded as the lord's property. Any attempt to control its supply therefore signalled disrespect and disobedience which were contrary to the patriarchalism of the elite.

Yet, in a very real sense, the problem was not with the supply of labour but rather with its demand. The early modern rural economy was incompletely attuned to the rhythms of a sequential labour process; instead, most work was task-oriented and tended to be arhythmic, irregular and, of course, seasonally-specific. On a daily basis, "most work was not geared to a machine, [so that] men did not exert themselves overmuch but adapted their pace to the long day ahead".[37] The legal fiction had it that the hours of work were regulated by the statute of 1495 and that they remained virtually unchanged until the nineteenth century. This law required that work was to begin at five in the morning in the summer (and "the springing of the day" between mid-September and mid-March) with a couple of breaks allowed for meals (and a "siesta" "authorized between 15 May and 15 August") before the end of the day.[38] Of course, the work-week was supposed to start on Monday morning and last until Saturday night but probably a half of the time was lost for a variety of reasons: first, the wet English climate washed out many days' work; second, the demand for labour was irregular and its deployment was insufficient and poorly organized; and, third, there were numerous holidays sanctioned by the Church.[39]

Sixteenth-century reformers were bedevilled by the "leisure preference" of workers and the only effective remedy seemed to be the cruellest, most hard-hearted one: the discipline of hunger. Most members of the upper classes regarded this insubordinate independence as the root of all social evil. Writing in 1509–10, Edmund Dudley suggested that "idleness" was the "mother of all vice . . . and lineal grandame of poverty and misery, and the deadly enemy of this tree of common-wealth". In Thomas More's *Utopia* begging was to be forbidden. Work was to be a civil responsibility. The moral value placed on work by religious reformers of all stripes in the sixteenth century cannot be over-emphasized. Another Henrician social ideologue, Thomas Starkey, echoed a representative view of both reformers and humanists in claiming that poverty "is their own cause and negligence that they so beg".[40] Magistrates expected a pliant, deferential and, above all, stable labouring population; their fear of vagabondage inspired a criminal code whose "objective was not simply to inflict punishment on actual criminals but, rather, to criminalize the transient poor".[41]

Early modern ideologues blamed the victim for the social crime of unemployment. Of particular interest in this regard are the laws which focussed on the growing restlessness of labour and its increasingly "insubordinate" ways. People who were unable to find employment and who were without property were forced out on to the highways and byways of the kingdom. They were subjected to a "merciless cruelty" and a "severe and terrifying . . . labour and criminal code". Peter Linebaugh further notes that "The laws against vagabondage provide us with a Foucault-like index of the growing attack on the corporal person." The curtain between the landed stability of the peasant and the landless instability of the proletarian was thin and fragile; in this maelstrom of social reconfiguration it is a spurious rigour which fixes a man or woman in a social category solely by his or her occupational title at one moment in time.[42] Labour was becoming insubordinate precisely because it was being removed from the orbit of patriarchalism and household government. At the heart of this phenomenon one can see the contradiction between the moral economy of patriarchalism and the political economy of capitalism. It is a reflection of this tension that the legislation which responded to the emergence of a proletariat was most viciously transparent. Thus we see a 1547 Vagrancy Act which enslaved those who refused to sell their labour at the behest of the natural governing class. Noting that later laws governing apprenticeship and life in a house of correction were very much like slavery, C.S.L. Davies suggests that "it was the name that rankled, rather than the actual condition of slavery".[43] This short-lived, draconian attempt to impose law and order at the expense of social justice set the tone for the following years when "sturdy beggars" were routinely whipped, their bodies branded, their clothing badged, their cottages pulled down and their personal lives invigilated with a ferocious intensity. The new code of social discipline was legislated by the 1563 Statute of Artificers which provided local authorities with the discretionary power to control labour markets and fix wages and it was re-inforced by the 1589 Act which empowered these same men to pull down cottages without the appurtenance of four acres. In this legislation the powers of the state to criminalize behaviour and those of the landowning class to manipulate local economic life were united. Political power is not exercised in a "neutral" fashion. The "Tudor Revolution in government" reconstructed the politics of social administration, thereby providing the cornerstone for a social formation which enhanced the wealth and privilege of those at the apex of the social pyramid.

The emphasis placed on "idleness" led reformers and ideologues to castigate the popular culture of the villagers. Much of this "reformation of manners" took place under the rubric of religion but its patina of spirituality was a thinly disguised form of hegemony aimed at the control over men's and women's minds and bodies. Insofar as this moral warfare was conducted at the level of the village community, it pivoted on the cultural distancing and socio-economic differentiation among the erstwhile peasants. Family units in medieval England were stratified by wealth and property but, as we have seen, rural society tended to be egalitarian in the sense that villagers belonged to the same moral universe. It was quite possible for medieval peasant families to be economically differentiated yet similar in their cultural orientation and material culture. The solidarity of the village community was the primary characteristic of rural society in medieval England.[44] This is not to claim that life went smoothly and was not conflict-ridden but rather that there was a substantial basis for common action which, in the final analysis, very substantially outweighed internal squabbling. Rich and poor peasants, freemen and villeins were united in resisting feudal exactions; in the early modern village one finds this kind of collective action with decreasing frequency.

Unlike the medieval community of the vill, the early modern village was subjected to the centrifugal forces of economic polarization and moral distancing. Capitalist farming practices and puritan attempts at moral reformation caused frequent grievances which stirred cottagers and labourers to action in order to defend communal rights and to maintain the sociability of the village. Capitalist farmers were not infrequently members of the same lineal families as the other villagers whose lives they now sought to change. Here, then, is the nub of the difference: just like a civil war, early modern social change set families and neighbours against each other and at each others' throats. The combination of these two forces was a new process; it had far-reaching effects.

The Essex clergyman Ralph Josselin gives us a remarkable peek into the implications of this process in dividing his parishioners into three groupings: first, "our society"; second, "sleepy hearers"; and, third, "the families that seldom heare". We see here another continuum in which a broad middle ground was occupied by people for whom the processes of stratification and differentiation could be forestalled, if not indefinitely avoided. Not yet proletarianized but hardly sympathetic to the moral reformation proposed by the village puritans, they assumed the protective colouration of indifference and simply got on with their lives. Their spiritual procrastination and behavioural backsliding infuriated the godly for whom nothing less than total commitment was satisfactory. Josselin's village of Earles Colne contained something like 1,000 inhabitants yet when the godly met for a communion service in 1651 they were able to muster thirty-four of the self-styled "better sort". Later, in the early 1660s, Church attendance rarely surpassed 10 per cent of the community.[45] In a neighbouring Essex village, Terling, the elite formed a tight congeries bound together by their wealth, social status, local political power and godliness.[46]

The protracted character of the transition

The sixteenth and seventeenth centuries, then, produced an uneasy accommodation between the "better sort" and the "ruder sort". It was not their preferred solution; in fact, it was the best they could achieve.[47] The first stages of the transitional period were thus characterized by the sub-atomic welter of conflicting, often contradictory, individual experiences. It is salutary to recognize the uneven, protracted nature of the transition from the independence of the cottager to the dependence of the proletarian. During the early modern period many people were caught between these two polarities so that their historical "moment" had the flavour of a prolonged period of suspended animation during which time the issue's resolution was still in doubt.

Because we already know the final upshot there is a tendency to assume that it was inevitable; such a tendency is mistaken in that it condescendingly rides roughshod over what, from our vantage-point, seem to be "minor", hopeless struggles for a different form of social organization. While the study of history is not directly concerned with "what if" questions, one can readily appreciate that the persistence of the *cottage economy* in England might have had profound repercussions, as it did in France. At the very least, the whole character of English political culture based on deference and aristocratic lese-majesty would have developed in a quite different fashion.[48] It is in this regard that the enormous significance of the ideology of legal equality and "British liberty" were important in cementing the political culture of the eighteenth century. Of course, "British liberty" meant one thing to the capitalist and quite another to the plebeian cottager.[49] The point is that this contradictory interpretation of "British liberty" was never generalized and only made sporadic and ineffective appearances in the countryside, where the bulk of the population still lived. Without their mobilization, political revolutionary movements were stillborn.

The kaleidoscope of experience was thus attuned to the specificity of time and place, the variability of demographic factors and family structures, and the imperatives of social formation and economic function.

History cannot be compared to a tunnel through which an express races until it brings its freight of passengers out into sunlit plains. Or, if it can be, then generation upon generation of passengers are born, live in the dark, and die while the train is still within the tunnel. An historian must surely be more interested than the teleologists allow him to be in the quality of life, the sufferings and satisfactions, of those who live and die in unredeemed time.[50]

Popular preference for the independence of the *cottage economy* was a persistent characteristic so that "To the extent that lifetime moves into the proletariat comprised the dominant process, we might expect a good deal of proletarian action to consist of efforts to retain or recapture individual control over the means of production."[51] It is in this sense that the agricultural proletariat c. 1700 was "Janus-faced": looking backwards to its roots in the *cottage economy* and looking forwards to its dependence on wage-labour.

The first half of the early modern period stretched the integuments of peasant society; the economic and demographic developments of the later eighteenth and early nineteenth centuries snapped them. During the century after about 1660 the social structure's respiration system was pausing to catch its breath before the final, withering onslaught on the *cottage economy* and its adherents. Between two bouts of frenetic activity, the first of which separated the vast mass from their property in land and the second of which ultimately disinherited them from their property in common rights, there was a period of social recomposition. During this intervening period the religious, moral and legal lineaments of the rural complexion were reconfigured. Although it did not occur overnight, the patriarchal politics of everyday life were being transmuted into class struggle.

Social distancing

The implications of social differentiation in the countryside were realized as the wealthier classes – gentry and yeoman alike – segregated themselves from the plebeians by erecting walls around their estates and parks. After 1750, farmers began to mimic their betters and to jettison the boarding-in servant in favour of wage-labourers whose rudeness could be kept out of sight from an increasingly polite society. Household government and personal supervision were being abandoned and, like a giant centrifuge, the dominant cultural forces created a huge gap between the classes and the masses. Family prayer and catechism, the centrepieces of the moral economy of patriarchalism, seem to have become a more exclusive, private practice around 1700.[52] Housing arrangements began to reflect demands for domestic privacy and social segregation on the part of the rural upper classes. Lawrence Stone has described the ways that country houses were rebuilt to accommodate the newly realized affective unit and so make its family matters private; M. W. Barley has found similar evidence for the gentlemen-farmers whose farmhouses separated family-space from servant-space.[53] In contrast to its predecessors, the rural elite of the eighteenth century began to adopt a studied style of social hegemony based on the majesty of the law and the theatricality of its highly articulated political culture.[54] From the mid-century, in particular, class attitudes towards popular recreations hardened and the game-laws were enforced with increasing ferocity.[55]

The human dimension of political culture, so characteristic of patriarchalism, was only very slowly supplanted by the arm's-length legalisms of the market economy. Social distancing entailed ideological distancing as the moral vision of patriarchalism came to be regarded as being deficient on utilitarian grounds. In the later seventeenth century "the

burden of defending legislative interference shifted, and the proponents of economic regulation had to make good their case".[56] In this
way the economic differentiation and social stratification of the first
century of the early modern period began to be assimilated into the
fabric of life. Intra-village struggles which had arisen from the *ressentimente* of those who were left behind by the advancing commercialization of social ties had been expressed within a common intellectual
framework.[57] The rise of mechanical philosophy and the laws of probability, preceding the Enlightenment, was very much a class-specific
phenomenon which left the lower orders behind. They retained the
older forms of common belief in magic, mystery and authority. Literacy
and rationality were only incompletely assimilated into their modes of
thought.[58] Social solidarity thus gave way to the intellectual and moral
distancing which came to characterize country life in Georgian
England.

The Old Poor Law: sturdy beggars and impotent beggars

At the heart of this new regime of social discipline stands the Poor Law
with its emphasis on the local control of labour markets. In the pithy
words of one contemporary, social welfare was meant to provide "work
for those that will Labour, Punishment for those that will not, and Bread
for those that cannot".[59] The solution was *optimum* in the sense that it
balanced the economic needs of agrarian capitalism with the ideological
requirements of the village patriarchs. In theory, the poor would be
invigilated by the local members of the upper classes and their welfare
entitlement would become a matter of magisterial discretion. Such a
system, it was hoped, would inure the lower orders to their station,
inculcate deference and punish transgressors and their families. Resistance was driven underground in an "Atlantic Diaspora" of the "active
part of the English proletariat".[60]

In the age of mercantilism the unwelcome hordes of masterless men at the
beginning of the century appeared to the most concerned of their betters
seventy years later as a pool of badly managed labor. What made the poor a
national issue in Restoration England was their tenuous position. They had
been expelled from a traditional order and as yet were only conditionally and
occasionally needed in the new economic structure growing up outside the
old.[61]

The preferred management solution was the creation of workhouses
which could "Manure and Improve the first Sprouts as they come into the
world" while also "reducing the wages of servants, labourers and
workmen of all sorts".[62] Labour was to be disciplined and regulated

through the administration of social policy directives rather than the personal intervention of local patriarchs. Such distancing demanded bureaucratic organization and it is not surprising that we find a series of initiatives on the part of "societies for the reformation of manners" dating from this period. The age of lobbying for sectional interests, rather than ordained prescription, was dawning.

The workhouses and special interest lobbies are important for what they tell us about management solutions to the problem of poverty in the Restoration and early eighteenth century; they are a less reliable guide to contemporary practice, particularly in the rural areas.[63] The workhouse itself was a permeable institution which was only used in times of extreme depression or cyclical unemployment by able-bodied males. E. M. Hampson's study of inmates in eighteenth-century Cambridgeshire workhouses did not turn up the hordes of masterless men who haunted the ideological nightmares of the mercantilists; rather, she found the old, the infirm and the helpless among whom one must number the substantial numbers of deserted women with their dependent children.[64] In her classic account on the subject Dorothy Marshall wrote that "as a rule, the workhouse was detested by the Poor, and people who before had asked for relief almost as their right, when a workhouse was built, preferred to manage anyhow rather than enter it if they could possibly make a living outside".[65] Conditions in the workhouses shocked contemporaries.

The I Edw. 6 [the 1547 Act which imposed slavery for vagabonds] wears indeed a more ferocious air, but it is not more barbarous and oppressive to the poor than this statute, which empowers the overseer to cram them into a narrow, nasty workhouse, and to contract with any person to lodge, keep, and maintain them. The fund of such House is not sufficient to redeem them from their filthy rags; nor the capacity of it to furnish them with convenient, decent, and distinct apartments; but the young, the old, the virtuous, the profligate, the sick, the healthy, the clean, the unclean, huddled together and inhaling a stagnant and putrid air, deplore their miserable existence; which receives its utmost aggravation from their immediate servitude to the Contractor, some low born, selfish, surly ruffian, from whose sordid tyranny there is no appeal, no redress, until the unhappy sufferers repose in the grave.[66]

Another pamphleteer claimed that "A short life with less Pain were to be preferred to this pining Death with Parish Allowance."[67] Mercantilists' attempts to set the able-bodied poor to work were abject failures so that "The chief virtue which the workhouses possessed in the eyes of eighteenth century administrators arose from their aid in reducing the [welfare] rates, by acting as a deterrent to people who would otherwise have asked for relief, the qualification for which was not so much absolute destitution as a very considerable degree of poverty."[68]

Servants-in-husbandry

The other force counteracting the Restoration theorists' demands for setting the poor on work came from the changing organization of the agrarian economy. As Ann Kussmaul has shown, servants-in-husbandry became more important in the 1660–1760 period than either before or afterwards.[69] Kussmaul identifies the period's slow rates of population growth in general, and the relatively "sticky" supply of wage-labour in particular, as the central factors in her equation. Labour in this intermediate period became relatively scarce and its price rose so that proletarians could take "advantage of their position by 'consuming' more leisure" with the result that "farmers [were] increasingly unable to rely upon the continuous offer of labour from day-labourers. The annual contracts of farm servants took the decision to enjoy more leisure out of the workers' hands, and guaranteed a continuous supply of labour during the contractual year." In this regard, it is interesting to note the contemporaneity between the exertion of the "leisure preference" among workers – many of whom were still members of the *cottage economy* – in the later seventeenth century and the rising cries against it on the part of mercantilist social theorists who wanted to find new methods of extracting labour power from its (relatively) unwilling owners. Soft cereal prices during this century provided farmers with an incentive to invest more heavily in animals and so required them to have a reliable supply of labour because "Their valuable investments in draught animals, fat and breeding stock, sheep and dairy herds needed constant attention."[70] In response to the low wheat prices which obtained for a century after 1660, even the cereal farmers of the south and east avoided disaster by incorporating some high-price livestock into their low-profit arable farms, thereby retaining significant numbers of servants-in-husbandry who would be quickly discarded when the terms of trade turned against this strategy and favoured cereal mono-culture. As long as population growth rates were sluggish and wheat prices low, a switchover from servants-in-husbandry (male and female) to male proletarians did not occur. But after 1760 all the evidence points towards rising levels of population, especially among the food-consuming industrial and commercial groups in the urban and quasi-urban areas, as well as declining wages for rural labourers alongside the intensification of arable farming in the south and east. It is within this framework that Kussmaul's model of agricultural organization explains the extinction of servants-in-husbandry in the arable half of the country after about 1760.[71]

Keith Snell's innovative work with settlement examinations enables us to go further in discussing the decline of service. In particular he has discovered that a very large number of these servants-in-husbandry before about 1760 were women. He suggests that "gender differences appear to have been almost a matter of indifference to employers". In addition he finds abundant supportive evidence that while these women seem to have specialized in dairy farming nevertheless "their work extended to reaping, loading and spreading dung, ploughing, threshing, thatching, following the harrow, sheep shearing, and even working as shepherdesses". Snell suggests that women were excluded from the agricultural labour force when large-scale capitalist farmers switched to cereal mono-culture in the boom years of the second half of the eighteenth century. Relying on the research of E. J. T. Collins and M. Roberts into the changing agricultural technology, he advances an explanation for the gender-specific unemployment among servants-in-husbandry in the cereal belt in contrast to the pastoral districts of the north and west. When the gravy train of profit was running full steam ahead, tenant farmers desired "to quicken the harvest and so catch the pre-harvest peak of prices". Women never used the heavier scythe – they remained with the lighter sickle – and when the terms of trade made it imperative to harvest quickly in order to maximize profits women were left with an obsolete technology and had to look for other work. In the event, as we shall see, the upshot was the creation of a huge, structurally underemployed *male* agricultural proletariat in those regions which specialized in cereal production. The small farmer employed servants-in-husbandry according to the demands of his own family-cycle. The persistence of the **cottage economy** was integrally related to its system of life-cycle proletarianization in which "lifetime moves" into and out of the proletariat were possible – and, indeed, likely – for people whose occupational title was connected to their age and marital status. Such "life-cycle proletarians" moved out of the proletariat when they were old enough to have accumulated stock and capital for the establishment of a family farm – to become "cottagers" in their own right. The forces which combined to slow down population growth in the century before 1760 – urbanization and colonial migration – intruded themselves in the lives of the most humble of the cottaging population because as long as agriculture was "depressed" (i.e. relatively unprofitable for capitalists) the peasantry held on to its way of life. As long as it did so "prospects of upward social mobility ... coupled with savings from farm service ... acted to delay marriage". The asymptotic state of the agricultural economy in the century after 1660 meant that the relentless proletarianization of the peasantry was stalled – perhaps even reversed in some areas.[72]

The changing character of patriarchalism

Capitalism is about capital accumulation; when capitalists see no advantage in investing in the tried-and-true ways then they deploy their money in other ways. In the hard times after 1660, when the market for agricultural products was flat, they invested in such objects of conspicuous consumption as colonialism, culture and country houses. At this time there was little sense in throwing good money after bad in the hopes of making profits from a buyer's market. The huffing-and-puffing of social ideologues thus appears to have had a marginal impact upon contemporary material conditions. It would therefore seem that their importance lies not so much in what they tell us about the organization of daily life as in the insights they give into the changing character of patriarchalism. In this sense, the passing of the household phase of patriarchal discipline pivoted on the distancing between master and servant. Much of the ideological baggage which invested everyday life with its social meaning relied upon metaphors of reciprocity which were increasingly devoid of meaningful content. Characteristically, the law mystified the transformation of patriarchy into contract by its insistence on quasi-feudal obligations on the part of employees while, at the same time, freeing the hands of employers. Social hegemony was slowly transmuted from an all-encompassing way of life to a strategy of control. The 1601 Poor Law had been designed to relieve *life-cycle* poverty, not provide work for the able-bodied. It is indicative of the deepening crisis of the *cottage economy* that, by the later seventeenth century, the Elizabethan distinction between the deserving and undeserving poor was revised to take into account the *life-long* poverty of the emergent proletariat. When Gregory King discussed his contemporaries he divided them into two groups: those who were productive and so increased the wealth of the realm, and those who were in receipt of welfare and so decreased its stock of wealth.

One of the main reasons why the number of able-bodied poor had risen so dramatically was that their entitlement to rights of common were under attack. As a provincial journalist wrote to his contemporaries in 1726,

there are a sort of Stewards in the World ... that cannot endure to see a little House or a little Farm, ... and have therefore of late Years perswaded their Lords and masters, that little Houses and little takings are every where detrimental to great Estates; and that there is more Charge and Trouble in supporting Cottages than they are worth; that they are impolitick harbours for poor People, and do even tempt them from other Parishes, to become troublesome, if not chargeable, to theirs: and in short, that it is therefore adviseable for his Grace, his Lordship, or his

Worship, utterly to abandon such Cottages, and let them fall; especially considering that thereby the Right of Common, belonging to such Cottages, (in some Places
not inconsiderable) will be sunk to the benefit of larger Takings.[73]

Here, we are told in no uncertain terms just what the transformation from
the Tudors' concern for "habitation" to the Hanoverians' desire for
"improvement" meant for those who were largely powerless.[74]

Enclosure and the collapse of the *cottage economy*

Enclosure by agreement in the period 1600–1750 appears to have doubled
the amount of land which was privatized. W. G. Hoskins writes:

We hear more in contemporary sources about the iniquities of the Tudor enclosers,
but it is more likely that there are more miles of seventeenth-century hedges in the
Midlands than sixteenth. It may be surprising to some who look upon the Midland
landscape as the undoubted product of the [post-1760] parliamentary enclosure
movement to know that even in Northamptonshire one half of the county had been
enclosed and transformed to a modern landscape before the first private enclosure
act; and in the adjacent county of Leicestershire three in every five fields had been
created before the parliamentary period. The enclosure of open fields into smaller
fields that form our familiar world today, and the reclamation of the wild lands,
had been going on intermittently and at a varying pace in every century. But after
the Restoration the government ceased to interfere with the enclosure of open field
by private landlords, and the pace of change quickened. Up to about 1730 most of
this enclosure was carried through by private agreements between the owners of
the land in question.[75]

Insofar as this land was taken out of the open fields and consolidated into
large farms in place of numerous smaller ones, such property, and its
attendant use-rights, were made permanently inaccessible to the poorer
members of the community. With the loss of common rights, the so-called
"patrimony of the poor", an important dimension of household self-
sufficiency, was lost forever.[76] In substituting exclusive legal title for
shared use-rights, Georgian magistrates, in their reverence for private
property, criminalized attempts to retain this inheritance.[77] "The rights
and claims of the poor, if inquired into at all, received ... perfunctory
compensation, smeared over with condescension and poisoned with
charity. Very often they were simply redefined as crimes: poaching,
wood-theft, trespass."[78]

The post-Restoration rationale for enclosure was to increase the efficiency of farms and there seems to be ample evidence to support the claims
made by its advocates.[79] Yet, in a most important way, this kind of
improvement is beside the point because, in Daniel Defoe's words, "of the
popular claim in England; which we call right of commonage, which the

poor take to be as much their property, as a rich man's land is his own".[80] In the terms of Georgian social commentary, one man's virtue was another's vice. Such an equation was a bitter pill for the losers to swallow. The expropriation of their use-rights meant that dependence on wages was heightened and their independence was commensurately diminished. The extinction of common use-rights pauperized the members of the *cottage economy*, who prized self-reliance, thrift and independnce, by making it impossible to provide "for one's own needs by one's own efforts, without the mediation of wage-employment".[81] Having to forsake their "social patrimony" meant that cottagers were proletarianized; they were also excluded from the material benefits which their labour was making possible and being downgraded into paupers, dependent upon charity and welfare to bridge the gap between wages and subsistence.[82]

The collapse of the *cottage economy* drew a fault-line through most rural communities. This social earthquake took place in a piecemeal fashion; it was a process, not an event. Modest population growth and relatively low food prices during the century before 1760 had put off the day of reckoning. The pauperizing implications of agricultural capitalism became painfully obvious in the later eighteenth century when increasing population levels, rising food prices, and the final stage of parliamentary enclosure combined to depress the real wages of agricultural labourers and inflate the parochial welfare rolls to levels which alarmed social commentators.

The agricultural proletariat and the political economy of capitalism

It was readily apparent that without their patrimony of common rights with which to robe themselves, cottagers were nakedly exposed to full-scale proletarianization. John Caird wrote that in many areas of the early Victorian countryside there was "a redundance of labour which oppresses property and depreciates wages".[83] Caird's point regarding the overabundance of labour and its lack of leverage in the marketplace is affirmed in Sidney Pollard's recent survey of labour conditions: "It was only when labour found its feet, in the second half of the nineteenth century, that a true labour market – one in which the supplier had at least a semblance of power – began slowly to emerge."[84] As we shall see, the way in which labour "found its feet" in the rural world was by leaving it behind. But for the generations living and dying in that late Georgian tunnel, the sunlit plains were a long way off. For them, the political economy of production in the cereal belt interacted with their own reproductive arrangements to produce a harrowing experience of structural unemployment, low wages and stultifying demands for deference. A kind of *demographic involution* existed in which the employing class could have it both ways – they profited from the capitalization of economic relationships and yet they still maintained a patina of patriarchal domination; the proletariat thus got the short end of two sticks. It is impossible to understand the demand for labour without paying heed to the reorganization of production in the cereal boom after 1760; equally, it is impossible to understand the supply of labour apart from the devolutionary reproductive regime created by the impact of patriarchal controls upon family formation strategies. We might telescope our discussion of this process by using the 1851 census data describing farm sizes and employer : employee ratios printed in the 1852–3 *Parliamentary Papers* to focus upon its implications, preparatory to discussing its social evolution. Highlighting the main contours of the social formation in the second decade of Victoria's reign should give an essential perspective within which to consider pauperization and proletarianization in the countryside.

The historiographical discussion of the statistical dimension of this "redundance of labour" is obscured by a somewhat simplistic method of counting. J. H. Clapham, in the classic statement of this position, merely divided the number of landless labourers by the number of occupiers listed in the 1831 census returns and declared that because the proportion was 2.5:1 the news of the rural proletariat's birth had been premature.[85] Yet one would hardly have expected to discover a single descriptive statistic with which to measure the categorical "existence" or "non-existence" of such a class across the length and breadth of a country whose agrarian history was heavily conditioned by the specificity of geographical context. The agricultural statistics derived from Victorian census enumerations need to be refined so as to acknowledge the basic divisions between highlands and lowlands, wood-pasture and arable, if not the exceptional diversity of local, mini-ecologies, before proceeding to compare farmers with labourers.

The summary tables derived from the 1851 census enumeration contain an enormous wealth of statistical information. Because of its great detail and attention to important categories, this census is more useful than its predecessors. Thus, we learn not only about the simple totals of farmers and labourers but about their working relationship to each other. In itself, this is a most valuable resource which immediately allows us to push the limits of our analysis much further than Clapham has done. In 1851 there were 223,318 men over twenty years of age classified as farmers and 724,839 who were agricultural labourers living-out. There were 183,839 labourers under twenty who lived-out and 189,116 living-in servants-in-husbandry.[86] One might first discuss these statistics by county, or groups of counties, as the Victorians who provided us with this record have done. In so doing we find that regional differences had a profound impact on the social structure. Thus, Yorkshire had 27,445 farmers and 57,283 male agricultural labourers over twenty; the employer:employee ratio was only a fraction over 1:2. In this large northern county one in five adult male labourers was a living-in, servant-in-husbandry. In the South Midlands (comprising the eight small counties of Bedfordshire, Buckinghamshire, Cambridgeshire, Hertfordshire, Huntingdonshire, Middlesex (extra-metropolitan), Northamptonshire and Oxfordshire) the employer:employee ratio was 1:7 (14,903:112,232) and just one in thirty adult male labourers was a living-in, servant-in-husbandry. The variability within England was therefore enormous and, indeed, even these rough measurements underestimate it because they do not account for women and young men who made up the prime servant groups. In the 1841 census enumeration, for example, women comprised 2.9 per cent of the labour force in the south and east – less than a third of the comparable proportion in the western counties. In Bedfordshire, women comprised only 0.6 per cent of the labour force in 1841. Most of these women were probably servants-in-husbandry – a vestigial category in the cereal belt but a vital one in the pastoral regions.[87]

Not only was there enormous regional variation but, hardly surprisingly, the landed proprietors were immensely differentiated in terms of the size of their holdings and the number of labourers they employed. This relationship was quite simple: the more land one held, *ceteris paribus*, the more labourers one would employ to work it. The 91,698 occupiers who employed no labour farmed a (median) average of 21.8 acres; the 7,622 farmers employing five labourers worked about 123 acres apiece; 8,632 farmers, with 241.8 acres, had between ten and fourteen employees; 850 employers, with an average of 568.4 acres, required twenty-five to twenty-nine workers; and the 132 men who employed fifty to fifty-four adult males had farms of 874 statute acres. It is obvious, therefore, that to refine our statistical picture further we need to discard from consideration those occupiers who held land but employed no labour. Elsewhere in the summary tables drawn up from the 1851 census we are presented with the information to do just this.[88] Across the countryside as a whole 40.7 per cent of all occupiers employed no labour (91,698:225,318); in Yorkshire 53.8 per cent of farmers were self-sufficient (15,506:28,825) while in Bedfordshire 11.1 per cent (161:1,449) worked the land without hired help.[89] Further more, it is clear from these tabulations that the concentration of land in large farms in the southern and eastern counties was accompanied by the employment of wage-labour on a very substantial scale. Referring again to Yorkshire and Bedfordshire makes the point. While the national figure for the (median) average size of agricultural labourers' gangs on the farms of men who employed wage-labour was 9.3, in Yorkshire it was 3.6 while in Bedfordshire it was 22.8. This statistic means that if we turn the usual proposition on its head and look at the phenomenon of wage-labouring in the countryside from the perspective of the proletarians, *not the farmers*, we get a radically different picture from Clapham's. For the majority of early Victorian agricultural labourers work was carried out in groups, not in the familiar setting of family farming.

The countryside was internally differentiated into three broad types of social formations. First, in a large section of the country wage-labouring was a highly organized activity which men undertook in gangs. This is not to say that all wage-labourers in the southern and eastern regions were so employed but it is clear that this form of production was predominant and defined the character of the rural scene across the length and breadth of the country's granary. Second, there was another large area of the country in which the family-farming economy, still employing servants-in-husbandry, persisted. Here, mostly in the north and west, farming was an extensive and·not an intensive activity. In these regions one finds that farming labour was organized in a way which was not markedly different from that of the Tudors and Stuarts. Third, there were other areas which occupied an intermediate position between these two poles and in which local conditions might have distinguished one village from its neighbour. Dennis R. Mills' work on landownership and rural population in Leicestershire makes it plain that local society was enormously variegated even within this one county located in the middle of England.[90] One should not get too carried away by the crazy-quilt of local mini-ecologies at the expense of seeing the more significant pattern. The historical novelty in the period after about 1760 was the increasing importance of the really large farm with its score of workers. To put the point in another parlance, the large farms with several hundred acres and a score of adult male wage-labourers was the leading-edge in this sector. The "redundance of labour" was of critical importance in maintaining traditional techniques at the expense of, first, "higher working capacity hand tools", and second, mechanization itself. "The years 1835–80 and particularly 1850–80 constitued the 'majority adoption' phase of the hand-tool revolution, in which small tools were almost everywhere superseded ... the scythe and the heavy hook gained ground much faster than the reaping machine between 1850 and 1880."[91] Moreover, the social obligation to employ agricultural proletarians played a crucial role in the cost-benefit equation of capitalist farmers when they considered the organization of production and their strategies for investment in their enterprises. One contemporary noted that farmers could not employ just a few labourers and feed them well; they had to maintain all in the parish, either in the field or in the workhouse.[92] Thus, in contradistinction to the position taken by Clapham, it seems clear that not only was there a most substantial agricultural proletariat but also that its very size had profound implications which impinged upon the mainsprings of the rural economy.

The political economy of agricultural proletarianization

The problem which remains to be addressed regarding this proletarian population is concerned with the socio-political implications of its massing in certain sections of the country. How and why did this mushrooming population emerge?

Industrialization and urbanization were predicated upon the growth of a surplus-producing agricultural sector. This is precisely what happened between 1750 and 1880 when agricultural output rose almost as fast as population. Even in the third quarter of the nineteenth century about four-fifths of the food consumed by an urbanized population was still home-grown.[93] The specialization of function inherent in the national division of agricultural labour meant that cereal production became the primary form of farming in a large part of southern and eastern England. In order to achieve rising production in conditions of relative technological backwardness there was a "bias ... towards products and processes needing large inputs of manual labour".[94] In particular, the harvest was both an unpredictable imperative as well as a bottleneck demanding a maximum supply of labour for a short period of time. Harvest labour demand fluctuated wildly. A large and extremely elastic supply of labour was therefore essential. If there was a simultaneity of crop-ripening over a wide area then inter-regional flows of labour would be seriously disrupted and could not cope with the convergence of a series of discrete local labour markets usually phased their demand for the harvesters.[95] Two complementary solutions were adopted by farmers to guard themselves against the dangers inherent in this labour-supply bottleneck: first, the whole society was mobilized for a short period of time by the payment of wages high enough to draw workers away from other pursuits, even from overseas; and, second, a substantial pool of indigenous labour was kept on hand so as to provide a base-line, over and above which seasonal workers could be recruited to meet the exceptional, marginal-demand schedule for harvest labour. There is every indication in the first phase of industrialization, through the 1840s, that urban and industrial labour still ebbed and flowed to the seasonal rhythms of the harvest, albeit in an attenuated fashion. In addition, the recruitment of men and women from Ireland, Scotland and the pastoral upland regions provided crucial seasonal additions to the resident proletariat in the granary of southern and eastern England.[96] In fact, we see here a kind of vicious circle leading to a form of **technical involution** in the agricultural sphere: because labour was inefficient, lots of it was needed; but because a large supply of labour was retained there was little economic or social incentive to engage in costly forms of technical upgrading. Therefore, labour remained underutilized and the harvesting technology was hardly upgraded before the middle of the nineteenth century. The impetus to transform the harvest technology came from outside this vicious circle when the usual supplies of seasonal labour began to dry up in the mid-nineteenth century.[97] For the hundred years before this time, however, there had been strong material incentives for the capitalist farmers of southern and eastern England to manipulate their local labour markets in order to retain a pool of largely *under-employed* adult male labourers (and *unemployed* women) whose presence was the *sine qua non* of cereal farming. For these reasons, enormous groups of predominantly male agricultural proletarians were enumerated by the early Victorians in counties like Bedfordshire.

Agricultural proletarianization: the final phase

From the middle years of the eighteenth century a series of forces interacted to bring about the final stage of differentiation, both between regions and within regions. No one factor can be given primacy; rather, it would seem that the critical mass was attained by something akin to spontaneous combustion. The causal arrows flowed in both directions: first, population growth drove up the price of food and drove down the cost of labour making it attractive for capitalist farmers to shed servants-in-husbandry in favour of labourers while, in the southern and eastern regions, concentrating their attention on the super-profits to be made in the grain market; and, second, the gradual expansion of a **proto-industrial** sector increased the numbers of people who married earlier, a process which was facilitated by the *relatively high* wages of industrial labour and the *relatively low* wages of agricultural labour, and so promoted the growth of a food-consuming population. In response to these new opportunities farm sizes increased and the employment of wage-labour became the norm. In grain-producing counties like Bedfordshire the preponderance of large units was emphatic: there, farms of over 100 acres accounted for 90.3 per cent of the land enumerated in the 1851 census and the really big farms of more than 300 acres occupied 42.8 per cent. In the country as a whole the proportion of the land occupied by large farms was still noteworthy but rather less than in Bedfordshire: those with more than 100 acres occupied 78 per cent while farms of over 300 acres accounted for just over a third of the whole. It should be noted that these national figures include counties like Bedfordshire, thereby raising the score and giving the misleading impression that large farms were everywhere dominant. In fact, in pastoral areas dominated by family enterprises the average farm was smaller and the likelihood of retaining servants-in-husbandry contributed to the survival of near-peasant conditions. There were also mini-regions, specializing in dairying, market gardening or fruit farming, which also retained a strong representation of smaller production units and frequently relied on family labour, aided by servants-in-husbandry.[98] The important point to be gathered from the foregoing discussion is not that there was a single type of farming which dominated the country as a whole but that, as a result of the national division of agricultural labour, the grain-producing areas fed most of the English population its daily bread. It was in these regions that agricultural capitalism meant the emergence of large farms employing wage-labour. In other, more labour-intensive forms of husbandry, the older tradition of family farming and servants-in-husbandry persisted well into the nineteenth century.

The final piece in the re-construction of the agricultural sector was provided by the parliamentary enclosure movement, 1760–1830, which involved nearly 3,000 parishes and

in the great majority . . . it was a complete transformation, from the immemorial landscape of the open fields, with their complex pattern of narrow strips, their winding green balks or cart-roads, their headlands and grassy footpaths, into the modern chequer-board pattern of small, squarish fields, enclosed by hedgerows of hawthorn, with new roads running more or less straight and wide across the parish in all directions.[99]

When added to the old-enclosed counties of Norfolk, Suffolk, Essex, Kent and Sussex, extensive parliamentary enclosures completed the proletarianization of farming in the English bread-basket. For the members of the *cottage economy* these private bills passed by a Parliament which was largely composed of landlords were as disastrous as the earlier enclosures by agreement had been – they lost their use-rights to the land and saw their preferred way of life disappear. The ideology of the day sanctioned enclosure in terms of the "rationality" and "efficiency" it would engender. This was a naked demand to end the cottager's independence and subordinate him to the dictates of agricultural capitalism. The attack on the *cottage economy* took away the villager's common rights and in losing them he lost his cow, an asset worth almost as much as his wages. Unable to supplement the family diet with home-grown milk meant that labouring children often had to do without valuable forms of protein and calcium in their growing years. Having lost the tenement garden meant that it was impossible for the *cottage economy* to survive in an attenuated form through a dependence on potatoes. The subsistence cottager was inevitably turned into a consumer of wheaten bread. Without the resources of the commons, the cottager had to purchase fuel to maintain a level of bodily warmth in the damp winter months. Is it any wonder that all commentators were appalled by the deterioration in the physical aspect of the labouring poor in the later Georgian period? Enclosure knocked the keystone from a way of life which then disintegrated.[100]

The Malthusian moment

Let us now turn to the social implications of agricultural proletarianization and, in particular, its concentration in certain sections of the country. In a very real sense, the social history of the agricultural proletariat between 1760 and 1850 is the history of the Old Poor Law. Unemployment became "structural"; that is to say, it was part-and-parcel of this system of production. The irrevocable disintegration of the *cottage economy* occurred in a political framework which gave the cottagers little chance of successful resistance yet they did not buckle under nor were they simply quiescent.[101] They struggled, but they lost hold over their way of life and were pauperized into the bargain. The welfare system was transmuted in order to bring it into line with the new reality of a proletarian labour force. Poor rates rose and so it is hardly surprising that alongside the cereal boom we find pauperization. Slowly but surely the very character of patriarchalism found itself in contradiction with the penny-pinching administration of the welfare system whose local overseers were caught between the *structurally induced* demands for assistance from the families of adult male wage-labourers and the indignant howls from local taxpayers.

This propertyless mass of agricultural proletarians had been created in order to provide the local pools of tied-labour without which the specialized cereal economy of the south and east could not have been developed. Meeting in 1795 at the Pelican Inn in Speenhamland, Berkshire, local magistrates devised a wage-subsidization scheme in response to the short-term problems engendered by rising grain prices and the local agricultural proletariat's demands for a "customary living wage". Essentially a stop-gap procedure, their solution neatly solved their problem of balancing the demands of farmers and labourers in a way that was blatantly prejudicial to the independence of the working class who were not only tied to their parish of settlement but also restricted in their ability to negotiate wages. In many ways the Speenhamland or "roundsman" system of welfare was an outgrowth of the older methods of local administration in which allowances in relief of wages were arranged in a discretionary manner by the local parochial officials. It emerged in a haphazard, situational fashion; it was not legislated in the provisions of any statute. As poor rates shot up during the cereal boom and the population explosion of the later eighteenth century, parochial officials used the Law of Settlement to prevent married labourers from becoming a charge on the local rates but if they were unable to do so then they seem to have conceded extra relief to their captive labourers, especially those with large families. The wage they paid to a married labourer was, thus, recognized to have been inadequate so that the social welfare system picked up the slack in a case-by-case manner.[102]

An emergency plan which developed in response to surplus labour, low wages and rising prices metamorphosed into a system of social reproduction in which the rationality, independence and self-control of the proletariat were devalued and, so Thomas Robert Malthus argued at the time, ultimately discarded. It was within this set of contradictions that Malthus addressed himself to the population question. Malthus saw the profits derived from the new mode of production but was appalled by its costs. Like so many who have priced the disintegration of the cottagers' way of life in a cost-benefit analysis, Malthus paid rather too much heed to the capitalists' benefits and hardly enough to the proletarians' costs. In so doing, he missed the obvious point that the capitalists' benefits *caused* the population problem by deforming the inherently homeostatic imperatives of the *cottage economy* and so destabilizing the demographic equilibrium which had hitherto existed.

The role of the simple-minded Malthusianism – the view that population growth, by itself, caused poverty – in bringing an end to the patriarchal organization of the village welfare system cannot be overemphasized. Nor, I think, can the influence of simple-minded Malthusianism be underestimated in considering the mean-spirited stinginess which characterized upper-class attitudes to the poor in Malthus' own lifetime. It was a result of this dyslexic view of social reality that the landowning class – for whom Malthus was so obviously a spokesman in his own time – blamed the poor for their poverty. In assessing the historical impact of the first edition of *An Essay on the Principle of Population* Gertrude Himmelfarb has written that Malthus

formulated the terms of discourse on the subject of poverty for half a century – and not only in respect to social policy (the debate over the poor laws, most notably), but in the very conception of the problem. It was Malthus who defined that problem, gave it a centrality it had not had before, made it dramatically, urgently, insistently problematic. Whatever difficulties there were in his theory, however faulty the logic or evidence, it gripped the imagination of contemporaries, of all ranks, classes, callings, and persuasions, as few other books have ever done.[103]

Malthus is hardly an heroic character, yet one cannot gainsay the impact of his insight into the relationship between the social organization of production and the private organization of reproduction. His importance in intellectual history lies in the singular fact that he was the one who put his finger on the linchpin of his contemporary social experience – without rapid population growth, sparked by earlier marriage and higher fertility, the expansion of the capitalist sector in agriculture would have been halting simply because the labour to harvest the production of larger and larger farms would not have been available. Without a steady supply of foodstuffs it is quite conceivable that the unleashing of the industrial Prometheus would have been restrained, urbanization would have been slowed down and the specialized division of labour – the creation of a tertiary sector serving agricultural and industrial producers – would have been constrained. In the historically contingent moment at which Malthus was writing, the homeostatic relationship between population and economy was metamorphosing into a dynamic one. Changes in production were creating the conditions within which strategies of reproduction were being reconsidered; population growth, in its turn, accelerated revolutionary changes in agriculture and industry by shifting the indices of supply and demand.

In his *Essay on the Principle of Population*, Malthus contended that

> The poor laws of England tend to depress the general condition of the poor . . . [because] a poor man may marry with little or no prospect of being able to support a family in independence. [For this reason,] If men are induced to marry from a prospect of parish provision, with little or no chance of maintaining their families in independence, they are not only unjustly tempted to bring unhappiness and dependence upon themselves and children, but they are tempted, without knowing it, to injure all in the same class with themselves.[104]

To the best of my knowledge, no one has ever suggested that when he wrote his famous *Essay* Malthus was aware of the more systematic applications of the allowance system that were being devised in the obscurity of the Pelican Inn in Speenhamland and adopted in a situational fashion by magistrates across the south and east. With remarkable prescience he pinpointed the pauperizing implications of the Old Poor Law's attitude to social welfare measures which were becoming generalized in a period of growing population *and* intensified cereal farming. In so doing, J. D. Chambers argues, Malthus "helped cement an alliance between vested interests and economic theory . . . [so that] the labourer was now separated in theory as well as in fact from all proprietary interest in the product of the soil which he tilled".[105] Malthus' explication of the struggle for survival inherent in the fertility of man prefigured social darwinism and offered, together with David Ricardo's law of diminishing returns, the intellectual basis of that kind of liberal economics which earned its nickname, the dismal science, from its pessimistic expectations.

In dispensing with Adam Smith's humanistic foundations, Malthus and Ricardo incorporated the lessons of Townsend's 1786 "Dissertation on the Poor Laws" in which the legendary goats and dogs on Robinson Crusoe's island of Juan Fernandez illustrated the axiom that "It is the quantity of food which regulates the number of the human species." Himmelfarb writes that "the 'historic' Malthus, the Malthus who had the largest historical impact in his own time and for generations afterward, was the Malthus of the first edition" yet it was a remark in the second edition – and quickly deleted thereafter from subsequent editions – which so aroused contemporaries. In it we can see both the clear influence of Townsend's deconstruction of the moral basis of economic analysis and the harbinger of social darwinism based on the iron laws of survival found in nature.

A man who is born into a world already possessed, if he cannot get subsistence from his parents on whom he has a just demand, and if the society do not want his labour, has no claim of right to the smallest portion of food, and, in fact, has no business to be where he is. At *nature's mighty feast* there is no vacant cover for him. She tells him to be gone, and will quickly execute her own orders, if he does not work upon the compassion of some of her guests. If these guests get up and make room for him, other intruders immediately appear demanding the same favour. The report of a provision for all that come, fills the hall with numerous claimants. The order and harmony of the feast is disturbed, the plenty that before reigned is changed into scarcity and the happiness of the guests is destroyed by the spectacle of misery and dependence in every part of the hall, and by the clamorous importunity of those, who are justly enraged at not finding the provision for which they had been taught to expect. The guests learn too late their error, in counteracting those strict orders to all intruders, issued by the great mistress of the feast, who, wishing that all her guests should have plenty, and knowing that she could not provide for unlimited numbers, humanely refused to admit fresh comers when her table was already full.[106]

This passage had an electric effect in transforming the paradigm within which the problem of poverty was to be understood at this time, the Malthusian moment.

The history of humans was thus a biological process albeit one which could, so Malthus repeatedly insisted, be controlled through the intervention of prudential rationality. Malthus makes a further point in his *Essay* which is supremely important in his criticism of the pauperizing implications of parish welfare: "The love of independence is a sentiment that surely none would wish to be erased from the breast of man, though the parish law of England, it must be confessed, is a system of all others the most calculated to gradually weaken this sentiment, and in the end eradicate it completely."[107] In contrast to the peasantry to whom Malthus ascribed a rational attitude to personal decision-making, the agricultural proletarians were being weaned from their birthright as Englishmen and losing their independence in domestic matters. He believed in providing education for the working class because it would instil in them that sense of moral restraint without which the prudential check could not operate. For Malthus, prudential behaviour was the rational expression of independence; the personal was political.

The Malthusian controversy thus brings the relationship between agrarian capitalism and family life into the spotlight. His powerful polemic makes us focus not only on the novelty of family formation strategies among the agricultural proletariat but also on their divorce from the earlier arrangements under which the peasantry lived. Most obviously, one can distinguish these two family systems by the simple fact that the peasantry owned land (or the rights to land) while the proletariat did not. This distinction had profound implications since families with land could and did bring a degree of control to bear on the personal lives of inheriting children which was fundamentally different from the interest which the parents of propertyless men and women could exercise. Thus, the process of proletarian family formation became an intensely personal affair between the partners as opposed to the peasantry's involvement in an orbit of social relations. In order to highlight the distinctions between these contrasting reproductive systems I will now propose a highly schematic dichotomy. On the one hand, the peasantry's decisions were usually their own because their property made them largely self-sufficient so that they were insulated from external pressures; whereas, on the other hand, the proletariat's intimate affairs not only were the object of concern for the local welfare officials but also were subjected to economic factors beyond their own control. Peasant marriages were social events concerned with the disposition of family property; proletarian marriages were private affairs, subject to external intervention. The exercise of prudence was internalized by the property imperatives of the peasant system whereas the exercise of prudence among proletarians was the object of social policy. From the Malthusian perspective, such social policies were successful if, and only if, proletarians exercised restraint in forming new families.

The contradiction between the thrust of social policy and the economic forces of pell-mell capitalist expansion of cereal farming in the century after 1750 unleashed those alarming powers of demographic reproduction which so frightened the magistrates who controlled the early modern system of social welfare that they brought it to an end. In its last years, the Old Poor Law became the target of those who misunderstood the contingent interaction between proletarianization and family formation in an age of nascent capitalism. The abandonment of the Old Poor Law radically transformed the social framework within which the agricultural proletarian family lived and introduced a new phase in its history.

Prudence and the proletariat

In the second half of this chapter we will, first, establish some basic facts about the demographic system and then, second, integrate them with the processes of proletarianization which impinged on the family formation strategies of the great mass of the agricultural population. Of course, demographic events did not occur in a vacuum or even in some sort of knee-jerk relationship with economic stimuli. The social and cultural environment was of great importance as Malthus recognized when he placed paramount emphasis on the prevailing prudence built into the traditional system of family formation. It is quite clear that social and cultural factors provided the essential framework within which people acted and that there was a remarkable consensus regarding what is now regarded as the English family system: nuclear family households set up by economically independent adults which implied a late age at first marriage for both men and women. Such a consensus is impressive but it is important to recognize the extent to which *play within the system* was possible. On the one hand, the family system enhanced the ease with which an essentially homeostatic demographic regime was maintained by the rough balancing of hands and mouths that resulted from the prudential assessment of economic independence. On the other hand, the recomposition of the agricultural population and its means of livelihood meant that slightly different, class-specific interpretations of deeply embedded cultural rules had considerably different implications when the class structure itself changed. Such is the thrust of Malthus' argument in his *Essay*; it is also the thrust of my position which locates this changing prudential rationality in the interaction of agricultural capitalism and its modes of labour organization.

The age at first marriage for women was the linchpin of the demographic homeostasis which aimed at balancing the hands of producers with the mouths of consumers. There is now ample evidence that the early modern peasantry married *relatively* late: the average age at first marriage for women was in the mid-twenties; for their husbands, a year or two later. Of course, it is also the case that the distribution of marriage ages discovered in family reconstitution studies tells us that about a quarter of the brides married three or more years earlier than the average while another quarter married three or more years later. Our measurement of central tendency both illuminates and obscures the process of family formation: it illuminates the quantitative dimension of prudence by giving us a single statistic with which to describe the workings of the system; it obscures the varied interpretations which were distributed around the average and this variety was itself an equally important characteristic of group behaviour.

The cornerstone of the peasant system of family formation was its land. It is not coincidental that a married peasant was a *husbandman*. Marriage was unthinkable without economic independence; economic independence was untenable without land; and land was usually transmitted at the death or retirement of the possessor and the assumption of adult status by his/her heir. The age at first marriage, then, was the product of social negotiations between groups of property-holders and familial negotiations between parents and children. Furthermore, it was itself conditioned by the availability (or scarcity) of the resources required to assemble the material underpinnings of economic independence. Almost everyone had to wait to inherit before becoming economically independent; for some this might have meant waiting for the family property to be handed down and for others it might have meant waiting for a niche in the village economy to become vacant. These years of prolonged dependence were usually spent in service during which time young men and women assembled a stock of capital which, for the poorer cottagers, might be used to buy into the bottom rung of the landholding system or, for the children of the wealthier peasantry, might be useful in counterbalancing the older generations' life-long monopoly on the family property. While the partners seem to have been free to choose one another there is still abundant evidence that they chose brides or grooms whose social station was roughly similar to their own. "Parity of age, status, wealth, reputation and religion, together with personal attraction made the perfect match."[108] Marriage was an act of social reproduction by which members of each group in society reconstituted themselves in the next generation. There is little evidence of parental arrangements although parental consent was eagerly sought out and valued, not least because an unfavourable match could jeopardize the inheritance which was technically at the discretion of the life-time holder of the property. This family system was frayed at its edges, lumbering in its movements, and operated through an unconscious rationality, with which members of the social order were inculcated through their formal and informal education.

Once the couple had selected one another and received parental consent, the marriage process swung into full gear and a relatively private courtship became a public affair whose bargain was cemented in full view of the community. The choice of partner was a largely private matter for the individuals to sort out for themselves but the celebration of the marriage was a communal event because marriage symbolized the transition from the dependence of youth to the independence of adulthood. The ritual publicity surrounding this transition is described in Miles Coverdale's 1541 translation of *The Christen State of Matrimonye*:

After the hand fasting & making of the contracte, the church goyng & weddyng shulde not be deffered to long, lest the wicked sowe hys vngracious sede in the meme season . . . for in some places the is such a maner, wel worthy to rebuked, that at the hand fastynge there is made a great feast & superfluous bancket, & even the same night are the hand fasted persones brought & layed together, yea certayne wekes afore they go to the church.[109]

The "big wedding" of the peasantry thus united familial concerns with the preservation of property and communal concerns with respectability ("honesty" in the parlance of the times). In so doing it looks back to the cultural homogeneity of the middle ages rather more than it looks forward to the social and cultural distancing which was to develop during the early modern period. The peasant system of family formation "both faithfully reflected, and served to perpetuate the social order: its privileges, its opportunities, its constraints and its injustices".[110] Because the peasant system of family formation was predicated on a specific series of material relationships, the foremost of which was the perpetuation of subsistence agriculture and the accessibility of land, it was subject to profound stresses and eventually broke apart when it became impossible to accommodate both the increasing capitalization of farming and the polarization of landholding. We shall treat this subject later when we come to discuss the emergence of a proletarian family system, but now we will turn our attention to the integration of peasant marital strategies with the larger demographic equation.

The *Peasant demography model*

Relatively late and relatively infrequent marriage were the distinguishing characteristics of the peasant demography system in England. Insofar as the access to economically independent positions (niches) was restricted through social and familial controls on marriage there was a built-in brake on the forces of demographic expansion. Demographic growth is usually caused by one of two factors: a rising birth rate or else a falling death rate. Either way, there would be more births than deaths, and the total population would have increased. This kind of simple arithmetic axiom was subject to several permutations but because marital fertility rates had little scope for growth and mortality rates had little room to fall, the major demographic variable was the age at first marriage for women and, to a lesser extent, the frequency of marriage (i.e. the proportion of all women who married).[111] Such an homeostatic system was inherently flexible in that, *ceteris paribus*, there were usually self-correcting responses to short-term dis-equilibrating pressures. Rising birth rates were often counterbalanced by rising death rates, the result being another kind of zero-sum-game. Demographic homeostasis was a delicate balance of forces in which small shifts in the levels of the equation's components could lead to a massive burst of energy. Malthus' dictum that the forces of population growth, when unleashed, could spark geometric increases must always be kept in mind.

The following model of marriage and family formation is static; it is useful because it highlights the lineaments of the family system, not because it faithfully describes historical reality. Indeed, that reality was so complicated that one is very likely to lose its essential features by concentrating too much on the overwhelming variations and permutations on its main theme. Modelling relationships is an essential first step in creating hypotheses which can be employed in answering the important questions such as how and why the increase of proletarianization made its effects felt in the demographic realm, and vice versa.

Each village population was to a certain extent a semi-independent sphere in which local conditions influenced the application of general rules. The age at first marriage for women in Terling, Essex, was 24.5 in the period 1550–1624; in Shepshed, Leicestershire, it was 28.5 during the first half of the seventeenth century. In Terling the economic structure of village life was "precociously modern" and it contained a high proportion of labourers while in Shepshed the classic English peasant society persisted.[112] The reason for such late ages at first marriage for women was that these villagers needed to achieve economic independence before marriage although, clearly, the ways that labourers in Terling and peasants in Shepshed did so was rather different in its demographic implications. One might suggest that the perdurance of family farming and family property in Shepshed meant that inheritance was more important there but, as we shall see, it is as likely that the causal arrows flowed in both directions at once because the local mortality regime had an impact on the reproductive strategies of a late-marrying population.

Though it does not appear that marriage was triggered by parental death in a direct or mechanical fashion, nonetheless there is a striking correlation between life expectation at the average age of parenthood and the age at first marriage for women.[113] Midway through their reproductive years, when husbands and wives were in their early thirties, the average person could expect to live for another twenty-five years. In a village like Shepshed where the life expectation of the parental generation was higher, the marriage age of the younger generation appears to have been rather later than the national average; in villages like Terling where the mortality of adults was higher, the marriages of their children took place earlier. Overall, then, the replacement of one generation by the next was a rather orderly process in most villages. Higher levels of survival and therefore excess population growth in the parental generation would very likely lead to increases in the number of never-married persons in the next generation unless there was some way in which the number of niches could be expanded to permit these excess men and women to achieve some sort of economic independence within the framework of the *cottage economy*. Inheritance, therefore, was at least as much a social as a personal event because, as E. A. Wrigley has shown with remarkable clarity, in the prevailing demographic system only about three families in five would have been survived by a male heir.[114] For this reason, above all, we would be well advised to see inheritance as the transmission of niches in a relatively stable economic structure. Some niches passed along the male line, others went down the female line, and still others reverted to collateral descendants when the family had no direct heirs. The fact that the access of economic independence could vary between villages by four or five years makes it clear that the demographic framework was not simply a dependent variable which was the object of external economic forces; in villagers' lives demographic conditions played a significant role in their application of social rules concerning economic independence and the establishment of a new household. Demography and economy were fused together and it is misleading to split them in an arbitrary manner; the nature of this fusion is a factor with a life of its own and served to distinguish local populations from one another, just as certainly as it demarked the individuality of family life. The key point is that no one strategy was paramount but that whatever strategy was employed was subservient to the reproduction of a social system predicated on the rule of deferred marriage and economic independence.

Fertility in the **peasant demography model** was *natural fertility*; that is to say, there were no attempts to restrict fertility after a certain number of children had been born.[115] Evidence drawn from family reconstruction studies has shown that both late-marrying and early-marrying women bore about the same number of children per unit of time when they were in their later thirties which suggests that there was no attempt to *target* a desired number of children and then stop. Women continued to bear children right up to the end of their physiological fecundity, about age forty.[116] Illegitimacy levels were low so that, on the average, natural fertility meant that there was a span of some fourteen years during which married women were "at risk" of bearing children.[117] The interval between births exhibited a tendency to become more prolonged as women grew older and had been married longer. Thus, first births often occurred within a year of marriage, with an average of 25 per cent of brides already pregnant at marriage and bearing their first child within the first eight months. Subsequent children were born at increasingly longer intervals, although there was a connection between the death of an infant and a shorter interval until the next birth. This shorter interval usually occurred because the infant's death interrupted maternal lactation and the accompanying postpartum amenorrhea. The premature resumption of ovulation meant that all things being equal, the subsequent birth would occur earlier than if the previous child had survived. In sum, there was an association between the duration of marriage and the marital fertility rate.

We might for the purposes of explication examine the interaction of nuptiality, fertility and mortality by proposing a rather stylized simulation of representative experience within the *peasant demography model*. Our peasant family would have commenced its reproductive history when the wife married at twenty-six. If the husband and wife had remained alive and marriage was unbroken by death or desertion throughout the fourteen years of the childbearing period then this family's fertility schedule would have looked something like this: in the first five years of marriage (26–30) there would be 2.25 children; in the second five years (31–5) there would have been another 1.50 live births; and in the final four years (36–9) maybe 1.00 more. In total, then, this couple would have produced 4.75 live births. But since few families escaped the ravages of mortality these total fertility figures should be revised downwards.

Epidemic and famine mortality have been largely over-rated in terms of their efficacy in halting population growth. There are two reasons for revising the view that the preventative check was dominant in the early modern period: in the first instance, the quantitative evidence is hardly compelling; and, second, even after crisis-level mortality cut swaths through populations, the losses were made up very quickly. Plague was endemic in London, and many smaller urban centres, during the sixteenth and for much of the seventeenth centuries but most of the English population did not live in the capital or any other quasi-urban setting – they lived in rural villages. These communities were not necessarily isolated from epidemic disease, although for the most part they did not suffer from recurrent crises. Aggregate-level surveys of 404 English villages are remarkably revealing in this regard: whereas most of the communities making up the sample did experience at least one year (between the onset of parochial registration in 1538 and its end in 1837) when the annual totals of burials was four times the normal level, only an exceptional minority were ravaged more than once.[118] Years of twice-normal mortality were much more frequent, but their impact was easily overcome. In Bottesford, Leicestershire, such twice-normal levels occurred twelve times in the 160 years before 1740 and once afterwards. In one of these years, 1610, there was a plague epidemic and one villager in six died.[119] The mortality rate tended to fluctuate randomly in non-crisis years so that there were some years when more than the normal level prevailed just as there were others when fewer died.

Healthy years often followed sickly ones and so they tended to cancel one another out. The parish register evidence suggests that this short-term balancing of demographic feast and famine, as it were, is precisely what happened. Years of elevated mortality were thus naturalized and played a role in the homeostatic equation's short-run application. By killing adult men and women, plagues and epidemics relaxed the normal sanctions against marriage, and it was usual for a sharp rise in the marriage curve to follow such crises. Niches were left vacant, but not for long. Moreover, the surge of new marriages probably depressed the age-structure of the total married population thereby leading to a short-term increase in the birth rate. In killing off children, plagues and epidemics made little impact since they were, in effect, easily replaced. Only recurrent, catastrophic mortality peaks could have had a long-run impact deleterious enough to produce population decline – this state of affairs seems to have obtained in the later fourteenth and fifteenth centuries across much of the country.[120] There is little evidence of a repeat performance of wildly fluctuating, debilitating epidemics in the early modern period. In fact, the evidence which has now been assembled by historical demographers provides little comfort for those who would argue that a high death rate in normal years and a remarkably elevated one in crisis years kept the population in check. Wrigley and Schofield have addressed this point in a most direct fashion: "England patently did not conform to the [mortality-dominated] high-pressure paradigm. An accommodation between population and resources was secured not by sudden, sharp mortality spasms ... England experienced a fertility-dominated low-pressure system."[121]

The development of family reconstitution has provided us with an exceedingly sharp analytical scalpel for probing the anatomy of historical populations. Its great virtue is that we can now substitute reasonably accurate statistics for the often grotesquely inaccurate surmises of contemporaries. In the case of sixteenth- and seventeenth-century England, the studies display a quite substantial degree of uniformity.[122] Infants died at the rate of about one in six; another one of the five survivors was likely to have died before reaching age twenty-five. Overall, then, two-thirds of all infants survived to their mid-twenties, the average age at marriage.

At age twenty-five life expectation was around thirty years for both sexes – women suffered excess mortality during their childbearing years but were rather better off after menopause. In round figures it would appear that one marriage in three was broken by the death of a partner before the end of the wife's fecund period. What did this adult mortality mean in terms of the total fertility level, 4.75, which was based on the survival of both partners? For adults, mortality was lowest in the early years of marriage when fertility was highest, it increased as births became more widely spaced, so that it would not be unreasonable to suggest that a fifth of the total fertility figure of 4.75 would have been wiped out by parental mortality. Our revised figure is therefore 3.80 children born to the typical married woman.

Before discussing the impact of mortality on infants and children, we must make some allowance for illegitimacy. In the early modern period there were a small number of such births – about 2 per cent of the total – and we must inflate our revised total fertility figure of 3.80 in order to allow for these additional, pre-marital births. If 3.80 children represents the 98 per cent of all births which occurred within wedlock, then the actual number of all births per woman would have been 3.89. Of these 3.89 actual births, about two-thirds, or 2.60, would have themselves survived until their mid-twenties.

Each first-generation couple would have had 2.60 surviving children; this sort of reproduction rate would therefore have implied that the second generation was 30 per cent larger than the first. However, we can accurately assess the rate of replacement only if we compare like-with-like and to do that we need to consider marrying children, not surviving children. The reason for this is that some of the survivors did not marry and, for the purpose of demographic replacement, were irrelevant. So, the penultimate stage in constructing our model of generational replacement is the determination of "permanent celibacy" ratios – in our model family about 90 per cent of the surviving children would have married. Therefore, 2.34 of the 2.60 surviving children themselves ultimately married and continued the process of biological reproduction. These 2.34 children were the replacements of the original husband and wife. Thus, the generational replacement rate derived from our simulation was 17 per cent. If each generation lasted for about thirty-five years such a simulation suggests an annual, compounded growth rate of about 0.4 per cent. Such a population would double in nearly two centuries. Such, then, is the statistical dimension of the *peasant demography model*. What did it mean?

The *urban counterweight* to the *peasant demography model*

It is generally believed that the population of England doubled between the 1520s and the end of the seventeenth century.[123] Precise figures are bandied about although it is hard to have much confidence in them; instead, the best that we can garner from this pre-statistical age is an approximate size. The same applies to the *peasant demography model* which also can do no more than approximate the relations between the various components of the reproductive equation. But even approximations are valuable, since they allow us to supersede the estimates that have been used before and to use them in constructing models that can test the predictive value of competing hypotheses and explanations. Seen by itself, the *peasant demography model* suggests that the doubling of the English population in these five generations could be largely attributed to the natural growth of the original population. However, such a deduction needs to be qualified. In particular, we must balance the growth of the rural population with the voracious appetite for new recruits displayed by the cities, London above all.

At the beginning of the early modern period the proportion of the English population living in urban areas, defined as places with populations of over 5,000, was 5.5 per cent; in 1700 the comparable figure was 17 per cent, three times as many. London's growth, especially, was explosive: it grew from around 50,000 in Henry VIII's reign to 575,000 at the beginning of the eighteenth century.[124] When the nineteenth century began the urban population of 2,380,000 accounted for about a quarter of the national total. While the process of urbanization will be discussed in more detail in a later chapter, the important point to be made at the present stage in our argument is that this growth was achieved at enormous human costs – E. A. Wrigley has suggested that about a half of the *national* excess of births over deaths was required to underwrite London's expansion. Throughout the first half of the early modern period urban areas in general, and London in particular, had *negative* rates of population growth and the shortfall could only be made up through migration from the countryside where a persistent surplus was accumulating. From 1750 the urban populations were at the least reproducing themselves but hardly making much of a contribution to their own skyrocketing totals.[125] Only in the last century of the early modern period could the rural–urban migration of the excess population from the countryside make a commensurate impact on the size of cities.

Considering the quality of life in the early modern city it is not surprising that urban mortality rates remained much higher than rural ones, even after the spectre of famine had vanished. Density bred the conditions of high mortality in built-up areas: poor sanitation, contaminated water and inadequate ventilation created a hothouse environment in which micro-organisms were easily transmitted between humans. It is striking that very small increases in density led to dramatic upsurges in mortality, particularly among infants who were the most vulnerable to both transmitted diseases and enteric fevers. The market town of Gainsborough, Lincolnshire, seems to have had a level of mortality that was more than 50 per cent above that of rural settlements like Shepshed or Terling. Within London, the wealthier parishes had infant mortality rates that were roughly double those of the rural villages, whereas the poorer parishes in the capital and the proletarian suburbs outside the walls lost even more infants and small children.[126] Thus, the demographic toll exacted by urbanization was immense; it cut deeply into the generational surpluses produced by the *peasant demography model*. Since these urban areas were growing, not just remaining at their original level, it is clear that their expansion represented an enormous drain on the potential growth of the peasant population. In effect, then, the rural excess of births over deaths must have been largely negated in the process of stocking the urban centres.

The *colonial counterweight* to the *peasant demography model*

English migration to the New World is more usually considered from the vantage-point of the receiving country rather than that of the sender. Historiographical biases have thus obscured its great importance to the social structure and the family lives of those who were left behind. The trans-Atlantic flow of young men and, to a much lesser extent, young women was part-and-parcel of the English economy's lateral growth in the first stage of its overseas expansion. The expropriation of the peasantry had expelled large numbers of young people from their niche in the *cottage economy*. These people, who had been called "vagabonds" and "sturdy beggars" in the Tudor period, provided a ready supply of labour power in answer to the dinning cries for "hands" emanating from the staple-producing colonies of English America and the sugar islands. Additional labour power was needed on the high seas; without the supply of such "deep-sea proletarians" it is quite inconceivable that Britannia would have ruled the seas. Absolutely enormous numbers were caught up in this trans-Atlantic traffic – Wrigley and Schofield's "back projection" procedure suggests that between 1630 and 1699 perhaps 850,000 left England; in the eighteenth century the level of out-migration seems to have been roughly similar. Of course, not all those who left Wrigley and Schofield's "observational universe" arrived safely or lived long after their arrival. To these premature deaths we must also add the unknown, but hardly inconsiderable, numbers of able-bodied mariners who died at sea and were buried in Davey Jones' locker.[127]

About one in two emigrants was an indentured servant; mostly young men, between fifteen and twenty-five.[128] David Souden's analysis of the Bristol servant registers for the later 1650s makes the telling point that there was a close fit between the characteristics of the overseas migrants and those who have been termed "subsistence migrants" by Paul Slack. When compared to young men apprenticed to Bristol merchants, not only did the overseas migrants come disproportionately from towns a long distance away but those who come from nearby were disproportionately from cloth-working towns in the "marginal forest areas", noted for their poverty and footloose populations.[129] Although a heated debate concerning the interpretation of surviving registers of emigrating servants' occupations has arisen because of the large numbers for whom no occupation has been given, it is still clear that almost all of these indentured servants can be embraced within the *cottage economy* paradigm used in this essay. In fact, these people were on the very margins of the *cottage economy*. It is therefore reasonable to argue that this colonial migration can be seen within the perspective of population movements in early modern England which has led David Galenson to write that "Instead of moving from one village to another to enter service, after 1607 English youths frequently moved to another continent."[130] When we view the migration process from this perspective it makes little difference whether the unknown residual in the servant registers were labourers or self-styled yeomen; whatever they chose to call themselves it seems perfectly clear that they emigrated because they were finding themselves adversely affected by the social and economic trends which attacked the foundations of their world, the world of the *cottage economy*, root and branch. The obverse of the emergent capitalist agriculture was the land-hunger which was, so Mildred Campbell claims, "rife among all classes" in the West Country from where so many of the Bristol emigrants originated. She also specifies depressions in the clothing trades, of both the West Country and East Anglia, and the severe dislocations occasioned by the Civil Wars among the factors pushing "middling people" to find a sanctuary in the New World.[131]

In addition to those youths who more or less willingly embarked on the adventure of a lifetime, one needs to add the substantial numbers who seem to have been kidnapped or misled by unscrupulous labour-agents. Souden's research into the Bristol records suggests that perhaps one in three of the indentured servants sent off to the colonies was sent across the ocean "under the aegis" of "larger-scale operators [who] were the least discriminating in hiring those they were to send to the colonies".[132] The notoriety of this practice is made clear from the prologue of a 1664 Bristol city ordinance which stated "many complaintes have beene oftentimes made to the Maior and Aldermen of the Inveigling, purloining, carrying and Stealing away Boyes Maides and other persons and transporting them beyond Seas and there selling or otherwise disposeing them for private gaine and proffitt".[133] The London "spirits" seem to have frequented Wapping, where the notorious press-gang also found its victims. The correspondence between the activities of "spirits" and the notorious press-gangs is obvious: the former played on the desperation of down-at-the-heel and out-of-work young people; the latter outfit simply cudgelled its victims before selling them off for the "king's shilling". Abbot Smith argues that "kidnappers and spirits instead of being deplorable outlaws in the servant trade were the faithful and indispensable adjuncts of its most respected merchants". Another group of migrants comprised those convicts and felons who received a form of judicial mercy by being sent into bondage rather than hanged. In the later seventeenth century there were some 4,500 transportees and maybe as many as 30,000 more in the eighteenth century.[134] Among the coerced emigrants, as among the indentured servants, men were preferred by colonial employers. The imbalanced sex-ratio in the colonies meant that "the Women that go over into this Province [Maryland] as Servants . . . are no sooner on shoar, but they are courted into a Copulative Matrimony".[135]

The out-migration of such a multitude of mostly young, mostly single males would have had profound repercussions; comparable, in fact, to the **urban counterweight** of these same years. Furthermore, as Souden's analysis makes clear the migration patterns of men and women were different: most of the female migrants came from close to the port town of Bristol, few came from far afield.[136] Thus Bristol, as other cities of the time, sapped up "excess" local women and exposed them to the tender mercies of its urban mortality regime. We might say that throughout the early modern period the **urban counterweight** operated by selectively skimming off excess women while the colonial haemorrhage overwhelmingly depleted the excess males produced by the **peasant demography model**. We might also note that the negative pressure exerted by urbanization and the sea-borne empire, both commercial and military, was more or less constant while the intense demand for migrants coming from the colonies was highly specific in terms of chronology. Let us pursue these points; first by considering their demographic implications and then their social structural ones.

In the decade 1600–9 the "back projection" estimates suggest a crude rate of natural increase of 0.96 per cent per year; in the 1670s, after a half-century of age- and, especially, gender-specific migration, the comparable rate was 0.07 per cent. Using the same cohorts we learn from Wrigley and Schofield's statistics that the annual crude marriage rate had fallen from 0.9 per cent to 0.7 per cent.[137] In a marriage-driven demographic system like England's, population ceased to grow when marriages did not occur. Because so very many young men crossed the sea alone, large numbers of young women were left behind with little or no prospect of ever finding suitable or even eligible mates. Furthermore, the fact that the positive forces of growth should have been thwarted *contemporaneous with* the rising secular mortality rate goes against the logic of a homeostatic demographic regime – in conditions of exogenously rising mortality such as prevailed in England after 1630 one would have expected, *ceteris paribus*, a reflexive increase in the birth rate through earlier and more frequent marriage. Since this is just the opposite of what happened, it is perfectly obvious that all things were not equal. The frantic expansion of commercial capitalism across the Atlantic wrenched young men from the **cottage economy** in England as a part of the process of linking the supply of hands with the unslaking American demand for labour to harvest sugar and tobacco as well as working on the grain-suppliers' farms in the middle colonies. Is it therefore surprising that the later seventeenth century witnessed the lowest rates of growth and the highest incidence of permanent celibacy among women in the early modern population history of England?

Contemporaries were not unaware of the ramifications which issued from the annual loss of some 8,000 "hands" in the seventeenth century and about 5,000 in the following period.[138] The most vital cohort, men aged fifteen to twenty-four, was sapped by the haemorrhaging consequences of the colonial labour demand. The English age-pyramid – at least the male side of it – became more wasp-waisted. Inevitably, the real dependency ratio must have been rather heavier than that suggested by the "back projection" estimates because this method adopts "a fixed age-schedule of net migration [which] inevitably means that the *timing* of surges in migration will not be accurately captured when the schedule varies even if the *total* net migration were correctly estimated".[139] The implications for the kind of argument which posits *favourable* dependency ratios in the later seventeenth century and *deteriorating* ones during the classic **Industrial Revolution** seems obvious enough.[140] Indeed, the writings of so-called "mercantilist" authors display their very keen eye for this particular aspect of their contemporary social world. The Restoration theorists' obsessive concerns with population policy questions strikes a resonant chord when viewed from a social-structural perspective emphasizing the previous generations' loss of some 332,500 productive "hands" who had crossed the Atlantic in search of land and a measure of personal liberty. Not surprisingly, some of the most cogent pamphlets of the later seventeenth century emphasized the labour problems derived from colonial emigration. It became something of a scapegoat. Mercantilist authors believed that their most pressing social concern was how to increase the inflow of bullion by increasing England's productive capacity which in terms of the productive organization of the time could only mean increasing its population. As Joyce Appleby has written:

The problems of the poor – their numbers, their habits, their opportunities for work and proper management – absorbed the attention of dozens of writers in the 1660s, 1670s and 1680s. The most significant change of opinion about the poor was the replacement of the concern about over-population at the beginning of the century with fears about a possible loss of people at the end. Where sending people to the plantations had been advanced at one time as a solution to the surplus mouths to feed, the colonial emigration was criticized more often than not after 1660.[141]

But, the government of the day turned a deaf-ear to these increasingly shrill cries because, so Campbell argues, "the shaping of colonial policy was in the hands of men who were themselves head over heels in colonial activities".[142] In 1721, when Sir Robert Walpole drafted the king's speech to Parliament, the Great Whig put the following words into the Hanoverian's mouth "It is very obvious that nothing would more conduce to the obtaining so publick a good, than to make the expectation of our manufactures, and the importation in the commodities used in the manufacturing of them, as practicable and easy as may be."[143] This great predatory politician, the hunter of hunters, spoke axiomatically not rhetorically. Commercial policy, the political economy of colonialism, by Walpole's time had been on the agenda for several generations. It had already sent shock-waves reverberating throughout the whole social system; a reorganization of production for exchange had made its impact felt on the reproductive strategies of the plebeians. Walpole and his cronies thought globally; members of the *cottage economy* acted locally.

The Janus-face of proletarian prudence

If we make due allowance for the *urban* and the *colonial counterweights*, then it is unlikely that adherence to the *peasant demography model* could have generated more than a small portion of the total growth of the English population. Furthermore, its relevance declined throughout the early modern period so that we must look elsewhere to discover why the English population grew in these years. My argument is that we shall find the mainsprings of population growth by clearly explicating the historical effects of proletarianization on family formation strategies. In contrast with the synchronic model of family formation already outlined, we must create a diachronic version to account for the dramatic impact of proletarian family formation strategies.

The expropriation of the peasantry meant that by Gregory King's time, at the end of the seventeenth century, there were likely to have been only a small number of families whose productive and reproductive strategies were organized in the ways that were normal during the reign of Henry VIII. Yet, and it is a big qualification, as long as the *cottage economy* persisted the old connections between *inheritance* and economic independence breathed life. To the extent that it remained autonomous, the Janus-faced, early modern proletariat was still connected to the peasantry's family formation strategies. Until the last century of the early modern period it was only in old-enclosed, proletarianized communities like Terling that a new system of reproduction was unveiled. This point is made with exceptional force by Ann Kussmaul in her discussion of the complementarity of agricultural service and late, deferred marriage as opposed to rural proletarianization and early marriage.[144] In much of the rest of the southern and eastern cereal belt, it was only when the agricultural proletariat lost its "social patrimony" of common rights that its members forfeited their prudence and traded it in for a new strategy of early marriage.

It should be pointed out that there was an *endogenous* decline of mortality in the later eighteenth century and, given the prudential imperatives of the *peasant demography model*, such an improvement in life expectation would likely have provoked a decline in the momentum of the marriage-driven reproductive system, not an increase. It may well have been the case that the initial increase in demographic growth rates during the third quarter of the eighteenth century, simultaneous with the first burst of parliamentary enclosure, was caused by *exogenous* shifts in the incidence of mortality. Population growth was a necessary pre-condition to social changes but it cannot be construed as a sufficient one. Equally, the expropriation of the peasantry did not necessarily mean demographic expansion without the realization of a quite different kind of family formation strategy. For these reasons my argument employs a feed-back mechanism joining together production and reproduction and weighing the impact of change against the considerable weight of the *status quo ante*.[145]

It is within the context of an integrative argument that we can appreciate the enormous force of Malthus' recognition: when the equilibration of the demographic system was simultaneously undermined by both *economic* and *demographic* factors, dramatic shifts in the rate of population growth ensued because whatever improvements in life expectation occurred were not counteracted by a compensatory response in the birth rate. In this regard Malthus pointed to the utter failure of the welfare system to maintain the traditional measures of prudential marriage which should have re-equilibrated population levels by recourse to deferred marriage. The ever-increasing – but frequently *situational* – resort to the allowance system of poor relief seems to have promoted a new and different family formation strategy. Malthus is well worth quoting on this very point:

The labourer who earns eighteen pence a day and lives with some degree of comfort as a single man, will hesitate a little before he divides that pittance among four or five, which seems just sufficient for one. Harder fare and harder labour he would submit to for the sake of living with the woman that he loves, but he must feel conscious, if he thinks at all, that should he have a large family, and any ill luck whatever, no degree of frugality, no possible exertion of his manual strength could preserve him from the heart-rending sensation of seeing his children starve, or of forfeiting his independence, and being obliged to the parish for their support. The love of independence is a sentiment surely none would wish to be erased from the breast of man, though the parish law of England, it must be confessed, is a system of all others the most calculated gradually to weaken this sentiment, and in the end may eradicate it completely.[146]

The rational man was therefore the prudent man and rational prudence existed within a longstanding cultural framework. For Malthus this cultural inheritance seems to have been fixed and so not subject to reinterpretation. He was wrong; profoundly wrong.

The *proletarian demography model*

What we are confronting is not, therefore, a simple choice between ideal types but something far more difficult to categorize: that subtle blend of change and continuity characterizing historical experience. We will, therefore, introduce the *proletarian demography model* in its starkest form to explicate the Malthusian prediction of geometric increases in population but we will then qualify its impact so as to bring it into line with our other knowledge. In this way we can assess the role of agricultural proletarianization on the one hand, and rural industrialization on the other, in promoting population growth in the early modern period. Such a plan is of value for three reasons: first, it provides a perspective on the interplay between modes of production and reproduction among the agricultural proletariat during the protracted decline of the *cottage economy* which has been the major theme in this chapter; second, it links this chapter with the one to follow by highlighting the importance of self-sustained demographic growth among the industrial proletariat; and, third, it enables us to look backwards to the previous chapter and fill in some of the blank spaces in its treatment of demography and economy in the feudal period.

The central feature of the *proletarian demography model* was earlier marriage. In addition to a three-year fall in the average age at first marriage for women there were three ancillary characteristics that contributed to the higher birth rate: more frequent marriage; higher marital fertility; and increased levels of illegitimacy. Mortality levels, by way of contrast, do not seem to have changed very much except for the fact that proletarianization and urbanization were frequently linked. In the rural areas there was no such connection, of course. At this point we might ignore rural/urban distinctions as well as the differential timing of proletarianization in agriculture and industry. We can return to these aspects of the larger process after we have considered the main statistical contrasts between the demography of the peasantry and that of the proletariat.

Proletarian men married earlier and, much more importantly, they married younger brides. In Shepshed, the early nineteenth-century proletarians' brides were 5.5 years younger than the women who had married seventeenth-century peasants; in Terling, where the proletariat had always been a considerable proportion of the village population, the historical changes were more muted – there, nineteenth-century brides were 1.5 years younger than their late sixteenth- and early- seventeenth-century counterparts. It is of more than passing interest that although the two villages had quite different paths to the proletarian demography regime they nonetheless arrived at much the same finishing point: age at first marriage for women was 22.6 in Shepshed and 23.0 in Terling. Wrigley and Schofield have reported much the same sort of decline from their sample of twelve reconstituted parishes – from 26.5 in 1600–49 the age at first marriage for women had fallen to 23.4 in 1800–49.[147] Their comment on these results is apposite:

Earlier marriage alone would therefore account for more than half of the rise in the GRE [Gross Reproduction Rate]. But there were other changes directly or indirectly linked to changing marriage age which between them suggest that a full under-standing of the behaviour of the marriage market in England would go far towards explaining changes in overall fertility, and thus in turn population trends generally, since we have already seen that fertility changes dominated the demographic scene.[148]

The English demographic system was therefore "marriage-driven". Let us now consider the magnitude of these changes within the parameters of our schematic categories.

Not only was marriage earlier among the proletariat, it was also more frequent: the proportion of permanent celibates was likely to have been halved.[149] Marital fertility rose a little, too. An examination of the demographic patterns in fourteen parishes has demonstrated the Malthusian connection between earlier marriage and rising marital fertility in the later eighteenth century.[150] Levels of bridal pregnancy and illegitimacy rates rose dramatically – the former probably doubled and the latter most likely quadrupled. Economic uncertainty, largely accounted for by involvement in the marketplace rather than subsistence production, often intervened between the initiation of sexual courtship and marriage. Such uncertainty frustrated marriage plans and it, not rampant promiscuity, was the reason why proletarians had more children out of wedlock. Not only were there twice as many illegitimate births in the proletarian family as in its peasant predecessor, but these births occurred in about half the time. Unmarried women were "at risk" for a far shorter time because the *pre-marital* period was reduced when their ages at first marriage fell. For this reason a rate of illegitimacy measuring the numbers of illegitimate births per unit of time is a more accurate gauge than a ratio measuring illegitimate births as a proportion of all births. The former takes into account the changing marital environment; the latter does not.[151] In opposition to these positive forces promoting the birth rate, we might say that mortality rose a little and that most of its negative impact devolved upon infants and children.

Let us now explicate the **proletarian demography model** to see the results of these changes in the reproductive system. Women married at twenty-three and had seventeen years of childbearing. During the first five years they would have had 2.50 births; during the next five years 1.60; in the third five-year period they would have given birth to 1.40 children; and in the final two years they would have had a further 0.40 live births. In all, then, the potential total marital fertility would have been 5.90 children. Given our assumption that adult mortality during the childbearing years among a proletarian population was little different from that experienced by a peasant one, the potential total fertility of the representative woman would have been reduced by a fifth – from 5.90 to 4.72. In addition to these children born after marriage, there were the pre-marital births; say, 4 per cent of all children were illegitimate so that the final score would have been 4.92. In the *peasant demography model* we estimated that two-thirds of all live births survived to the average age at first marriage for women, twenty-six; in the *proletarian demography model* we might estimate that 65 per cent reached the now-earlier marriage age of twenty-three. So, 3.20 children reached their early twenties of whom 95 per cent eventually married. The original proletarian couple was replaced by 3.04 marrying children.

The replacement rate of the *proletarian demography model* was far above that of the *peasant demography model* – each generation of proletarian demography meant a 52 per cent increase in the base-population as opposed to a 17 per cent rise in the peasant model. Since proletarian generations were shorter, because earlier marriages meant that the length of a generation was reduced, the compounded effect was dramatic. Whereas the peasantry required about 200 years to double themselves the proletariat could do so in 52. In 300 years a proletarian population of 100 would have grown to 6,000; a similar peasant population would have reached 300. Parenthetically it might be remarked that the medieval population probably grew three-fold between the Norman Conquest in 1066 and the Black Death in 1348 – i.e. a trebling in about three centuries. Such a coincidence between the theoretical model explicated in this chapter and the state-of-the-art position must cause one to ask if some variant of the *peasant demography model* was in place during the high middle ages, even before the massive dislocations of the plague and the ensuing devastation.[152] An English population of 2.4 million in 1524–5 which adhered to the *proletarian demography model* would have doubled, redoubled and so compounded itself to 1,920,000,000 in 1851 – i.e. double that of the Chinese population in 1980. In point of fact the 1851 English population was about 17,000,000 – somewhat less than 1 per cent of the hypothetical projection.[153]

The previous exercise is of value because it provides a material point of reference to the Malthusian argument regarding the "prolific power" that could be unleashed when traditional social norms, prudential checks on reproduction, were discarded. It should be borne in mind that the 800-fold increase achieved by the unrestricted application of the *proletarian demography model* for the eleven generations between the reign of Henry VIII and Victoria was *not* the result of a wholly different form of reproduction but rather a mutation of the older system. The earlier age at first marriage for women in the *proletarian demography model*, it must be stressed, was *within* the parameters of the older system's distribution of marriage ages. The distribution itself shifted but not to such an extent that it became unrecognizable. One did not necessarily forfeit one's "Englishness" by marrying some three years earlier. Indeed, given the fact that marriages in the early twenties were *always* within the bounds of expected behaviour, what had changed was not the system but its interpretation, largely because the interpretors saw the system rather differently than their predecessors. Such a transformed social hermeneutic would have had profoundly explosive and completely unexpected results. This exercise in simulated historical demography emphasizes the implications of dis-equilibration on a population organizing itself according to homeostatic principles. As long as the birth rate and the death rate were part-and-parcel of an equation which was internally self-governing, the English population was largely able to maintain a balance between production and consumption.

The contingency of the *proletarian demography model*

The resilience of the *cottage economy* in the early modern period was the central historical problem of the first two centuries; thereafter, its breakdown defined the agenda of the rural political economy. In the first half of the early modern period the rural proletarians grew from about 125,000 adult males to 204,000 while the number of peasants declined from 375,000 to 225,000. Between 1688 and 1851 the number of agriculturalists more than doubled, from 449,000 to 1,125,000, mostly as a result of the growth of the proletarian component from 204,000 in 1688 to 902,000 in 1851. These statistics beg an important question which has been the main concern of this chapter and can now be addressed directly: was proletarian growth the result of population transfers from the expropriated peasantry or was it the result of its own internal dynamic? As a corollary to this main point we will want to know for how long the *peasant demography model* was dominant and when it was superseded by the *proletarian demography model*. In fact, there is no single answer because the trajectory of change was not constant over the whole of the early modern period. The population history of rural England in the first two centuries of the early modern period can be understood within the explanatory framework provided by the *peasant demography model* and its *urban* and *colonial counterweights*; the final century, 1750–1850, can be understood within the explanatory framework suggested by the *proletarian demography model*. During the first two centuries the agricultural proletariat grew mainly because of the expropriation of the peasantry. This was a slow, protracted process and one which was inimical to significant long-term population growth because the reconfiguration of the political economy quite literally consumed the rural surplus. After 1688 the four-fold increase of the agricultural proletariat, from 204,000 to 902,000, was almost completely concentrated in the years after 1750 when the *proletarian demography model* was unleashed in the countryside. The three generations living between 1750 and 1850 quadrupled their numbers so that the whole observable increase in the agricultural proletariat is therefore explicable by the transformation of family formation strategies. As Malthus realized, the "distortion" of the traditional prudence was an integral factor in the emergence of new systems of agricultural production and the novel arrangements for its reproduction. This feedback between production and reproduction was set in train by the reconfiguration of the agrarian political economy. It can be plausibly argued that without the expropriation of the peasantry and the dismemberment of the *cottage economy* the vast increases in productivity which characterized English agriculture would have been impossible. The creation of a national division of agricultural labour – pastoral north and west and a southern cereal belt – was, therefore, a singularly important factor in the emergence and rapid growth of a disproportionately proletarian, urban–industrial society.[154] The transportation revolution in the nineteenth century – railroads and steamships, building upon the infrastructural framework of the eighteenth-century turnpikes and canals – created a division of agricultural labour which broached national boundaries thereby allowing the Malthusian day-of-reckoning to be forestalled.[155] Industrialization – in particular, the mature industrial economy built upon the coal mines and the railroads – thus provided an answer to the problematic posed by human fecundity during the Malthusian period.

When Malthus wrote his famous *Essay* he quite simply had no idea of the ways in which his world – the world of 1798 – were changing. Growing up in the cereal belt of southern England, educated to be a cleric at Cambridge University, becoming first a country parson and then an imperial civil servant; these were not factors conducive to comprehending a new mode of production at the moment of its birth. He had no idea that the English imperium would effectively extend the available land mass with which a burgeoning industrial population could be fed. He seems to have been largely unaware of the radical transformation – a quantum leap, in fact – in the labour process which the application of steam-power was then making possible. He did not understand that steam power could be substituted for human labour power so that productivity, too, could be enhanced at a exponential rate of increase. Although he lived well into the nineteenth century, even Malthus' later writings do not suggest that steam power was of much significance to him. He thought in the idiom of a commercialized society of simple commodity producers and traders. In commenting on the historicity of Malthus' analysis of the relationship between economy and demography, Wrigley and Schofield have written: "by an ironic coincidence Malthus has given pungent expression to an issue that haunted most pre-industrial societies at almost the last moment when it could still plausibly be represented as relevant to the country in which he was born".[156] In fact, Malthus did rather more than that. Unlike Malthus, we are all believers in the inevitability of scientific and technological progress – can we be so certain that he has had his final say on the subject? His belief that there were limits to growth has the most suggestive resonances for our experience. He may not have completely grasped the social and economic experience of his own time but that misunderstanding should not discount his profound insight that there exists an integrated relationship between humans and their ecological system – a system they create and of which they are creatures. Malthus left us with an appreciation of the elemental fact that while humans may be social animals, humankind is subject to biological imperatives. The *systematic* character of that interaction operated at the level of rational individuals acting upon their own interpretations of the material world. He demands that we pay at least as much heed to cultural expectations as material ones. Thus, Malthus provides us with an acutely contingent form of historical analysis in which social forces – economy and demography – were interpreted in different ways by different groups *for their own reasons.*

During the early modern period – 1500–1750 – the problem which has had to be explained is not simply how the population grew but, rather more, why its growth was so slow and, additionally, why the secular growth curve shot upwards in the later eighteenth century after a century of spluttering along at about the level of replacement. Agricultural capitalism was a necessary factor in the disintegration of the *cottage economy;* the demise of the English peasantry reverberated in the establishment of new productive and reproductive relationships. But by itself, it cannot explain the massive increase of the proleteriat. To explain this really radical departure in the political economy of English population history, therefore, we have to turn our attention to the emergence of the world's first industrial economy. The historical contingency in which industrialization confronted the *cottage economy* frames my explanation for the radical discontinuity of population growth rates in the age of Malthus.

3

The industrialization of the
cottage economy

*Unbinding the Industrial Prometheus; or, the Englishness of
the First Industrial Revolution*

Industrial proletarianization preceded the factory. In this chapter, which
largely deals with *proto-industrialization* – "pre-industrial" industrial
production – my main interest will be to describe the lineage of the
industrial proletariat in the industrialization of the *cottage economy*. To
my way of thinking, *proto-industrialization* refers to the industrialized
cottage economy. Like the latter concept it has fhe enormous value of
implying a shifting set of strategies that allowed those involved to have
had, and to have exercised, the power of choice in their own productive
and reproductive lives. Just as the *cottage economy* was earlier described
as a *catch-as-catch-can family economy* so, too, was its *proto-industrial*
step-child. A point of clarification needs to be made here since it is
germane to my account but will not figure in it in any obvious or explicit
fashion. I am not a rigid believer in any "theory of *proto-industrialization*" but I do believe that the concept has some value if we allow it to be
both loose-fitting and general. *Proto-industrialization* has gained an
historical vogue in the last fifteen years yet it has proven to be almost
impossible to specify what *proto-industrialization* was; it has been easy to
suggest alternatives to any schema which has been offered.[1] Such complexity does not bother me. I do not want to propose a self-contained
schema but rather I will use the term adjectivally in that loose-fitting and
general way which would see it as a Janus-faced *stage in the process* of
transition from feudalism to capitalism – a halfway-house looking forwards to industrial proletarianization and backwards to a world of
independent petty commodity producers.

The practising historian may ask questions which are social-scientific in
their thrust but the practising historian does not expect to produce answers
which lead to "theory". On the contrary, the practising historian expects
to produce answers which lead to knowledge. Historical knowledge

is anti-theoretical in the sense that it is non-predictive; historical knowledge is not concerned with prognosticating the future but rather with explaining how the past evolved to create the present. In that process of evolution there were no ordained choices, no prescriptions, no formulae, no instructions, and absolutely no foreknowledge – the historical present was contingent. There was no goal – no *known* terminus – towards which these historical actors were consciously moving even though we can interpret *their* motivations within *our* mental paradigms. This point is of the greatest significance because on it hinges our viewpoint as historians seeking to interpret the actions and motivations of predecessors who had neither the benefit of our hindsight nor foresight of their own. Therefore, the **Industrial Revolution**, like all revolutions in history, can be seen as historically determined only after the fact. Historians, though, have a privileged position – we can benefit from our hindsight and make use of it in fashioning *our* explanation of *their* behaviour. Historians can distinguish *facts of history* from insignificant and unhistorical facts which are also known about the past. As an historian of England, it is my task to explain why "pre-industrial" industrialization in England culminated in the **Industrial Revolution** at a specific point in time. As an historian of England, it is my task to explain the specific interaction of production and reproduction during the process of industrialization – i.e. the "pre-industrial" period of *cottage industry/proto-industrialization* – in producing an historically specific form of industrial society in England. As an historian of England, it is not my task to explain why other "pre-industrial" social formations did not lead to the same result at the same time elsewhere. Or, perhaps, it might be more correct to state that as an historian of England it is most decidedly not my task to explain why England was the first industrial nation when superficially similar sets of circumstances – i.e. *cottage industries/proto-industrialization* – *seemed* to exist elsewhere. As far as I am concerned, the issue of comparison is interesting and sometimes illuminating but it is also essentially beside the point. Because of this intellectual orientation towards the historically contingent political economy of English population history I want to retain a loose-fitting and general terminological usage for *cottage industry/proto-industrialization*; that seems to me to be the only way to reconcile it with an historical explanation. Finally, it has to be kept in mind that across the length and breadth of early modern England *cottage industries* waxed and waned. Success in one region was often being achieved at the expense of another's contemporaneous failure. For this reason, too, I do not think that *proto-industrialization* provides us with a useful "model" of industrial growth. No "theory" can be employed satisfactorily to encompass the bewildering complexity of the industrialization and de-industrialization of the *cottage economy* before the **Indus-**

trial Revolution. The preceding has been a long-winded way of saying that the *Industrial Revolution*, like all revolutions in history, occurred in an unexpected and unpredictable manner. As far as I am concerned, the crucial point is that England experienced the first *Industrial Revolution*; that fact occurred within a specific nexus of production and reproduction and its explanation is what sets the rest of this book in motion.

England was the first industrial nation but the *Industrial Revolution* was not an event. Industrialization was a lengthy social process. Industry in the medieval countryside and handicraft artisanal activity in the corporate towns was almost completely small scale. Most industrial proletarians in the "pre-industrial" period were frequently part-timers and not infrequently contract workers (or sub-contractors). They were preponderantly self-employed. Most worked at tasks servicing local markets although some were involved in the production of luxury goods for distant consumers. Such people – men and women worked at these activities – were petty producers. Their industrial commodities were usually sold in the marketplace or their skills were usually employed at the job-site. In all these ways they had far more in common with the independent peasant (the petty agricultural producer) than with the industrial proletarian who sells his or her labour power but who has no control over the process of production. Over the course of the early modern period the balance between "independence" and proletariani-zation – strictly defined in its ancient usage as one who served the state not with property but with offspring – was a precarious one. On the one hand, the logic of capitalist expansion brought workers into a condition of dependence upon a nexus of cash relations. On the other hand, there is substantial evidence to suggest that for a great many members of the *cottage economy* industrialization was a buttress *against* proletariani-zation. As I will stress throughout the following discussion, this strategic defence against proletarianization was first thwarted and then cruelly deranged in the wake of the population explosion of the Malthusian period.

The period before about 1780 was not therefore "pre-industrial"; it was *proto-industrial* as a result of the industrialization of the *cottage economy*. There is an element of hair-splitting here because for me the issue is not to distinguish one social formation from another by the presence (or absence) of industry but to situate the protracted character of this transformation in the social reproduction of new productive relationships. Here, I think, the Marxist formulation with its emphasis on the political economy of the labour process is more useful than a neo-classical emphasis on exchange relationships between "factors of production". Seen from the Marxist position, full-blown industrial capitalism has had two predominant characteristics: first, the worker is separated from ownership of the means of production; and, second, he or she loses control over the labour process and becomes an extension of a machine-tool which regulates the pace of work. Yet, an emphasis on the labour process is by itself too narrow. It concentrates on the *demand* for labour power but does nothing to tell us about its *supply*. Without the reciprocating interaction of demand and supply – production and reproduction – the character of English population history would have been one-dimensional. That is to say, the causal arrows would have only flowed from production to reproduction. If that were the case then English population history could be encompassed with a rather straightforward narrative account. Such an argument will not be advanced in the pages which follow. To my way of thinking the crucial factor is the interaction of these two variables in historical time. For this reason, above all, we need to pay heed to the chronology of industrial growth and its interaction with demographic factors.

The forces of production and reproduction – the main concerns of this essay – were set in motion by, and have to be placed in the context of, the specific political economy which characterized England during the transition from feudalism to capitalism.[2] In this way of seeing we can chart the protracted transformation of an isolated and economically backwards part of Europe and its emergence as the centre of the world economy in the period before the **Industrial Revolution**. In this way we can understand how the onset of full-scale industrialization in England was the product of a concatenation of forces – some local, some global. And, in this way, we can understand the contingent context of labour supply and the destabilizing impact of proletarianization on family formation strategies. We might begin our discussion from the position that as long as most industrial production was carried out in a "pre-industrial" manner by "pre-industrial" workers the **peasant demography model** was applicable. For our present purposes, then, the question at issue concerns the passing of this "pre-industrial" mode of industrial production – that is to say, the timing of industrial proletarianization. We will locate that chronology in the demise of the characteristic form of nascent capitalist industrial organization, the **proto-industrial cottage economy**. It, too, was a process – not an event.

King Coal's kingdom

England is built upon an underground mountain of coal. Its exploitation was the motor-force in the revolution in production that created modern industrial society. Without coal the **cottage economy** may have undergone quite complete **proto-industrialization** but it was the utilization of these vast reserves of cheap coal which distinguished the early modern English economy from that of its major competitor, the Dutch Republic. There, too, the early modern period was marked by a thoroughgoing commercialization of all economic activities and a major expansion of traditional cottage industries in response to buoyant demand from its urban population and specialist agricultural producers. Dutch industrialization was largely concerned with a highly complex form of barter in which the products of agricultural specialists and urban services were taken in trade for the products of its rural producers. The Dutch industrial sector did not revolutionize production even if it did transform the character of consumption patterns by enhancing the size and complexity of commercial society. Without the development of coal-based heavy industries, one can easily envisage a similar pattern of specialization of function, without the revolutionization of production, occurring in early modern England. English industrialization had reached an asymptotic state in the early nineteenth century from which it could not have extricated itself without coal. Although there is a substantial teleological element in such an analysis, one cannot understand the emergence of industrial society in England without appreciating the absolute centrality of the coal industry. England was the first industrial society because it was the first fully to exploit inanimate energy sources for powering machinery. Without a coal-based economy such an *Industrial Revolution* was unthinkable; without a coal-based economy the involution of the *proto-industrial* mode of production was inevitable. Here, then, is the crux of the issue. While one may over-emphasize the role of mining in the early modern economy such an over-emphasis is both understandable and justifiable in the sense that without it one cannot delineate the forces distinguishing English economic history from that of other countries. The coal industry's importance to economic development extended far beyond its direct share in the statistics of economic growth. Without its expanded supply at virtually constant prices, most other sectors of the economy would have been hamstrung and their progress would have been halting.[3]

Coal mines at the time of Henry VIII were technologically primitive and quantitatively insignificant. 200,000 tons of coal were produced in the mid-sixteenth century; 2,500,000 tons in 1700; 27,000,000 in 1830; and 287,000,000 in 1913. During much of England's industrial history the north-eastern coalfield, in Northumberland and County Durham, dominated the national scene; it yielded something like 40 per cent of the total output c. 1700 and even as late as 1830 it still accounted for about a quarter of the market. As one puffed-up Newcastle patriot had it:

> England's a perfect world!
> Has Indies too!
> Correct your Maps!
> New Castle is Peru.

Allowing for poetic licence it is, in truth, the case that contemporaries thought that coal mining was the most striking aspect of the early modern economy in England.

whereas when we are at London, and see the prodigious fleets of ships which come constantly in with coals for this increasing city, we are apt to wonder whence they come, and that they do not bring the whole country away; so, on the contrary, when in this country we see the prodigious heaps, I might say mountains, of coals, which are dug up at every pit, and how many of those pits there are; we are filled with equal wonder to consider where the people should live that can consume them.[4]

Daniel Defoe's wonder is almost palpable; this brilliant sentence captures the essential relationship between consumers and producers. In it, too, the symbiotic complementarity between London and Tyneside is effectively underscored by the elegant structure and ornate balance of his writing.

For much of the early modern period coal was prized as a fuel for domestic heating, especially in the London market; its industrial utility was secondary. But the balance was continually shifting in favour of the latter use; four-fifths of all coal in 1550 was used for domestic purposes but in 1700 the comparable figure was only two-thirds. "What is astonishing is the great quantity of coal burned in industry a century before the Industrial Revolution is supposed to have taken place."[5] It was used extensively in limeburning, smithying and metal-working, salt- and soap-boiling, starch- and candle-making, brewing and malting, food processing and sugar refining, textile processing, smelting, brick- and tile-making, and glassworks as well as in the manufacture of alum, copperas, saltpetre and gunpowder. Coal from the north-east was of more lasting value to the English people than all the silver in the New World was to the Spanish. Coal provided the sinews and muscles of a nascent industrial economy while the silver mountain of Potosi was frittered away in the Quixotic ambitions of the Spanish Crown. Contemporaries knew perfectly well that the wealth derived from the coal mines, principally situated in the north-east, was a critical element in the strength of the English economy." 'It cannot be doubted' said one of them, 'but that it is the coal-mines which worked so many miracles ... There necessarily results from this multitude of workers, ceaselessly active, a mass of wealth, equally advantageous to the state and to individuals, who owe this condition of comfort to coal.' "[6]

Industrial consumption had been next to nothing in the sixteenth century, it had risen to about 1,250,000 tons c. 1700, and around 10,300,000 tons in 1830. The age of iron and steel had a long lineage in the process of industrialization before the *Industrial Revolution*. It was one of the triumphs of England's industrial history that in a few generations, between 1700 and 1830, "the British economy had passed from dependence on human-, horse-, wind- and water-power for its energy needs to a high degree of dependence on coal". There is no question that this change was economically advantageous; the fact that it derived from sheer necessity is immaterial in assessing its ultimate impact.[7]

The industrial proletariat: a quantitative discursus

When Sir Thomas More saw a world in which sheep ate men he was describing the contemporary orientation of the English economy towards the provision of staples, not finished products, for foreign markets. Of course, the woollen trade provides an exception to this generalization but, in the main, the relationship between late medieval England and the developed world was that of periphery and centre. In this sense, the England of Henry VIII looked backwards to the feudal, agrarian world rather more than it looked forwards to the capitalist, industrial one. Yet, by Gregory King's time more than one family in eight was headed by a male worker in "manufacturing trades" and in 1851 there were four times as many industrial workers as agriculturalists. England's green and pleasant land became, in the space of eleven generations, the undisputed workshop of the world. When R. Dudley Baxter anatomized English social structure in 1867 he determined that 81 per cent of the male population belonged to the "manual labour class".[8] He understood, as did his contemporaries, that in contrast to the owners of capital, the bearers of labour were a different species.

In Henry VIII's reign very few householders were full-time industrialists although every community had its share of craftsmen who provided essential services for the mass of peasant farming families. Such, too, had been the situation in the middle ages when the division of labour called forth specialists. Almost every sizeable village had its smiths, carpenters, tilers, millers, spinsters and weavers, and some even were the home for hucksters and chapmen. But, as R. H. Hilton suggests, "the village craftsmen tended to identify themselves with the peasant communities to which they belonged".[9] When we ask how many industrial workers were to be found in the early sixteenth century it is almost impossible to gain any kind of satisfactory answer simply because most industrial work was carried out *in conjunction with* agricultural activities. Only in a few, selected areas were there concentrations of people whose incomes were completely, or even largely, derived from industrial activity. During Henry VIII's reign most of these people would have been found in the three textile regions: East Anglia, the West Country and the North – south-east Lancashire and the West Riding of Yorkshire. Even there, the inter-penetration of agriculture and industry was a marked feature and the balance, in Tudor times, was on the side of farming.

For the purposes of comparison with later statistics, we might therefore consider that Henrician England was truly "pre-industrial"; when placed next to the later seventeenth-century occupational distribution which Lindert has derived from tax and burial registers, its industrial component was quite literally next to nothing. Peter Lindert, the most recent student of the socio-occupational structure of early modern England, has argued that in contrast with the sums of his famous predecessor "England and Wales were almost surely more industrial and commercial in [Gregory] King's day than he has led us to believe."[10] There appear to have been some 272,088 families (out of a total of 1,390,586) headed by a man who was described at death as having an occupation in either manufacturing, the building trades or mining. In considering these statistics it must be pointed out that Lindert's analysis focusses on the occupations of dead men; it does not take into account the working experience of living women, youths and children nor does it allow for the possibility that wives and/or children of non-industrial workers could themselves be engaged in industrial tasks nor, in fact, does it consider that men described with one occupational title might be engaged in several differ-ent activities while being described in terminology appropriate to an essentially rural and still largely agrarian society. What Lindert's analysis provides might be considered as a base-line of non-agricultural economic activity across the length and breadth of "pre-industrial" England. By the end of the seventeenth century, however, this society was "pre-industrial" only insofar as manufacturing was overwhelmingly carried out with human labour and dispersed in the workers' cottages or their small workshops instead of being driven by inanimately powered machines located in factories.

Lindert's analysis of late seventeenth-century tax and burial registers estimates that one in eight families c. 1700 (179,774:1,390,586) was headed by a male worker in "manufacturing trades"; this figure represents a fortieth of the total industrial population (non-mechanized handicrafts and factory workers) reported in the 1851 census. Lindert also estimates that at the same time there were 448,306 family heads who were agri-culturalists, either employers or labourers; in the 1851 census 1,790,000 agricultural workers (farmers and labourers) were enumerated. The agricultural sector had grown by a factor of about four in the same period that the industrial population had grown forty-fold – thus the industrial-ists had grown ten times as fast as the agriculturalists.[11]

English industrialization: combined and uneven development

The continuities were, perhaps, more important than the changes in the first phase of industrialization. Because of the tendency to hyperflate the period of the classic **Industrial Revolution**, economic historians have generally tended to over-emphasize the impact of changes occurring during the first phase of industrialization at the expense of the more far-reaching developments after 1850. Yet, such a concentration on elements of change at the expense of those of continuity is dubious in that "much of the England of 1850 was not very strikingly different from that of 1750".[12] The uneven development of mechanization in the first phase of industrialization is an important theme of Sir John Clapham's classic *An Economic History of Modern Britain*. He remarks that "Because no single British industry had passed through a complete technical revolution before 1830, the country abounded in ancient types of industrial organization and in transitional types of every variety."[13] The diversity and dispersal of rural handicraft manufacturing in the "pre-industrial" period has acquired new emphasis with the recent publication of econometric analysis by C. K. Harley and N. F. R. Crafts.[14] In revising the earlier work of Phyllis Deane and W. A. Cole, Harley concludes that "the industrial sector in the eighteenth century was nearly twice as large as previous estimates estimated and that its subsequent tranformation was less dramatic".[15] Given this elevated starting point, it would appear that between 1770 and 1815 growth was a third lower than the Deane and Cole estimate of aggregate output. N. F. R Crafts also found that their estimate for the rate of growth during the last years of the eighteenth and first years of the nineteenth centuries was overly optimistic. In both Harley's and Crafts' revised chronologies, growth was not only slower, it started sooner too. Of particular importance to this revisionist argument is the fact that as late as the 1840s over 75 per cent of British manufacturing was in "diverse, dispersed and unspectacular industries" – i.e. neither cotton nor iron and decidedly not steam powered. Moreover, when one looks closely at the deployment of steam power in the first phase of industrialization we immediately see that its use was very narrow and of importance mainly in cotton spinning, blast furnaces and coal mining. Furthermore, in mining it was only employed in shifting the black stuff about since "In 1830, as in 1700, coal was brought down from the face by pick, wedge and hammer . . . human muscle was as necessary in 1830 as in 1700 to cut coal . . . [so that there were] few major advances in the productivity of face workers."[16] Therefore, anticipating Harley's argument, Clapham claimed that it would be a mistake to concentrate too much on "the industries, or sectors of industries, which were going through rapid metamorphosis".[17]

The perdurance of handicraft skills during the nascent age of steam casts a different light on the revolutionary character of the first *Industrial Revolution*. Vast increases in output were frequently accomplished by keeping each worker at one constant, repetitive, high-speed task instead of allowing him/her to maintain control over the whole production process. Speed-up was more typical than the introduction of complex machinery. Greater efficiency was achieved by working workers for longer hours and allowing them fewer rest days. The employment of women and children increased the accessible supply of labour. An intensified division of labour requiring more hands, not elaborate machines, offered very large opportunities for outwork, in the workers' homes. In permitting large fluctuations in output without corresponding capital costs for the employer, this system of handicraft manufacturing was able to resist competition from improved machine technology. As Sidney Pollard writes, "There is . . . an impressive degree of agreement among observers of the British industrial revolution that it was characterized by low wages and abundant labour, and that the cheap and elastic labour supply itself played an instrumental part in the progress of industrialization."[18]

The years after 1780 did not just simply continue earlier forms of domestic outwork. Indeed, as Eric Richards has written, there were "substantial changes in employment in the traditional sectors of the economy – some of which declined rapidly in the early phases of the Industrial Revolution, others which expanded at unprecedented rates until perhaps 1830 and then withered away, and others which carried on much as they had been in the previous century".[19] Not only was hand labour often preferable to the adoption of machinofacture but its output was capable of increased·productivity through either the development of new tools or the more systematic exploitation of older methods of production. British industrialization, then, was a process of combined and uneven development in which production was largely based on human energy and human skill. The vast increase in supply of these humans was part-and-parcel of the process of social reproduction which formed the essential complement to the developments in production we have discussed so far.

The transition from handicraft processes to machinofacture was not, therefore, an overnight occurrence. In point of fact, quite the opposite appears to have been the case. The factory's triumph over older forms of industrial organization was protracted. It was not until the last decade of the nineteenth century that it became the dominant form of organization in a majority of industries. The 1851 census returns of "Masters and Workmen", an obviously incomplete return which was biased towards the larger units of production, provides a useful method of crudely quantifying the workers' experience of Victorian industry.[20] Only those employers who specified themselves to be "masters" were considered in this tabulation; together, these 87,270 masters employed 727,468 workers – a fraction of the whole population of the 7,200,000 workers in manufacturing industry. It would seem that the vast reservoir of domestic labour went completely uncounted and so, too, must a great many others who worked in small units overseen by garret-masters. Still, this return is extremely revealing in that it probably represents a "best-case scenario". Among the observed fraction of the manufacturing population, employed by self-styled "masters" in what must have been the most advanced sites, the median workplace employed around thirty-five hands. In order to contrast this figure with a "worst-case scenario" we can add all the unenumerated manufacturing workers (men, women and children) to the lowest rungs on this ladder – working for masters employing under five workers. It is then clear that the median employment experience in the middle of the nineteenth century was in this group of employees. "The great majority of workers in manufacturing industry ... were not employed by great capitalists in larger factories but by innumerable small employers in small workshops."[21]

The first phase of industrialization was characterized by handicraft manufacturing, powered by human energy and requiring little in the way of fixed capital assets. Predominantly, the first phase of industrialization had been based on the extensive exploitation of family labour rather than the intensive exploitation of adult males; as a corollary one might also note that the desire of industrialists to dictate the pace of production by abridging the workshop control exercised by skilled workers led to the transformation in manufacturing processes that we know as the *Industrial Revolution*. This is not to belittle the importance of the developments in coal, iron and steel so much as to insist on the way in which the first phase of industrialization was experienced by most of the workers. It is clear that the years after 1770 also witnessed the growth of forces that ultimately led to an *Industrial Revolution*. These years, between 1770 and 1850, witnessed a final Indian summer for the human-powered handicraft mode of production. For inasmuch as the historical process proceeds unevenly, one would expect the rise of industrial society to overlap with the final stages of the *proto-industrial* mode of production. Moreover, the rise of one was predicated on and produced the demise of the other. This diminuendo was played out at an excruciatingly slow pace as the agonies of the handloom weavers, framework knitters, nailers, colliers and shoemakers all testify.

Industrialization was a process rather more than the *Industrial Revolution* was an event. Whatever date we choose to mark the transition between the first and second phase of this process is necessarily and inevitably arbitrary. In fact, one could just as easily describe the middle half of the nineteenth century, 1825–75, as one long transitional period during which time a new industrial order was slowly being born. In terms of the "Janus-faced" metaphor which was employed earlier, the backwards-looking face was more important in the first half of the nineteenth century; thereafter, the forwards-looking one became more prominent. E. J. Hobsbawm suggests that the building of the railways, and especially the "mania" of 1845–7, inaugurated the second phase of industrialization.[22] It provided stimulation at just the point in time when the bloom was fading from textile industrialization. Gareth Stedman-Jones has seconded Hobsbawm's point that "railway-building is what, more than anything else, resolved the capitalist crisis of the thirties and early forties. It lessened the impact of cyclical crisis, stimulated coal, iron, steel and machine production and resolved the crisis of profitability. More than any other single factor, it assured the successful transition to a modern industrial economy."[23] From this time on the economy was re-oriented and the age of coal and iron and steel began in earnest. The later nineteenth century, then, was the period "in which the Industrial Revolution really occurred, on a massive scale, transforming the whole economy and society much more widely and deeply than the earlier changes had done".[24]

Thus, there is some justification for choosing the middle years of the century as the turning-point in terms of the history of production; there is rather more justification for its choice in terms of the history of reproduction. As David Vincent has written:

At any given moment an artisan might appear to be enjoying an assured prosperity, but the image dissolves as we look at the [working-class] auto-biographers' accounts of their lifetime patterns of employment. Not until the establishment of the major capital concerns of industrial Britain, in particular the railway companies, could an artisan expect an occupation to provide him with a safe and predictable source of income.[25]

It seems to me that an emphasis on the centrality of the labour process is of particular importance in understanding the difference between "pre-industrial" and "industrial" society because of its concern with the organization of production and the reproduction of these material forces in the family lives of the working population. Moreover, such an emphasis on the *phases* of development serves to distinguish an economy based on family labour from its successor which was largely dependent upon the income generated by the principal breadwinner. English industrialization can best be understood as a piecemeal process of combined and uneven development; the vast increase in the supply of these humans was part-and-parcel of the process of social reproduction which formed the essential complement to the emergence of an industrial economy.

Given the centrality of dispersed handicraft manufacturing in the first stage of English industrialization, we need to consider further how this labour process was integrated with the family economy of the producing hands. Robert Malcolmson has written that "this family economy was not normally centred around a single breadwinner: rather, it was assumed that the family's sustenance would depend on the productive contributions of all its members, each of whom helped to sustain the whole".[26] In terms of the *cottage economy* paradigm which has been used throughout this essay, the first phase of industrialization represented continuity just as much as change. The peasant family economy was industrialized in response to its declining agricultural fortunes. Thus, the emergence of an industrial economy cannot be understood outside of, or apart from, the transformation of agricultural labour – the two processes were inextricably joined. Furthermore, the monetization of women's and children's labour draws our attention to the salient point that whether paid individually or as part of the family's piece-rate, the additional labour inputs provided by wives and children were crucial determinants of proletarian incomes and proletarian family formation strategies during the first phase of industrialization. It is therefore chimerical to chart the living standards of the *proto-industrial* population by relating it to an index of real wages. Such statistics as are presently available rely on the wage-rates of male, building-trades workers. It is a major act of faith to employ real wages (of men) as a proxy for wage-earning families. No such reification of the historical context will be provided here. Rather, the burden of my argument is that the first phase of industrialization involved the whole family while the second phase increasingly reconstructed the labour force's focus upon the breadwinner. The changing organization of production had profound implications for the reproduction of the bearers of labour. The rest of this essay is concerned to explicate how this interaction worked itself out in history.

The complementarity of industry and agriculture

The geographical distribution of rural industry was very much the obverse of cereal farming. The spatial location of industry is hardly surprising: first, because the preponderance of pastoral farming in the dispersed upland settlements created conditions in which a "dual economy" could flourish with little land; and, second, because the social economy of the closed, nucleated village grew increasingly antagonistic to any form of competition in the local labour market as a result of the pre-eminent importance attached to bringing in the harvest at the lowest possible cost. The national division of agricultural labour, remarked upon earlier, was balanced by a national division of industrial labour in which the largely pastoral north and west garnered the lion's share of manufacturing. Joan Thirsk has written that

In pastoral regions farming combined with industrial employment was almost common form. The combination was well integrated into a life focused on the family as the wage-earning group. Indeed, the use of the term 'by employments' for industrial occupations of pasture farmers may convey a false impression. They were not accidental or subsidiary, secondary, or a miserable makeshift. They were an integral part of the pastoral way of life. [so much so that] . . . the peasant-worker . . . must have comprised somewhere near half the farming population of the kingdom [in the seventeenth century].[27]

The transformation of the "dark corners of the land" into William Blake's "dark Satanic Mills" is of profound consequence. It provided the material foundation for the proletarian family but, equally, the origins of industry in the loosely governed forest/pastoral regions meant that the imprint of patriarchal authority was less pervasive and more easily ignored than in the cereal belt. Here, then, we have another polarity within which to frame our account: the rural industrial regions were largely free from magisterial domination whereas the agriculturally specialized areas were marked by the presence of landlords and the moral economy of patriarchalism. As one nineteenth-century writer expressed it, when comparing this life favourably with that of the inhabitants of the squire's village,

"a dominant and resident landowner was the centre of intelligence, of charity, and of social life," but for these advantages there was a social price to pay. "It is as true in the parish as in the nation that a paternal government makes a childish people. A man whose brothers and neighbours are dependent upon him is prone to become overbearing whilst the neighbours and even the brothers are apt to become obsequious."[28]

Thus, rural industrialists enjoyed a personal liberty largely unknown to their counterparts in the closed village. This last factor meant that industrial proletarians were able to go about their lives in a pro-active manner whereas agricultural proletarian life was constricted and largely reactive. We shall return to this point.

When Daniel Defoe toured around the whole island of Great Britain between 1724 and 1726 he was struck, over and over again, by the relationship between manufacturing and population concentrations. His observations on the relationship between population density and domestic industry in the parish of Halifax in the West Riding are justly famous and must be quoted extensively:

and so the nearer we came to Hallifax, we found the houses thicker, and the villages greater in every bottom [i.e. valley]; and not only so, but the sides of the hills, which were very steep every way, were spread with houses, and that very thick; for the land being divided into small enclosures, that is to say, from two to six acres each, seldom more, every three or four pieces of land had a house belonging to it. Then it was I began to perceive the reason and the nature of the thing, and found that this division of the land into small pieces, and scattering of the dwellings, was occasioned by, and done for the convenience of the business which the people were generally employed in, and that, as I said before, though we saw no people stirring without doors, yet they were all full within; for, in short, this whole country, however mountainous ... is yet infinitely full of people ... we found the country, in short, one continued village ... hardly a house standing out of a speaking distance from another, and (which soon told us their business) the day clearing up, and the sun shining, we could see that almost at every house there was a tenter, and almost on every tenter a piece of cloth, or kersey, or shalloon, for they are the three articles of that country's labour; from which the sun glancing, and, as I may say, shining (the white reflecting its rays) to us, I thought it was the most agreeable sight that I ever saw, for the hills, as I say, rising and falling so thick, and the valleys opening sometimes one way, sometimes another, so that sometimes we could see two or three miles this way, sometimes as far another ... yet look which way we would, high to the tops, and low to the bottoms, it was all the same; innumerable houses and tenters, and a white piece upon every tenter. But to return to the reason of dispersing the houses, as above; I found, as our road passed among them, for indeed no road could do otherwise, wherever we passed any house we found a little rill or gutter of running water, if the house was above the road, it came from it, and crossed the way to run to another; if the house was below us, it crossed us from some other distant house above it, and at every considerable house was a manufactory or workhouse, and as they could not do their business without water, the little streams were so parted and guided by gutters or pipes, and by turning and dividing the streams, that none of those houses were without a river, if I may call it so, running into and through their work-houses. Then, as every clothier must keep a horse, perhaps two, to fetch and carry for the use of his manufacture, (viz.) to fetch home his wool and his provisions from the market, to carry his yarn to the spinners, his manufacture to the fulling mill, and, when finished, to the market to be sold, and the like; so every manufacturer generally keeps a cow or two, or more, for his family, and this employs the two, three, or four pieces of enclosed land about his house, for they scarce sow corn enough for their cocks and hens; and this feeding their ground still adds by the dung of the cattle, to enrich the soil. Having thus fire and water at every dwelling, there is no need to enquire why they dwell thus dispersed upon the highest hills, the convenience of the manufactures requiring it. Among the manufacturers' houses are likewise scattered an infinite number of cottages or small dwellings, in which dwell the workmen which are employed, the women and children of whom, are always busy carding, spinning, &c. so that no hands being unemployed, all can gain their bread, even from the youngest to the ancient; hardly any thing above four years old, but its hands are sufficient to it self. This is the reason also why we saw so few people without doors; but if we knocked at the door of any of the master manufacturers, we presently saw a house full of lusty fellows, some at the dye-fat, some dressing the cloths, some in the loom, some one thing, some another, all hard at work, and full employed upon the manufacture, and all seeming to have sufficient business.[29]

Defoe's marvellously insightful account describes the symbiosis of agriculture and industry, the complete exploitation of potential sources of labour ("even from the youngest to the ancient"), and the classical sense of proportion in Halifax's social relations which were based upon the replication of its countless units of production ("innumerable houses and tenters, and a white piece on every tenter"). Halifax was at the centre of the most symmetrically balanced *proto-industrial* region in the country; Defoe writes that "this one trading, manufacturing part of the country supports all the countries round it, and the numbers of people settle here as bees about a hive".[30] If other areas did not quite achieve the involuted regularity of the West Riding, there is no doubt that it was a tendency to which they were susceptible. In the middle ages these wood-pasture districts with their extensive rights of common had provided a *locus* for industrial by-employments. The presence of both fuel and raw materials was seen as a potential source of employment by members of the *cottage economy* hard-pressed to balance hands and mouths. Such industries as forestry, woodworking of all sorts, charcoal preparation and iron working, limeburning, pottery and glassmaking were all located in wood-pasture regions with extensive commons.[31] In the early modern period these peasant-industrial regions witnessed the most remarkable population growth.

The dual economy of the "mere village"

When he visited Manchester, "the greatest mere village in England", Defoe wrote "as the manufacture is increased, the people must be increased of course". When he visited Leicester he took the opportunity to write that "one would scarce think it possible as small an article of trade [knit stockings] could employ such multitudes of people as it does; for the whole country seems to be employed in it".[32] Defoe's perception that small articles of trade, and particularly consumer goods, often lay at the heart of rural industrialization has found a resonance in the research of Joan Thirsk. She has written that although it has become commonplace to treat the mass market for consumer goods as a product of the *Industrial Revolution*, and therefore insignificant before the later eighteenth century, the seventeenth-century evidence for the production of such articles as knitted stockings, knitted caps, cheap earthenware, nails, tobacco pipes, lace and ribbon proves the existence at a much earlier date of a mass market for consumer goods. Her research has thus countered the argument that demand built up first, and was met first, among the middle class, and then only gradually filtered down to the working class. In contrast, so Thirsk claims, there was a perpetual restructuring of the consumer industries which was forced upon them from without by the "fickle" demands of consumers. The discrimination and satisfaction of buyers intensified specialization and encouraged producers in each branch of the same industry to strive for higher standards. English industries selling overseas for the most part succeeded best with cheap consumer wares. Rural populations were more fully employed in the seventeenth century than at any earlier time because these consumer industries exploited underemployed rural labour, especially but not entirely in pastoral regions. Furthermore, they absorbed a large share of extra manpower made available by natural increase, expropriation and internal immigration. Fixed capital requirements were minuscule; the largest expense was the cost of labour. At the same time that these consumer industries were multiplying in pastoral areas, they were spreading extra cash throughout rural society. So, Thirsk notes, purchasing power and productive capacity were thus mutually sustaining. It was the wages earned by wives and children, added to that of their husbands, which most impressed economics writers and prompted their praise for new consumer industries, and therefore the wage-rates of men tell us nothing about the earnings of families.[33]

In the metal-working hinterland of Birmingham, the Black Country, the industrialization of the *cottage economy* was similarly at work according to Robert Plot's 1686 *Natural History of Staffordshire*. Two thousand nailers "reckoning boys as well as men" lived in Sedgley parish, just south of Wolverhampton.[34] While these metal-workers had comprised a very small minority of the rural population of south Staffordshire in the later sixteenth century, Pauline Frost's study of probate inventories suggests that "the poorer, landless families ... took up subsidiary crafts, particularly nail-making and other small metal manufactures, to supplement their income sufficiently to buy corn". What began as a reasonably satisfactory "dual economy", in which metal-working was a supplementary activity to stock-raising, became after 1650 an increasingly bifurcated social structure in which "a vista of increasing dependence on a cash income from forge products was opening up".[35] In southern Yorkshire, around Sheffield, there was a similar "dual economy" of farmer/cutlers and farmer/nailers although when Arthur Young visited the community of Ecclesfield in 1769 he remarked that the villagers practised "very bad husbandry". Clearly, the balance between the agricultural and industrial components in the local "dual economy" had decisively shifted in favour of the latter.[36] When Robert Brown visited the West Riding of Yorkshire for the Board of Agriculture, about seventy years after Defoe's *Tour* brought him to Halifax, he found that land "was solely farmed by [the clothiers] as a matter of convenience or amusement" and that they had "little if any pretensions to the character of farmers. The speculations, the interruptions, inseparable from trade, call for all his capital; and ... his

time, his circumstances and interest conspire to prevent him from following up both professions at the same time." He found the clothiers not much
interested in discussing farming with him at all but "speak of spinning
jennies and mills and carding machines, they will talk for days with you".[37]

The availability of easily divisible land in such *proto-industrial* communities not only engendered the morcellization of holdings among the
natives but it also attracted immigrants who, in the words of the preamble
to the 1662 Act of Settlement, moved from parish to parish "to settle
themselves where there is the best stock, the largest commons or wastes to
build cottages, and the most woods for them to burn and destroy".[38]
Again and again scholars have shown that arable, closed villages were
smaller and grew more slowly than pastoral, open villages.[39] Most rural
industrial communities were really overgrown villages since it was usual
that rising population densities accompanied the dispersal of manufacturing in the countryside. Around 1800 the "mere villages" of Birmingham,
Manchester and Leeds were as much as a collection of contiguous
settlements as ordered urban spaces. "The most common industrial
configuration of the early 19th century was a commercial or manufacturing centre which served as the hub for a circle of straggling industrial
villages. As the villages became suburbs, and the farmlands were covered
over with brick, so the great conurbations of the late 19th century were
formed."[40] Outlying villages – the home for nailers, framework knitters,
handloom weavers, cutlers and other species of *proto-industrial* workers
– grew because the logic of the first phase of industrialization underwrote
the multiplication of nearly identical household units of production. The
Black Country, the West Riding and south-east Lancashire, which had
been peripheral, pastoral regions in Henry VIII's time, developed in just
this way to become three of the five major urban agglomerations of
Victorian England.

It was only well after 1800 that the industrial town became the typical place of the
new employment. It possessed external economies, a competitive environment,
and above all, a flexible labour supply, including an industrial reserve army of
Irish, unemployed, and other submerged groups, for whom the employer was not
responsible in any way except when he wanted their services. The rate of growth,
wholly unplanned, of cities like Manchester (17,000 in 1760 to 180,000 in 1830),
Liverpool (25,000 to 165,000), Birmingham (30,000 to 140,000), or Leeds (14,000 to
120,000) has never been repeated and could probably not have taken place in any
other social context.[41]

"Its hands are sufficient to it self"

Perhaps the most important point is the most obvious one – the family
work unit was composed of men, their wives and their children. In

particular, the labour of youngsters was an extremely elastic resource; its deployment was of great importance simply because of its sheer weight. Wrigley and Schofield's "back projection estimates" suggest that children aged 5–14 comprised between a little over a sixth (17.63 per cent, 1671–75) and about a quarter (24.41 per cent, 1826–30) of the total population.[42] For children, labour began at an early age. It was both a moral and material duty. Neil McKendrick has commented that "It was a commonplace of sixteenth- and seventeenth-century morality that a child should be set to some useful occupation by the age of six in order to avoid 'the sins and pitfalls of sloth and idleness'."[43]

The family was, by itself, a variable of immense experiential significance in differentiating the seeming homogeneity of class. One must always be aware that, swirling around the central tendency of a seemingly immutable series of life-cycle stages, there were a whole range of forces which could puncture the best-laid plans and deflate the most cherished hopes. Those whose parents died unexpectedly left school abruptly; only with the greatest sacrifice and a steely determination were they able to gain a basic level of literacy. Margaret Spufford's sensitive analysis of seventeenth-century spiritual autobiographies makes it clear that children were expected to start working at an early age. From her familiarity with these sources, "It looks very much as if seven was thought to be the age at which a child could cope with a full working day and start to earn a wage which began to be significant."[44] Spufford's work describes how those whose parents survived had early working experiences quite different from those who were orphaned or half-orphaned early. In an age of unpredictable mortality, family life was a fragile tissue. But for all its fragility, it was highly prized and cultivated. For many, the option to family was charity and the stigma of the workhouse. In these circumstances it would be hardly surprising that every effort was made to incorporate the labour of children into the creation of a common fund. To be sure, the individuality of the family's members was a centrifugal force but, *more than equally*, the logic of the family mode of production created centripetal pressures which bound the domestic commonwealth together in its struggle to subsist. David Vincent's humane and perceptive study of early nineteenth-century working-class autobiographies suggests that "Throughout their time as members of their parents' family economy, the child-labourers were deeply aware that their contributions, no matter how small, could make a significant difference to its well-being."[45]

Those activities which had no obvious monetary value attached to them were nonetheless prized for their "substitution effect" enabling their parents to do other work and so facilitating the reproduction of the whole family's labour power. Six-, seven- and eight-year-olds could gather dung and firewood, sweep the floor, clean pots and pans and dishes and cutlery, carry water, look out for and play with their younger siblings in close proximity to their mother and/or father, prepare foodstuffs by chopping and peeling as well as going out of the home on short errands. Nine- through twelve-year-olds could spin and knit as well as mending clothes and socks in need of repair. They could attend the fire in the hearth, wash and dry clothing and bedding, herd and milk domestic animals, watch the poultry and arrange for their food. These intermediate children could be left in sole charge of their younger siblings and be given some simple responsibilities for marketing. Young teenagers (twelve to fifteen) would be able to take on greater responsibility in regard to caring for their siblings and also to marketing, they could be given more difficult and arduous jobs and could even be expected to earn some money outside the home at harvest. They might be in charge of some animals or chickens and have some specific agricultural tasks – collecting eggs or growing potatoes, for example – as well as playing an ever-greater role in the preparation of food. Children over fifteen would be very nearly "adult equivalents" even if they might require several years to reach their full physical maturity and a few more after that to gain the requisite skills and to command an adult wage. It would, therefore, be a profound mistake to overlook the use-values derived from these little people's labour within the *cottage economy*. It would be an ever graver error to assume that because their monetary earnings were slight and may not have completely compensated the household for their consumption they were a marginal cost, a drag on the family economy. Children were part of a team; a team that worked together, a team that was more than the sum of its parts. When we get inside the logic of reproducing this family labour power we can then understand that children created an economic resource which could be expanded or contracted in a situational fashion.

The fact that children could and did begin to "pay their own way" from an early age meant that, for handicraft families, the impact of high dependency ratios (of non-productive "mouths" demanding support from the labour from few "hands") was a short-lived part of the complete family cycle. The benefits accruing to the handicraft family when this "dependency hump" was traversed were obvious enough when many mouths were being supplied by the income generated from the labour of almost as many hands. Families engaged in industry were less likely than agriculturalists to see their teenaged children leave home and embark on an extended sojourn in service. Having paid the cost of raising children, industrial families enjoyed the benefits of their labour. It seems that teenaged children in industrial households made a substantial monetary contribution to the common fund. They frequently turned over most of their earnings to their parents, even when they were paid separately.[46] Early industrial society therefore had its own reserve army of labour and most of the bottlenecks in the economy bore more heavily on the demand for this labour than its supply.[47] As far as the merchant entrepreneur was concerned, "the *obvious* way of industrial expansion in the eighteenth century was not to construct factories, but to extend the so-called domestic system".[48]

Involvement in industrial activity led to the intensification of women's and children's labouring experience. Neil McKendrick has argued that not only are daily wage-rates notoriously misleading indicators of the annual total income of the male family head, but they also obfuscate the contribution of working wives and children when "one wife and one child, in those industries which paid the wife two-thirds and the child one-third of male rates, or one wife and two children, in those industries where the wife received a half and the children a quarter of the male rate, could double a working man's take-home earnings".[49] There was an additional tendency for this family-wage system to undermine the prudential check on fertility within marriage because larger families earned much more than a single male. As the children grew up and earned higher wages, the family reached its peak earning capacity. Because of the long period during which children stayed at home – there were, of course, a large number of such children – the family wage was optimized over an extended period, not just during the breadwinner's peak earning years. Rarely were women and children independent wage-earners. More usually their wages were subsumed within a larger family income which was paid to the male "head" of the family unit.[50] Hans Medick has argued that "The decisive marginal work effort of the family ... remained underpaid."[51] There was thus an inherent tendency for the family to exploit itself which was built into the system. Among the *proto-industrial* framework knitters in the east Midland counties of Nottingham and Leicester,

Vast numbers of women and children are working side by side with men, often employed in the same description of frames, making the same fabrics, and at the same rate of wages; the only advantage over them which the man possesses being his superior strength, whereby he can undergo the fatigues of labour for longer hours than the weaker physical energies of women and children enable them to bear; and therefore he earns more money, by turning off more work.[52]

Of course, not all industrial activity before the *Industrial Revolution* was family-based; there were very significant sectors in which males were the main form of labour and the chief source of income for their families. Heavy industry – coal mining and navvying in particular – was characterized by the employment of adult males whose wages were usually higher, if rather less predictable, than the average for cottagers, whether in *proto-industry* or agriculture. One might postulate that the family organization of such workers was less egalitarian than that of their counterparts in *cottage industry*, being more focussed on the chief breadwinner. Such families were also less likely to have integrated an agricultural component with their industrial activity; this is not to say that they had no connection with the land but rather that they did not have the sort of "dual economy" of the sort Defoe described as being common in Halifax and which Frost and Hey have also found in the Black Country and south Yorkshire, respectively.

In addition, the early modern economy was characterized by the "honourable" trades – mercantile activity of all sorts and the whole, bewildering panoply of services which made life before the revolution so extravagantly pleasant for the owners of capital. Among these groups the traditional systems of apprenticeship and restrictive marriage persisted. Village craftsmen – millers, brick-makers, sawyers, cabinet makers, coopers and turners, wheelwrights, blacksmiths, saddlers, tailors, shoemakers and specialized building-trades workers of all sorts – grew in numbers right through the first phase of industrialization, to 1851, as the countryside became the site of a sophisticated division of labour. They were obliterated in the second phase of industrialization, after 1851, when the railways broke down rural markets and made England a single, truly integrated economic unit. In fact, it is probably specious to pinpoint the moment of change with any certainty; instead, we can only suggest tendencies and it is in this way that we have to see the perdurance of the "honourable" trades and village crafts as a brake on the *proletarian demography model* outlined earlier. Still, the overwhelming emphasis in the first phase of industrialization was towards the breakdown of older systems of control over the labour process by individual skilled workers and their replacement with cheaper alternatives. And, as we have seen, such changes in production had complementary implications for reproduction when the whole family was drawn into the labour process.

A resolved conundrum re-solved

"The whole Industrial Revolution of the last 200 years has been nothing else but a vast secular boom, largely induced by the unparalleled rise in population."[53] The argument put forward in this essay is quite different from Sir John Hicks' aside. Before turning to the feedback between production and reproduction, which is central to my argument, it is first necessary to consider the present state of our knowledge regarding the mechanisms of demographic change in English population history. E. A. Wrigley suggested that as a result of his research with R. S. Schofield on the population history of England a new conundrum has arisen to replace the old. The discovery that fertility was the dominant influence on population growth rates but that nuptiality changes account almost entirely for the great increase in fertility immediately suggests the need for a better understanding of the determinants and concomitants of nuptiality. One good conundrum, one might say, begets another.[54]

The growth of population during the **Industrial Revolution** has been solved, according to Wrigley, firmly and unmistakably on the side of the birth rate. Perhaps the single most important contribution of Wrigley's article is the comparative perspective with which he introduces his data. From it we learn that England was principally distinguished from its continental neighbours during the 1680–1820 period by its vigorous birth rate.[55] The new *problèmatique* which demands scholarly attention has been changed, at a stroke, so that "we should now look to changes in nuptiality as the principal immediate reason for the acceleration [in population growth rates during the 'long eighteenth century' – i.e. between 1680 and 1820] which occurred".[56]

As Malthus recognized, and Wrigley quotes, the cultural inheritance of the English was quite different from that of the Chinese.[57] Marriage, the linchpin of the English family's cultural inheritance, was generally late – the average age for *both* men and women was in the mid-twenties, it involved the formation of a separate nuclear family household, and it was predicated on the establishment of some form of economic independence by the young couple. While much recent work in historical demography has concentrated on the fine detail of the measurements of central tendency in the distribution of marriage ages, there has been relatively little investigation of the implications of variation about this average. This point is important precisely because there was no "average" experience; rather, the average is the sum of a whole series of competing – and often contradictory – interpretations. Thus, while most English people behaved in conformity to the English "economic demographic system", they did so for their own reasons. Their specific socio-economic circumstances would have been enormously diverse which would have led some to marry rather earlier than average and others to marry rather later than average.

The pattern of these individual decisions can be represented by the distribution of marriage ages. Statistically, we can then examine this pattern by concentrating on just the measurement of central tendency or else we can focus on the patterns of variance and give as much weight to the "mean" as to the "standard deviation" or the "inter-quartile range". The latter two characteristics measure the spread of the distribution. They are unfortunately neglected too often and so we are usually not told that fully a quarter of the population in question married several years earlier than the measurement of central tendency while a quarter would have married several years later. And, moreover, the fascination with the "average" means that we are not told that such early-marryers and late-marryers were just as much a part of the English population as those who hit the magic age for their cohort.

Let us pursue the implications of this line of thought a little further. Wrigley writes that "Age at first marriage [for women] dropped by about 3 years from 26 to 23 years" over the course of the "long eighteenth century" (i.e. 1680–1820).[58] There are several ways to interpret this simple statistic. First, we might just say that the English people all moved in the direction of earlier marriage in response to a long period of buoyant real wages and that this measurement is sufficiently comprehensive to capture their diverse interests. Second, we might say that, as the English population grew, those who were early-marryers and were therefore more prolific became preponderant while those who were late-marryers became less so. Third, we might look at the social composition of early- and late-marryers in the first period and then link our explanation to the growing importance of those groups which had always married at young ages. Fourth, we might argue that as a result of social and economic changes new groups were emerging which favoured an "early marriage strategy" and that older groups favouring a "late marriage strategy" were declining so that the apparent statistical result is really a compositional change in the characteristics of the population under investigation. Fifth, it would seem that social and economic change impinged upon the decision to marry by inserting itself *into* the marriage process and accelerating the prospect of independence while also separating that independence from the biological rhythms of the family cycle. Finally, we might propose an answer which makes use of all these perspectives to explain a shift *within the parameters of the older system*. Although tracks get covered and caveats are amended to their account, the main thrust of the Wrigley/Schofield explanation of rising fertility during the "long eighteenth century" is tied to the first of these five alternatives. Because of their real-wage-based argument, they are led to consider the prince with the pauper, the peasant with the proletarian, and the city-dweller with the countryman as a single entity – the English people. And yet, manifestly, the local ecology of social life varied immensely between a landlord-dominated village and a *proto-industrial* one. This being the case, it is surprising not that "the English" differed so much in their nuptiality practices in the "long eighteenth century" but that they were so comparable – at least in demographic terms so far as we can measure them. Here, then, is the nub of my disagreement with the real-wage-based model of demographic behaviour – obviously the behaviour of the English people, whether prince or pauper, peasant or proletarian, city-dweller or countryman was informed by a common cultural inheritance which distinguished them from the Chinese (*pace* Malthus) and, equally obviously I think, the use of a single measurement of central tendency allied to an outmoded and inadequate series of real-wage data can do little to capture the historically specific decisions of men and women.

What is needed is the incorporation of other forms of evidence which might enable us to consider the sub-populations which are joined for purely heuristic purposes into a whole. Thus, it was the case that most of the English people during the "long eighteenth century" married in their twenties, but they might have done so for a whole series of different reasons. They were all acting on a different set of assumptions from those which motivated the Chinese; nevertheless it is a mistake to claim that they were all therefore motivated for much the same set of reasons. Rather than proposing an explanation which highlights the comparative homogeneity of the English experience in a vast trans-national perspective, it makes much more sense to understand their activity within a specific historical grid of experience and cultural expectations. They might have all done much the same thing – at least so far as we can measure it and then boil that measurement down to its residual essence – but they might have each been doing their own thing for their own reasons. Social life is very much a balance of forces – on the one hand, we have the anarchy of individual behaviour based upon individual perceptions of interest and, on the other hand, we have the group-defined norms which provide limits within which individuals act. The "English negative feed-back economic-demographic system" can be construed as the latter side of the balance but any account which does not explain the other side of the equation is going to be unstable and incomplete. My disagreement with the Wrigley/Schofield form of explanation stems from its failure to consult social-historical materials and so to broaden its explanatory system. By considering the first stage of the industrialization and proletarianization within the same framework as that which is used to analyse the earlier, "pre-industrial" age, their account flattens the historical landscape. While it may be objected that my emphasis on the novelty of ways of life and thought which were associated with industrialization and proletarianization errs in the opposite direction, it is my opinion that in order to remain true to the complexity of the historical past we must reject neo-classical abstractions of it.

The burden of my position is not that there were immense differences in the *ages* at which the English people married over the course of the "long eighteenth century", it is rather that new and different groups continued to marry within the parameters of the old system – albeit rather earlier than before – in novel ways and for quite novel reasons. Thus, people may have been doing much the same thing at much the same age but these people were doing so for wholly new reasons. Who were these "new people"? The answer to this question is, in a nutshell, the proletariat. The population which was growing in the "long eighteenth century" was becoming disproportionately proletarian. These people not only married earlier than their predecessors but also married in novel ways and for quite different sets of reasons. Let us therefore turn to this aspect of the social history of marriage in the "long eighteenth century".

The labour process and the pro-active family

The crucial point to explain is not how population grew but why it did so. To address this question we must explain why, in a long period of improving life expectation, the homeostatic demographic regime of the peasantry was cast aside so that the birth rate rose at the same time the death rate fell. We need, therefore, to explain why the cultural imperatives of the *cottage economy* were superseded. Any such answer must focus on which groups grew and when that growth occurred. The lineaments of such an answer have been already indicated; it is now time to show how the *proletarian demography model* played itself out during the first phase of industrialization.

Given the massive increase in the demand for and the supply of labour in the first phase of industrialization it is necessary to consider nuptiality changes within a framework in which the imperatives of the family economy have pride of place. Concentrating on the simple, standardized measurement of the real wage (for men) is likely to be an inappropriate method for analysing the changing fortunes of the industrialized *cottage economy*. Even though the agricultural component in the domestic economy declined, family incomes most likely rose or at the very least remained stable when women's and children's labour was monetized. As we have already argued, during the first phase of industrialization the earnings of women and children became a central component of the family wage for a vast section of the population. "For not only were women and children earning high wages, but far more women and children were working. Both are notoriously characteristic of the British Industrial Revolution – and there is a massive literature on the increase in employment possibilities for them and the increase in the numbers actually employed."[59] Neil McKendrick's point is well taken but his focus on the period of the **Industrial Revolution** is too limited because this process of monetizing the labour of all members of the *cottage economy* was a central feature of the *whole* first phase of rural industrialization.[60] So, the increased demand for labour, its declining cost and the employment opportunities offered in the handicraft industries combined to create a massive rise in labour-force participation. If one were able to construct an index to calculate the maximum supply of labour – of men, women and children – its utilization would probably have reached its apogee in the early industrial period.

The industrialization of the *cottage economy* was a potent force in the plebeian's pro-active interpretation of the prudential check on marriage. The diminution of patriarchal controls over courtship was a characteristic of the industrial and/or staple-extractive villages. Hans Medick suggests that "Marriage and family formation slipped beyond the grasp of patriarchal domination; they were no longer 'tangibly' determined by property relationships, but they did not lose their 'material' foundation in the process of production."[61] Insofar as earnings, not property, became the pre-requisite for family formation and marriage, a family economy emerged. The labour of wives and children as well as that of the husband were crucial. Sons and daughters were kept at home instead of being sent out to service because their earnings were a crucial component of the family income and the attendant strategy of reproduction. The reconfiguration of the family economy affected its internal relationships so that "patriarchal authority, if not displaced, was modified. The peasant practice of betrothal agreements between families lapsed wherever young people had their own earnings and thus were able to accumulate their own marriage portions."[62] Furthermore, the density of relationships among the industrial villagers and a tradition of communal involvement meant that it was not unusual for "kinfolk and friends [to stage] a public bridal for their benefit or the young people used their own entrepreneurial talents to make a big wedding for themselves".[63] The requirement that marriage be preceded by the accumulation of a dowry was relaxed in the circumstances of what might be termed "public accumulation". Such customs as the "bride ale" and the "bidding wedding" to which guests brought useful gifts were "a form of mutual aid" and were abetted by the practice of building "so-called 'one-night houses', squatters' cottages made of wood or sod, which, if they could be built undetected on waste or commons, gave the new couple the right to a house and some small land".[64] Life in a *proto-industrial* community was public and the "publicity" surrounding this festive sociability was an integral component of social reproduction. "Festivities did not just serve the purpose of shared pleasure. They expressed and affirmed the solidarity of the social cohesion of the village community."[65]

The *proto-industrial* family not only supplied labour but it also absorbed a substantial portion of the costs of production. It usually supplied its own tools and therefore obviated the need for entrepreneurs to engage in fixed-capital expenditures. The merchant could therefore keep his capital liquid and profit from its circulation. For these reasons, extending the domestic system was the path of least resistance; "the *obvious* way of industrial expansion". That this practice was both long-lasting and not confined to the textile industries is evident from Eric Hopkins' study of the labour process in Birmingham in the second quarter of the nineteenth century where "a very large proportion of work was paid for by piece and was given out to be executed in the homes of the work people" and "As far as the smaller workplaces are concerned, the factor or middleman in all probability was simply not interested in changing the old routines as long as he got the work in on time and at the right price or wage."[66] Not only was the putter-out relatively uninterested in the organization of work but he was also loathe to intervene in its practice. In outwork and even smaller workshops the labour process was completely controlled by the workers. "Wherever unmechanized small workshop production remained then Saint Monday might accompany it: in Birmingham, in the gun trade, in pearl-button making, and among tool-makers; in Leicester workshops; among Scottish handloom weavers and Whitby jet-ornament makers; among woodworkers and tailors everywhere."[67]

The handicraft family manufactured a marketable product in exchange for its subsistence; in adverse conditions it did not hesitate to exploit itself and work longer hours. It was thus enormously flexible and particularly well adapted to the requirements of merchant-capitalists who were interested in having a relatively stable source to supply them with industrial products. On the other hand, in prosperous conditions *proto-industrialists* often invoked their "leisure preference" to the exasperation of merchants who saw the prospect of inflated profits slipping through their fingers. The organization of production in the *cottage industries* created the material conditions within which the "English" attachment to prudence was re-evaluated. The peasant world was essentially restrictive and based on its limited horizons and relentless struggle to subsist; in contrast, the industrialization of the *cottage economy* introduced a totally new element into the domestic equation and turned its traditional inwardness inside out. It became increasingly likely that the factors influencing the demand for their products were being determined outside the locale. These exogenous influences began with the withdrawal of the industrial segment of the English population from the relatively self-contained world of the *cottage economy* and its integration into a national or even world-wide pool of labour. Thus, the well-being of rural proletarians could be determined by trade fluctuations, distant climate conditions or, more ominously, by the vagaries of international diplomacy and its logical extension, war. The demographic importance of this development is obvious – control over the marriage process was being displaced in the sense that it was coming to be determined by conditions beyond a betrothed couple's control and understanding.

In these circumstances couples not only married earlier but the "eroticization of relationships began even before serious courtship".[68] Pregnant brides and bastard-bearers became commonplace. From 1680 to 1800 the proportion of pre-nuptial pregnancies rose from 15 to 35 per cent. The illegitimacy ratio rose from 1.5 to 5 per cent during the same period. "Since first births were approximately a quarter of all births, the two categories between them comprised a half of all first births."[69] Close analysis of illegitimacy in four communities has shown a very direct connection between rising prices and skyrocketing annual illegitimacy ratios, suggesting that the issue was not so much promiscuity rampant as marriage frustrated.[70]

It has been argued that, in contrast to the peasantry, the rural industrial population was freed from the patriarchal control of its social superiors and largely ignored by its economic masters. Although, we should note, there was no significant change in the household structure of the cottage industrialists – almost everyone still lived in nuclear family units – there were important changes within the home itself. In the *proto-industrial* centres the household (i.e. the "cottage") became a focus for production in a way that it never was for the agricultural labourer. Domestic outwork gave the worker control over the pace of production and, to a considerable extent, ownership of the means of production. Household units, like the ones in Halifax described so vividly by Defoe, were multiplied in an effort to raise the volume of production. But the worker himself dictated the pace of his work and the number of hours his wife and his children were required to assist him in producing the weekly product. The three-day weekend, with intermittent bouts of furious labour, was a possibility during periods of high prices. At other times the family exploited itself, as it were, by working longer hours to maintain the accepted level of subsistence.[71] In many trades – textiles and small-metal goods, in particular – the older children were kept at home so that they could contribute to the family's pooled income. At critical stages in the family cycle when a surplus of infants threatened to sway the balance between mouths and hands, it was not unknown for apprentices and servants – often orphaned paupers – to be brought into the household to restore the equilibrium. Ann Kussmaul's work on servants-in-husbandry makes it clear that the pastoral sections of the country, where there was a complementarity between industry and agriculture, long remained the stronghold of this institution. How many of these so-called "servants-in-husbandry" were, in fact, employed in the households of farmer-weavers, farmer-nailers and other members of the "dual economy"?

In many ways, therefore, the domestic economy of the *proto-industrialists* resembled that of the Russian peasantry described by A. V. Chayanov in the first part of the twentieth century.[72] Although they produced industrial products, the cottage industrialists' working lives were determined by their own inner rhythms, not those of a modern economy.

The worker's labour effort, or standard of output per unit of time, was also determined by custom rather than market calculation, at any rate until he began to learn the rules of the game. The ideal of 'a fair day's work for a fair day's pay' had, and has, little in common with the ideal of buying in the cheapest and selling in the dearest market.[73]

E. J. Hobsbawm makes this point in a discussion concerning the entrepreneurs' ignorance of "the potential economies of really efficient labour exploitation". He goes on to write that employers were tempted by "cheap labour economy" which made them not only tolerant of inefficient organization and administration but equally intolerant of more "intensive" exploitation of labour. Moreover, the essentially conservative nature of employers meant that they felt safer with old-fashioned "extensive" modes of appropriation. This extensive form of labour deployment was prized by cottage industrialists and merchant-capitalists alike. There were few external demands to change its internal configuration. When, after the Napoleonic Wars, major economic adjustments forced employers in a corner, because of pressure on profit-margins and increased competition, their response was to fall back on the "extensive" form of appropriation by extending hours and cutting money wage-rates. It was only at the mid-century that "intensive" modes of labour utilization were beginning to be substituted for "extensive" ones; while it was in the last decades of the nineteenth century that so-called scientific management led to the substitution of rational for empirical strategies.[74]

The proto-active family makes itself

During the first phase of industrialization, then, the family budget of most rural industrialists balanced the costs of partial dependence on wage-work with the benefits of vestigial household production of subsistence needs. The social relations of production resonated in the personal lives of the proletariat; they were not passive, inert objects of change. Nor did they simply inherit their culture from an earlier age, unmodified and in an unquestioning manner. If the working class can be said to have made itself in the "conflict between alternative ways of life, not just between the middle and working classes, but within working-class communities themselves",[75] then it is equally important to appreciate the impact of this struggle within the personal realm. Family life was not insular; it, too, was caught up in the historical process. Ideological and intellectual currents, just as much as economic and social ones, were at work in the dissolution of the *cottage economy* and its replacement by the wage-nexus of urban, industrial society. The *proto-industrial* labourer was the master of his own household, responsible for organizing its production and socializing his children. Another way in which the freedom of the ***proto-industrial*** family differed from that of the agriculturalist was linked with the dispersed settlement patterns of the rural industrial communities. Usually, domestic industries sprang up in forest settlements, freehold villages, pastoral uplands and urban suburbs which all lacked strong patriarchal domination, making it possible for these households to pro-liferate. The social and political implications deriving from this lack of supervision were of real importance.

It has been argued that non-conformist religion and its Halevyian antithesis, radical politics, flourished in a seed-bed of independent mechanics.[76] A very great many of the people attracted to the Methodist revival had been released from the patriarchal politics of the closed village and had their own space in which to work and think. They could interpret the world according to their own notions without the stern supervision of the old priest or new presbyter. The radical religion of the lower classes stressed free will and individual responsibility. Not surprisingly, John Wesley found some of his most enthusiastic converts among West Country and Yorkshire cottage industrialists, Cornish tin miners and the north-eastern colliers. The opportunity for intellectual independence afforded by this ***proto-industrial*** mode of production was crucial to the emergence of a world-view that was not interpreted according to the patriarchal organization of knowledge. E. J. Hobsbawm warns us that we should not over-emphasize the role of religious *observance*, at least insofar as we gain an insight into it from the 1851 religious census:

Broadly speaking ... The large cities and some, but by no means all, of the backward mining and iron areas were relatively unreligious (that is to say, less than 25 per cent of the *total* population attended divine service on the census Sunday). The Church of England was not merely a minority group in most [industrial areas], but was completely outclassed [by non-conformists].[77]

While attendance (or non-attendance) may have been highly variable and the strength of working-class apathy – and, indeed, antipathy – great, the impact of non-conformist religion cannot be distilled into a simple measure focussing on one moment in time. The great strength of E. P. Thompson's discussion of proletarians' attraction to the Methodist camp is in its recognition that the egalitarian universality of grace offered something almost tangible to people whose social world was in a state of flux:

it remains both true and important that Methodism, with its open chapel doors, did offer to the uprooted and abandoned people of the Industrial Revolution some kind of community to replace the older community-patterns which were being displaced. As an unestablished (although undemocratic) Church, there was a sense in which working people could make it their own; and the more closely-knit the community in which Methodism took root (the mining, fishing or weaving village) the more this was so.[78]

Additionally, the tendency for Methodism to splinter suggests very strongly that for all Wesley's authoritarianism he could only lead those who wished to follow his particular creed. Furthermore, one can understand that Wesley's great charisma may have mesmerized men and women, boys and girls, into following him; the same argument becomes less tenable after his death in 1791 as the remnants of camp-meeting evangelicalism were institutionalized when the Methodist Society was transubstantiated into the Methodist Church.

The Methodist movement is of particular interest because it may have been the first serious attempt to convert the labouring class as opposed to coercing them into formal acceptance of outward observances of religion.[79] Arnold Rattenbury has written: "The eighteenth rather than the nineteenth century clangs and rattles with Methodism." He goes on to claim that "The 60,000 Society members of 1791 signal perhaps millions not only touched but infected by Methodism" because "The 60,000 is that proverbial tip of an iceberg – an image apt enough since, if you follow me, Wesley had for fifty years been trying to freeze the passion in human relationships."[80] Elie Halevy, in his largely ignored essays in the *Revue de Paris* (1906), argued that

The very organization that Wesley imposed on the Methodist Society, which it has kept to our time, seems to have been based upon the organization of the industrial society of the time when Wesley went preaching from town to town. The Wesleyan minister corresponded to the merchant, to the employer; he was established, as it were, in the central town in the region, the "circuit". In the surrounding villages, "local preachers", individual lay men, exerted upon smaller groups of the faithful an authority comparable to that exercised by the rural manufacturers, subordinates of the merchants, upon the common day laborers. In both schemes of organization, the similar hierarchical orders corresponded to the half-urban, half-rural distribution of the population.[81]

The success of "pope" Wesley and the Methodist Church in sublimating revolutionary impulses may have been overdrawn by Halevy but his corollary point remains – adherents internalized personal discipline. The pro-active proletariat was confronted with the choice between the chiliasm of "emotional and spiritual paroxysms" and the adoption of "a methodical discipline in every aspect of life."[82] The choice of the one did not preclude an occasional flirtation with the other, although most people were likely to have oscillated within the mid-point range between these two extremes. The ambivalence and indeterminacy of this psycho-social landscape itself interacted with the changing configuration of the material world. We might model this interaction in the following manner: to the extent that the worker was his own master but subject to the external unpredictability of commercial capitalism, the cathartic energies of evangelical religion (Thompson calls this "a ritualized form of psychic masturbation") held sway; but when the worker was the more closely integrated with the warehouse and factory, thereby seeing the disposition of his own labour-time inexorably pass out of his own control, inner repression and the privatization of the emotions became the more dominant characteristic. During the first phase of industrialization the former set of characteristics were the more dominant; with the switchover to more intensive forms of exploitation, the latter congeries of personal attributes gained the centre-stage. Of course, there is a strong element of reductionist functionalism in such modelling and yet it bears a strong relationship to the historical evolution of labour discipline in general and English Methodism in particular. Is it so surprising that the mentality of the early nineteenth-century "Methodist political rebel [who] carried through into his radical or revolutionary activity a profound moral earnestness, a sense of righteousness and of 'calling', a 'Methodist' capacity for sustained organizational dedication and (at its best) a high degree of personal responsibility"[83] became the attributes so prized by the *respectable* working class and its trade union leaders in the quite different climate of the later nineteenth century?

Rational illiterates

It is often suggested that literacy and schooling, like religion with which they were so clearly associated in the early modern period, provide a touchstone revealing a deeper set of inter-related mental characteristics.[84] The literate members of the commons are thought to have learned to read in order to participate in activities which would otherwise have been inaccessible. In this way literacy served to sharpen a division within the working class itself, corresponding to the moral and intellectual distancing between the classes and the masses. Popular literacy is thus thought to have driven a wedge through the working class, distinguishing its rough from the respectable members.[85] Thomas Laqueur, a notable proponent of this view of "working-class demand" for literacy, further argues that in this way, and for these reasons, "There is little doubt that literacy alters the personality structure of those who possess it in ways congruent with the requirements of industrial society."[86] Yet, doubts remain about the kind of argument in which states of mind and *mentalités*, cut off from material conditions of life, are thought to reflect the mainsprings of a modernizing popular culture.

Working-class experience with literacy during the first phase of

126

industrialization seems to have been every bit as equivocally indetermi-
nate as its experience of evangelical religion. Working-class autobiographers were ambiguous and confused by their relationship to the
disintegrating pre-industrial popular culture. They can be best understood as explorers pushing forward the process of secularization and first
encountering developments which would eventually reconstruct
working-class culture. Experiencing such changes meant that the readers
were bound to be dislocated and, as David Vincent is at pains to point out,
the pursuit of really useful knowledge was and has remained a minority
tradition within the working class. Artisan readers rarely shared their
literary predilections with those amongst whom they lived and worked.
Artisan readers felt separated from, and often in conflict with, their
families and workmates.[87]

In addition, up to and during the period of Chartism, working-class
radicals had an educational agenda which was starkly antipathetic to the
"provided", clerically dominated system of schooling. Radical, alternative
goals suggested the use-value of education as a political strategy to rebel
against an oppressive system of production in which capitalists set
workers against each other, driving down wages and depriving them of
their independence. It was this mentality which led a Birmingham radical
journalist to write, in 1829, that "Labourers must become capitalists, and
must acquire knowledge to regulate their labour on a large and united
scale before they will be able to enjoy the whole product of their labour."[88]
A great deal of working-class activity was thus defensive, seeking to
stabilize social relations upset by the incursions of starkly competitive
industrial capitalism. Inheritors of the egalitarian traditions of the ***proto-
industrial*** village, the outworkers fell back upon their cultural inheritance
based on the self-sufficiency of the family unit of production, the integrity
of a communitarianism and spontaneous mutual aid which were all fast
receding in the new conditions. The followers of Chartism and Owenism
were split between these older traditions and the newer proletarian
movements which struggled for sectional gains. This split was characterized by the emotional commitment of the former groups and the
analytic clarity of the latter. "Both radicalism and Methodism attempted to
tame the emotional expression of their adherents and tie it to ideologically
sound and organizationally sanctioned occasions" so that "it can readily
be asserted that the proportionate influence of these 'nonrational' but
ordered aspects of social life declined, and with the decline, some of the
strength of the mobilization was sapped."[89] The price of this organizational success was high. ***Proto-industrial*** workers had failed to stop the
Industrial Revolution in its tracks whereas the new agenda of piecemeal,
ameliorative reform was open-ended and acknowledged the "rules of the
game". It was within this transformed political arena that radical attitudes

to state education were gradually shifting towards accepting "in a very sharp form, the child-adult divide, the tendency to equate education with school, the depoliticization of educational content, and the professionalization of teaching. In all of these ways the state as educator was by no means a neutral apparatus".[90]

The argument that education was a "modernizing" force in working-class life seems to be further contradicted by three rather important sorts of quantitative evidence. First, industrial regions not only attained literacy levels below the national average but they may have even declined for a couple of generations when the twin forces of industrialization and urbanization were experienced with the greatest intensity.[91] Second, even among rural industrial framework knitters in Shepshed, Leicestershire, there seems to have been no strong positive correlation in inter- or intra-generational literacy. Thus, while fathers may have been literate their sons were not necessarily so; similar differences prevailed between siblings.[92] Third, among these same villagers, there was clear evidence that illiterate proletarians were as capable in adjusting their reproductive strategies to meet adverse material conditions as those with the supposedly "modernizing" characteristics associated with literacy.[93]

The answers of these quantitative studies seem to me to be as ambivalent as Vincent's analysis of those exceptional individuals, "a distinct unit within the working class", who were usually isolated from their fellows because of their solitary habits.[94] Moreover, the only study which has analysed the way that this supposed touchstone of a new, different moral and intellectual world was transmitted within families has concluded that few literate workers seem to have been able to arrange that all their children learned to read and later to write. Indeed, only a very tiny minority appears to have made sure all their sons and daughters were literate. The implications of this research are important for "popular demand" theories of educational history.

The relationship between working-class schooling and working-class culture can only be understood within a grid which encompasses both the demand for and the supply of working-class scholars because, irrespective of all the well-meaning energy that was invested in the supply of schooling to working-class children, it only had a resonance when it was met with an equally energetic demand. The perdurance of child labour and the unpredictability of the family economy in the first phase of industrialization meant that working-class demand for schooling was a material problem which was quite obviously as complex as the moral one. Many people clearly did want to have their children learn to read and write so that they could "improve" themselves in prescribed ways, but I think that there is equally abundant evidence that many were frustrated before they could reach their goal by a combination of poverty and family circumstances. Such frustration must have blunted not the demand for schooling, which could persist even when it was frustrated, so much as the achievement of the new forms of behaviour thought to be associated with "introspection, literacy and privacy [which] form a single affinity group of characteristics".[95] Here again, perhaps, the voices that made most noise, that were the most insistent, have had disproportionate access to the historian's attention. It may be that historians of working-class education have paid far too much attention to what some people said, to the exclusion of what at least as many people were able to do. This kind of argument calls into question some of the central premises of modernization theories of social differentiation and, in particular, the role of educational attainment as a proxy-variable for "rationality". In fact, the whole conceptual construct which opposes rationality and tradition seems to me to be open to doubt insofar as it presumes that tradition is irrational.

The reason of rationality; or, the rationality of reason

In the centuries following the Reformation a gigantic effort was made by several generations of English reformers and divines to wean the common people from their traditional habits of time and work. This reformation of manners was intimately concerned with the persistence of popular mentalities which opposed both "rationality" and "modernization", although this is not to say that they were irrational. Far from it. What we see, therefore, are two quite distinct forms of rationality opposing each other: the rationality of the market and the rationality of the *cottage economy*. Because they disagreed on ends it was inevitable they would be in conflict over means. The first phase of industrialization thus presents us with a heightened sense of paradox in that almost all aspects of the political economy were "modernized" while continuing to co-exist with the remnants of a popular cultural world derived from the pre-industrial epoch.[96] This popular mental world does not appear to have declined in the eighteenth century but rather it became separated and isolated in a giant centrifuge of social distancing. We have already seen that the decline of magical beliefs was a class-specific phenomenon. While their betters were attracted to a latitudinarian scepticism, most plebeians continued to be ruled by a potent brew of magic, mystery and authority that was occasionally supercharged with a heady admixture of evangelical piety. The development of "rationality" and "modernity" cannot therefore be neatly pigeon-holed in the chronology of English history.

Our conceptualization of demographic history is shifting its emphasis so that the heterogeneity of reproductive systems antedating the "demographic transition" (to controlled fertility) has come to the forefront. Local "eco-systems" were subject to substantial variations within the over-arching framework created by the laws of biology and the cultural demands of the English family system. While there was a general assent to the imperatives of prudential marriage, its intepretation was subject to quite substantial local differences. In stepping back from the grand theories of economic development and cultural "modernization" by beginning to study ground-level behaviour, there has been a growing recognition of the primacy of local factors in the explanation of reproduction of local social systems. Work at the grass-roots has revealed a welter of contradictory patterns. In an attempt to come to grips with these islands of seemingly sub-atomic activity it is as necessary for us to break with general theories as it was for Max Planck and Werner von Heisenberg. The fit between the world of the large and the world of the small is inexact and, hence, problematic. The explanation itself becomes a theoretical problem and we are required to devote intellectual energy to a consideration of the appropriate level of analysis. The upshot of such an exercise has been a renewed emphasis upon discontinuity, unevenness and differentiation. In such a world of pullulating forces, individuals are assumed to make strategic decisions for their own reasons, in order to optimize their perceived circumstances. Such strategic decisions are *not* over-determined by the cultural milieu as "modernization" theorists would have it but are themselves part of a continuously evolving definition and re-definition of their relationship to their cultural inheritance. Men and women are understood to interpret cultural norms in terms of their own experience. Thus when ***proto-industry*** began to reconstitute the labour process within the ***cottage economy*** the prudential check on marriage was re-evaluated. A reduction of two, three or even four years may have still kept the age at first marriage within the parameters of the normal distribution of marriage ages by shifting the central tendency, but such a shift, *within* the parameters of accepted behaviour, had an explosive effect on the rate of replacement in the absence of any countervailing reduction in fertility or a rise in mortality. These developments were confined in neither time nor space in the so-called "pre-industrial" world; nor did they work solely to produce faster rates of growth since some ***proto-industrial*** areas were superseded and reverted to a later age at marriage and a more prudential replacement rate.[97] The point of this slight diversion has been to reiterate the heterogeneity of pre-transition demographic systems in England. It should also serve to emphasize the *situational* nature of my argument which lends such heavy weight to unevenness, discontinuity and differentiation. To the extent that this argument is based on a model of the home economics of fertility which stresses the integrity and independence of the nuclear family unit, it joins the history of production and reproduction and demands an explanation in which changes in the labour process

130

had contemporaneous resonances in the family formation strategies of the emergent proletariat.

The reproduction of the pro-active proletarian family

A quadripartite periodization is proposed to give some sort of structure to the shifting forces of production and reproduction.

1500–1780   the industrialization of the *cottage economy*
1780–1815   the efflorescence of *proto-industrialization*
1815–75   the proletarianization of the *cottage economy*
1875–1939   the breadwinner economy and the fertility decline

I have selected this chronology because it seems to represent the best fit between the process of industrialization, particularly as it was experienced by the working-class family, and the demographic statistics which Wrigley and Schofield have presented in *The Population History of England 1541–1871*. It should be emphasized that it is probably of value only for heuristic purposes since the ebbs and flows of the historical process are always too complex to allow for much more than an awkward and frequently inelegant fit. Nevertheless, if we are to overcome the tendency towards historical nominalism in which one thing can only be followed by another, it is necessary to provide some sort of structure to the train of events.

The real question which concerns me is not the description of these statistics – or even the fine detail of their periodization – but their explanation in the context of evolving material conditions. My explanation connects fluctuations in the rate of replacement with *contemporaneous* prospects for the establishment of a new family. It is therefore quite different from Wrigley and Schofield's explanation, which they term "dilatory homeostasis", linking changes in the real wages of men in one generation to much later shifts in the demographic behaviour of their children or grandchildren.[98] We are all in agreement, however, that the English demographic system was marriage-driven; our disagreement stems from our different explanations for this locomotion.

Pro-active interpretations of the prudential check made a mockery of the demographic equilibrium so that the populations in rural industrial communities reproduced themselves rapidly. Even in the absence of any significant improvement in life expectation, higher levels of pre-marital fertility acted together with declining ages at first marriage for women to produce a population explosion. The cohort which married in the early 1790s achieved the highest levels of reproduction computed by Wrigley and Schofield. The fertility of all married couples, during the five years 1810–14, was the highest recorded during the whole parish register period. Then, after Waterloo, the rate of replacement fell precipitously, stabilized for a generation and finally, after 1870, the "fertility decline" transformed the reproductive habits of the English proletariat by ending the reign of natural fertility which had been the common behaviour since time out of mind. But before we turn our attention to the recomposition of the proletarian family during the second phase of industrialization it will be necessary to look more closely into the destabilization of the demographic equilibrium which had characterized the peasant world.

The expropriation of the peasantry set in train a series of forces which not only transformed the organization of material life but also family life. The industrialization of the peasant family's *cottage economy* was of primary importance in this regard. This was not so much a revolutionary development as a changing emphasis which occurred because the older form of inter-penetration became untenable. The causal arrows flowed in both directions: the process of expropriation created an increasingly vulnerable peasantry while the industrialization of the *cottage economy* provided a respite which, in the nature of things, led to population growth that intensified the pressure on existing landed resources and so made the family economy even more dependent upon its non-landed sources of income. We might suggest, therefore, that the "dual economy" so characteristic of the earliest stages of rural industrialization did little to upset the prudential demographic regime of the peasantry. In fact, it may have reinforced it at least insofar as it became more accessible in those areas of cottage industrialization where the population may have grown as much by natural increase as by the immigration of new families. Certainly the evidence of "subsistence migration" in the early modern period provided by Paul Slack implies that whole families were on the move, looking for a place to settle, a niche of their own.[99] These dispossessed peasants were frequently able to set up an independent household – often a miserable hovel – on the commons or waste and eke out a living on the income derived from small-scale manufacturing and cottage husbandry. The nature of the *proto-industrial* mode of production meant that the replication of these separate, independent units was also encouraged by merchants who controlled the circulation of goods and money which made the system work. Their small credit advances, and communal support-systems such as "bidding weddings", were all that was needed to float a new enterprise, a new household. The labour of the family – husband, wife and children – provided the day-to-day income while the largely unregulated access to commons allowed for important non-waged supplements to this industrialized *cottage economy*.

The proletarianization of the industrialized *cottage economy*

During the first stage of the industrialization of the *cottage economy* the problem is not why the industrial population grew but, rather, why its growth was so slow. Bearing in mind the earlier simulations of a *proletarian demography model* we need to explain why this scenario is so plainly inapplicable until the last years of the eighteenth century. It would seem that the midddle of the eighteenth century marks the point in time when the rural industrial family lost the ability to balance its sources of income and became proletarianized. We have already seen evidence of this process from Staffordshire and Yorkshire and might dwell for a moment on the framework knitters of the East Midland counties, particularly the villagers of Shepshed and Wigston Magna in Leicestershire.

The expansion of this family-based, labour-intensive system of production was extremely rapid.[100] In 1660 there were only fifty frames in Leicestershire whereas by 1795 an estimated 43 per cent of the country's population depended on some branch of the trade.[101] In the 1680s there were fewer than a dozen frames in Leicester but by 1714 an estimated 600 were located in the mercantile centre of the county.[102] In Wigston Magna the industry seems to have been firmly established as early as 1698–1701 when about 16 per cent of the villagers were described in the parish register as framework knitters.[103] Perhaps Wigston's proximity to Leicester, the distribution centre, sparked its precocious industrialization. In Shepshed, the industry is first mentioned in 1655 when Thomas Trowell, "Silkstocking wever", was buried. It is perhaps significant to note that Trowell had come to Shepshed as an adult; there is no mention of him in either the marriage or baptismal registers. At the beginning of the eighteenth century just 4 per cent of the Shepshed villagers mentioned in the parish registers were *proto-industrialists* but within twenty years, in the period 1719 to 1730, this figure had jumped to 25 per cent. In each of these instances the rapid growth probably coincided with the industry's transition from a journeyman's trade to one in which capitalist relations predominated and cheap labour was a critical factor.

In Shepshed the age at first marriage for men and women remained high until the 1750s when it plummeted so that by the 1790s both men and women were marrying about five years earlier than in the seventeenth century. In the seventeenth-century village more than a quarter of all brides were over thirty, but after 1825 just one in eleven was this old. On the other hand, in the seventeenth-century village just one bride in fifteen was under twenty whereas after 1825 this proportion had risen to one in four. Accompanying this decline in average age at first marriage was a substantial compression in the distribution of marriage ages (as measured by both the inter-quartile range and standard deviation) so that, as demographers would say, nuptiality became not only more precocious but also more intense.

Land in Shepshed was morcellated; in 1832 the Land Tax returns reported that there were 250 separate owners although half of the tax was paid by one man. Many of these people held tiny parcels, often less than 1 acre, and by 1832 there were about twice as many landless proletarians as dwarf-holders, although as we shall argue this landlessness was probably a reflection of the more recent history of the village and cannot be read backwards to describe Shepshed's social structure several generations earlier. Evidence for landholding in eighteenth-century Shepshed is lacking, but W. G. Hoskins' sensitive study of Wigston Magna fills this void. *The Midland Peasant* is a magnificent piece of historical craftsmanship which details the evolution and final destruction of the commons over several centuries. Its long time-frame is important and for our purposes, as we shall see shortly, it represented a particular variant on a much larger theme. It should be borne in mind that Wigston is located on the Midland Plain; most of its land was heavy alluvial clay. Almost all of the village lands were incorporated into the common fields, there was little waste and the commons were meadows. Its local ecology distinguishes Wigston Magna from nearby Shepshed, located on the edge of Charnwood Forest, which was by far the more typical rural industrial location because of its wood-pasture agrarian economy. In this case, as in so many others, I have identified one example from the distribution of possible variants because it proves a point, not because it is in any way representative of the whole distribution. Indeed, Wigston's experience presents us with a more dramatic and revolutionary change in the balance between agricultural and industrial components of the *cottage economy* than would be the case in other villages such as Ecclesfield in south Yorkshire, Sedgeley in the Black Country or even nearby Shepshed. In the following discussion, therefore, it should be remembered that the social changes in Wigston Magna, which Hoskins details and whose main points I shall recount, were telescoped. Wigston's social drama was focussed more sharply on a particular event – the enclosure of the common fields – than was the case in other communities which featured dispersed settlements and wood-pasture economies.

The seventy households of the later middle ages had doubled by 1625. When Charles Stuart was putting his head beneath the Crown of England, some twenty-four years before he laid it out on the executioner's block, Wigston Magna was still a peasant village, farmed by middling and small landowners who worked the common fields unencumbered by the demands of a single dominant landowner. Poverty was a life-cycle phenomenon; it was, as Hoskins writes, "*incidental*, a matter of individuals (the old, or the orphaned, the maimed or the sick) rather than of *the poor* as a class". There was substantial stratification, to be sure, but most people lived in the prescribed fashion of the peasant economy in which thrift and self-subsistence were the keynotes. By the time of the Hearth Tax assessment of 1670 the old egalitarian structure of village life was crumbling: landownership and movable wealth were now markedly concentrated and fully a quarter of all householders were judged by their neighbours to be too poor to pay any tax at all. Yet the old village families persisted, even if some had fallen on hard times and slipped into poverty. Perhaps the most remarkable feature of the seventeenth and early eighteenth centuries was the emergence of what Hoskins calls the "peasant gentry", some of whom were absentee landowners. It will be recalled that in countless other villages across the south and east of England these years were the final stage in the history of the *cottage economy*. There were many thousand paths through the transitional thicket, yet there seems to have been but one destination – the proletarianization of the great mass of the population. No matter how unique Wigston Magna's experience may appear through the historical microscope, it looks quite different when viewed through the historical telescope. Students of history need to keep both modes of analysis at their disposal in order to see both the structural change and its experiential resolution.

On the eve Wigston's enclosure, only 30 per cent of the villagers were landholders, of whom a number farmed so little land that they had to work as labourers, craftsmen or *proto-industrialists* in order to make ends meet. About three families in four were largely divorced from the land although a great many would have been employed to work on it, both casually and seasonally. It was within this disintegrating peasant economy that rural industry came to the village and was welcomed by those villagers whose hold on the ancestral land had become tenuous or non-existent and whose domestic economies could only be stabilized with welfare payments. Thus, those members of the village community Gregory King would have considered to be "decreasing the wealth of the realm" provided the militia of *proto-industry*. The complement of rural capitalism in Wigston Magna was, then, rural industrialization.

Wigston Magna was enclosed by private parliamentary act, in 1764, and the award was made 17 November 1766. The agreement of perhaps a tenth of the village families was sufficient to meet the guideline that four-fifths of the landowners were required to consent. A tiny majority of the larger landowners were thus able to set the machinery of parliamentary enclosure into motion and doom the self-contained world of the *cottage economy*. On the eve of the enclosure award half of the villagers were still immediately connected to the land as either farmers or labourers. Two generations later, in 1831, ninety-three of 483 village families – about one in five – could be so described. Of these, a quarter were farmers, the rest were labourers. The 1851 census tells us that two families of big farmers worked about 40 per cent of the parish while the rest of the land was farmed by tenants, newcomers to the village. The capitalist agrarian economy specialized in meat production, requiring little labour. Only forty labourers were needed for the efficient cultivation of this pastoral economy, the other thirty probably were kept down on the farm by the operation of the poor laws. In contrast to the open-field system of peasant farming, the impact of parliamentary enclosure and capitalist agriculture reduced the local labour requirements by about two-thirds or maybe three-quarters. The peasant system, then, had completely vanished; in its place the census described the capitalist system of large farms, absentee landlords, tenant-farmers, and, of course, a host of labourers. The majority of the village families in Wigston were irrevocably divorced from the land, now chiefly engaged in industry or trade. Unlike most other Midland villages enclosed in the later eighteenth century, Wigston Magna's population went on increasing even after its tillage decayed.

Enclosure transformed Wigston Magna's physical landscape and altered its farming almost beyond recognition; it also changed the entire culture and habits of the peasant community. The domestic economy of the villagers was radically altered. Enclosure had obliterated the peasant's common rights and thrown him/her into a money-economy, bereft of money and possessed of precious little else. Right from the start he/she was loaded with debts to pay for legislation he/she did not want. The monetization of the *cottage economy* meant that agricultural labourers and *proto-industrialists* were transformed into shoppers. Almost everything they needed had to be bought and in this way "peasant thrift was replaced by commercial thrift". For the proletarian descendants of the Midland villagers of Wigston Magna every hour of work came to have a money-value. Money became the one thing necessary for the maintenance of life. In Wigston Magna parliamentary enclosure signalled the destruction of an entire society with its own economy and traditions, its own way of living and its own culture.[104]

Hoskins' insistence that a whole way of life was transformed is the crucial part of his account. In Wigston Magna the enclosure of the common fields proletarianized those members of the peasantry who had, until the later eighteenth century, held on to their patrimony in the *cottage economy*. Enclosure disinherited them. Elsewhere, this disinheritance was neither so summary an act nor so clearly an act of aggression by the class of capitalist farmers against their fellows in the village. In a village like Shepshed, as in South Staffordshire, the West Riding of Yorkshire and the Sheffield region, it would seem that the crucial factor at work in the proletarianization of the *cottage economy* was natural increase which inexorably changed the balance within the domestic economy so that dwarf-holders could hardly rely on their agricultural incomes as anything more than a supplement; many, indeed, had no land at all even if they might have enjoyed some "traditional" and unwritten common rights.

It is now appropriate to re-consider Charles Tilly's very important point concerning the strategic response to proletarianization on the part of members of the *cottage economy* which was quoted earlier: "To the extent that lifetime moves into the proletariat comprised the dominant process, we might expect a good deal of proletarian action to consist of efforts to regain or recapture individual control over the means of production."[105] In rural industrial villages it was possible to resist the full implications of proletarianization until the later eighteenth century when their own natural increase combined with the specialization of labour to transform the underpinnings of the *cottage economy*. When this happened, as Pollard writes, "the process [of domestic industrial work] was being changed in a fundamental sense, turning from a family-based occupation – allowing some degree of independence, and integrated with the domestic duties of the housewife, with a small plot of land, or with the harvest cycle of the surrounding countryside – into full-time dependence on a factory or a warehouse."[106] In this way the *Industrial Revolution* was experienced as a revolutionary change in the lives of the men and women, boys and girls, whose labour was its most critical component. This transformation in the very character of domestic production was of epochal proportions; it must be linked to the shift in reproduction, mainly earlier ages at first marriage among women and higher rates of bridal pregnancy and illegitimacy which unleashed the *proletarian demography model*.

The *proletarian demography model* and the Malthusian moment

Whether as a result of enclosure or their own natural increase, the full-blown industrialization of the *cottage economy* marked a decisive historical moment. Labour was monetized and the ability to employ wives and children meant that for many workers the first years of the classic *Industrial Revolution* were generally prosperous ones for the family economy. In the textile industries the mechanization of spinning had created a bottleneck in the weaving or knitting branches and so momentarily swung the balance in the domestic labourers' favour. The widespread adoption of steam-pumping in the eighteenth-century coal mines meant that coke-smelting could supersede the more traditional method of charcoal-smelting and the rapidly expanding metal-working trades were provided with reasonably stable energy and material costs. Here, then, we can see the material forces which inspired the proletarian family to re-interpret the prudential check. Cut off from the *cottage economy* and brought face-to-face with their proletarian condition, the surging demand for industrial labour was met with an increase in supply of hands sufficient to extend and even upgrade the low-wage technology on which the first phase of industrialization was predicated.

The *proletarian demography model* which was simulated earlier probably comes close to describing the demographic reality of these years, the Malthusian moment at the turn of the eighteenth and nineteenth centuries. The age at first marriage for women dropped across the whole of the industrialized economy. It was dropping in the agricultural economy, too; though for a wholly different set of reasons, as we have seen. In fact, one should link the peculiar demo-economic system engendered by the Old Poor Law with the demand for food coming from the exploding industrial population; equally, one should link the peculiar labour process in the Indian summer of the first phase of industrialization with the expanding food supplies which, for all the horrors of short-term fluctuations, enabled a fast-growing industrial population to be fed with domestic grain and meat at prices which never seriously drove up the cost of its labour. Wrigley and Schofield's measurement N.R.R. (Net Reproduction Rate) captures the broad outline of this great transformation – among the cohort marrying in the quinquennium 1751–5 it stood at 1.384, for those who married after the start of the *Industrial Revolution* it peaked at 1.624 for the 1791–5 cohort.[107] These figures represent the difference between slow growth, comparable to that for the *peasant demography model* outlined earlier, and explosive growth which might lead to enormous accumulations of population if continued over several generations. Statistically, they lend credence to the point derived by Malthus concerning the homeostatic relationship which had hitherto existed between the social controls on marriage and the biological limits to population growth. As was obvious to Malthus, who had an excellent mathematical education, if you change one part of a simple fraction while keeping the other part stable then the result is liable to change in a dramatic fashion.

Yet, this level of explosive population growth was only maintained for a short period. One is naturally led to ask what was so special about these years and how did this unique configuration translate itself into an explosive demographic reality. The answer, of course, is that the material basis for family formation was revolutionized. A rising proportion of people married – the cohorts born between 1736 and 1776, who married between 1760 and 1800, had the lowest rates of permanent celibacy estimated by the "back projection".[108] The number of illegitimate births skyrocketed and when marriage did take place these cohorts, especially in the industrial regions, had children who provided not only a contemporaneous source of income to defer the costs of their maintenance but also a built-in pension scheme for their old age. In the nature of things the Old Poor Law was far less effective in mushrooming industrial centres than in relatively settled agricultural villages where it was still financed disproportionately from the rates on agricultural land. Thus in Wigston Magna, and other Leicestershire industrial villages, land values fell and rentals were jeopardized.[109] For those in receipt of such welfare, it was inevitable that this pinched tax-base could hardly provide an adequate source of income at those moments in their life-cycle when they turned to the parish for assistance. Thus, there was a positive incentive to have children right through the whole of a wife's childbearing period. The last children, born when a woman was approaching menopause at around forty, were thus crucial for the parents' provisions for their final years. At the other end of their reproductive lives, involvement in rural industry encouraged them to begin courtship earlier and/or enabled them to set up their own independent, nuclear family household with a minimal accumulation of capital. It is in the light of these relationships that we can appreciate Neil McKendrick's point that "the crucial difference between the industrial period and the pre-industrial was the earning potential of both wives and children. And, of course, the family household generated demand for manufactured goods, as well as generating the income to pay for them."[110]

The contradiction of the Malthusian moment

The rate of replacement reached its peak in 1815 and for a generation it fell precipitously, then it stabilized for another generation at very near the level obtaining before the 1780s, before the momentous break with the age-old regime of natural fertility began in the 1870s. Why? Before advancing an explanation for this relative and absolute decline in the rate of replacement during the middle years of the nineteenth century it might be helpful to integrate it with some further detailed historical context within which these events occurred.

The generation of 1793–1815 had lived through the Napoleonic Wars during which time a very substantial section of the economy had been devoted to the demands of this conflict. The rhythms of war and peace were akin to the later surges of boom and slump that plagued the business cycle of the early nineteenth-century economy. The cessation of hostilities after Waterloo immediately cut back demand for a wide range of products and, by itself, would have had a profoundly depressive effect. What over-determined this historic reverse was the demobilization of 400,000 men between 1814 and 1817 at just the time when the total population was growing at the fastest rate ever attained – in 1814 the crude rate of natural increase was 19.2 per 1,000. The population was growing by 200,000 per annum. A huge scissors – plunging demand for labour and the exploding increase of its supply – cut into the personal lives of the working population.

On top of this short-term crisis came a more ominous force: these years witnessed the restructuring of the labour process in the outwork industries. In response to factory industrialization, domestic production was reorganized, its labour processes subdivided and its subordination to the warehouse and factory intensified. *Proto-industrialization* had reconfigured the homeostatic demographic regime of the *cottage economy* but, equally, the causal arrows did not flow in only one direction. There was a reciprocal response as population growth influenced the organization of production. Not only did workers replace themselves at a rapid rate but any sustained period of prosperity for the family economy occasioned an increasing number of marriages and therefore a replication of household units of production. For these reasons, then, labour costs were kept low. As long as labour was both cheap and plentiful, there was no imperative to undertake capital investments in order to raise productivity. Low wages meant that primitive techniques were still profitable so that, in turn, cheap labour was of critical importance. In effect, such conditions created the kind of vicious circle of self-exploitation that I will call *industrial involution*.

In the hosiery districts of Leicestershire and Nottinghamshire, for example, it now became common for small middlemen to set up "frame shops" in which a group of separate operatives were brought together in an effort to intensify labour discipline and tighten co-ordination between the capricious market for fashion and producers.[111] A shift away from household production occurred in the early nineteenth century although these "protofactories" were still dependent upon human-powered machinery. The labour process in these co-ordinated workshops was geared to batch, not flow, production; it was decidedly not automated and can be said to represent an inner colonization of the labour process through intensified exploitation. On this point Sidney Pollard writes that it was "a way of drawing forth labour whose existence had not been suspected – labour, moreover, that was paid either at cut rates or not at all". Most contemporary observers did not recognize this form of intensive exploitation "Yet it was a major factor in filling the demand for labour in the industrial revolution without driving up its price."[112] For the London tailors the competition between the "independent" artisan and the dependent supplier to wholesale warehouses led to the emergence of "the metropolitan armies of needlewomen" whose labour was orchestrated by "slop masters". In this instance, piece-work and sub-contracting transformed an "honourable" trade into a "dishonourable" one through the specialization of functions and the displacement of skilled workers.[113] Among the journeymen of the London trades – tailors, shoemakers and weavers above all – "the traditional craftsman had made economic independence the condition of conjugality, those involved in the piece-work labour of London's vast putting-out system reversed the priorities. Living with a woman now became their hope of gaining autonomy." A family wage economy, based on the combined earnings of both partners, was substituted for the older system of inheritance and guild privilege.[114] For the handloom weavers of Lancashire these years brought their confrontation with the factory to the forefront just when the historical defeat of Luddite resistance was making it evident that their now-traditional *proto-industrial* way of life was doomed.[115] A relative surplus of labour and vast expansion of production had created the conditions in which the repetitive crises of overproduction would be visited on the domestic outworkers. Is it any wonder that the primary economic goal of early nineteenth-century political radicalism was the eradication of competition and its replacement with co-operation?

The politicization of private life

The spasmodic, lurching growth of the early industrial economy left the handicraft worker on the horns of a terrible dilemma: on the one hand, labour and skill were not yet completely superseded nor were they obsolete, unimportant or valueless; while, on the other hand, the age of machinofacture had not yet arrived and so there was relatively little opportunity for occupational mobility from sectors employing older technologies to those in which the newer processes of production were becoming dominant. The spasmodic economic life of the period only heightened the inevitable agony associated with the demise of their way of life. It was a time of diminishing hope and rising anger. With the benefit of hindsight we can see this course of events in stark relief but for those caught up in the business of daily life such vision was less clear. Events themselves were in the saddle and rode them mercilessly. "The great mass of men and women are like corks on the surface of a mountain river, carried hither and thither as the torrent may lead them."[116] This lack of control was over-determined, as it were, by the visitations of boom and slump plaguing the early industrial economy in the generation after Wellington's victory at Waterloo.

The fading Indian summer of domestic manufacturing began to fore-close the opportunity to establish a new household on the prospect of family earnings while at the same time heightening the importance of the wage component in a young couple's strategic decision-making. In the factory town of Preston, contemporary moralists complained of "insubordination" among foot-loose teenagers and the dissolution of family ties and paternal authority. Michael Anderson is at pains to show that not only were most teenaged lodgers rural immigrants to the town but that among local youths a minuscule proportion could be found who had deserted their family.[117] But if the children of the Preston proletarians did not desert their homes to live in lodging houses, which many contemporaries thought to be "hotbeds of promiscuity and . . . bastions of antifamilistic and other antisocial values", they still seemed to have exercised the leverage their earnings gave them: "early independence, coupled with the fact that subsequent expectations were likely to be of a fall rather than any much greater rise, of wages, seems to have persuaded most that it was safe and even best to marry young".[118] In a similar vein John Gillis argues "The peasant practice of betrothal agreements between families lapsed wherever young people had their own earnings and thus were able to accumulate their own marriage portions." The plebeian public bridal was in its heyday during the later eighteenth century. It continued until the second quarter of the nineteenth century although its material base was then dissolving fast. There was no place for a "one-night house" in the huddled streets of the mushrooming cities. In place of the publicity surrounding the plebeian wedding, "The marriages of the urban proletariat were likely to be hurried and truncated affairs."[119] Urban workers were comparatively isolated and their lives relatively privatized in contrast to their predecessors who lived in rural industrial and staple-extractive villages. The intensive work regime of the factories and large workshops began to divorce work and leisure. The involution of the first phase of industrialization began to reorder the working lives of men, women and children. It also began to reorder their private lives.

It was within this context of diminishing hopes, recurring crises, rapid urbanization and utter dislocation that there was an abrupt reversal in the pattern of population growth rates. The highest rate of reproduction in modern English history had been achieved by the cohort who lived most of their married lives during the Napoleonic Wars. For those people who married after 1815 the decline was swift. In the thirty years after the end of the Napoleonic Wars the demographic surplus, over and above simple replacement, was halved.[120]

By the mid-century the process of recomposition was about to achieve its major victories. Factory production was now pre-eminent in certain sectors of cotton textiles and the "railway mania" of 1845–7 promoted a tremendous boom and laid the basis for the maturation of a different kind of industrial society based on coal and iron and steel. General improvements in living conditions among the working population date from this time and male wages began to increase steadily for the first time in living memory. Political opposition to the new industrial order and its social imperatives, which had flourished in the 1830s, had burned itself out around mid-century. A period of stasis ensued, laying the essential cultural foundations for the final part of our story which played itself out after 1875.

A most important feature of this recomposition took place at home. Commenting upon this development, Barbara Taylor has written that "The idea of a domestic, dependent, private 'women's sphere', rigidly segregated from the male sphere of work, politics and public life, became for the working class, as for the middle class, central to their concept of social respectability." This hardening "sexual apartheid" emerged first among the *respectable* strata of the working class in response to the "fundamental changes" which disintegrated the more egalitarian family economy so characteristic of the first phase of industrialization.[121] Women accepted this new segregation of sex roles because their prospects outside marriage were deteriorating and the inadequacy and hard-heartedness of the welfare system made single-parenthood a nightmare. As Taylor writes, "it is not surprising that women themselves tended to look towards a home-centred existence, supported by a reliable male bread-winner, as a desirable goal. Or perhaps more accurately, they found it impossible to imagine any real alternative, except the current reality of economic insecurity and overwork."[122] Male workers' demands for a "living wage" have to be seen in this perspective. They not only struggled so that their women could be freed from employment to elevate the private sphere but also fought to have them excluded from the public sphere so that they could not be used as a "cheap labour" form of competition. If women could be freed from a "double day of labour" to concentrate on domestic tasks then one could only hail this as a victory, albeit one which was achieved at the cost of women's liberty. This ambiguous victory took place within a redefined oppositional politics in which "the strategic shift away from the struggle against proletariani-zation to the proletarian struggle meant the political marginalization of all those who were not, scientifically speaking, proletarians".[123]

The industrialized Parthenon

The English population became rapidly urbanized in the first half of the nineteenth century. As late as 1800 over half of those living in towns of over 20,000 inhabitants were residents of London. The early nineteenth-century English urban population, outside the capital, expanded at a very fast pace: in 1831, the proportion of English people in towns of over 20,000 was a quarter (of 12,990,000); in 1841 over a third (of 14,860,000) were city-dwellers; and by mid-century the proportion had risen to a half (of 16,760,000) and was rapidly increasing. The representative Briton became a city-dweller during the course of a couple of generations so that "by 1881 perhaps two out of every five Englishmen and Welshmen lived in the six giant built-up areas ('conurbations') of London, south-east Lancashire, the West Midlands, west Yorkshire, Merseyside and Tyneside".[124]

Urbanization might be crudely equated with the final stage in the process of proletarianization. The urban worker had nothing but the market economy to define his family's relationship to and dependence upon the wage-nexus. Use-rights were lost forever. The income supplements of the *cottage economy* – a garden, cow-, pig- and poultry-keeping – vanished. These residual sources of income had continued to play an important part in the family economy, cushioning the reliance on wages even when the cottager was seemingly landless. With urbanization they were lost. The urban worker more usually sold his labour, not the product of his labour – a distinction which would be especially critical in times of economic downswing when the handicraft worker would watch his income diminish as piece-rates dropped, whereas the urban proletarian watched his income vanish when he was fired. The generation after Waterloo lived through the worst years in modern English history. "Cyclical unemployment was super-imposed on the evils of casual work and structural unemployment; and above all it is most unlikely that in the past there had ever been such a large proportion of the population exclusively dependent on income from market-oriented industry."[125] Nowhere was this process more dramatic than in Manchester.

"The greatest mere village in England"

When Daniel Defoe visited sprawling Manchester in the 1720s he had encountered "the greatest mere village in England"; when the twenty-four-year-old Friedrich Engels arrived in Manchester at the end of November, 1842, he first encountered its industrial satellites – "all towns of thirty, fifty, seventy to ninety thousand inhabitants . . . almost wholly working-people's districts, interspersed only with factories, a few thoroughfares lined with shops, and a few lanes along which the gardens and houses of the manufacturers are scattered like villas" and only then arrived at the heart of this vast integrated region of factories and workshops.[126] In the space of the eleven generations, between the reigns of Henry VIII and Victoria, Manchester had grown from an unimportant country town to Cottonopolis – the industrial Parthenon at the heart of a vast hinterland stretching along the western foothills of the Pennines. By Engels' time the population of south-east Lancashire had grown forty-fold – to one million – mostly in the previous four generations. The reason and nature of the thing was that here the final phase of *proto-industrialization* was super-imposed on the first flight of the Unbound Prometheus, factory-based industrial society.

Even in the 1720s, so Defoe thought, only a fifth of these Lancashire *proto-industrialists* could have scratched out a subsistence without their industrial incomes; as time passed the fraction with any connection to the land plummeted and the *cottage economy* disintegrated. So, the classic conditions of rural industrialization already existed in Lancashire: an over-extended population of poor cottagers provided a tempting source of cheap labour. In the middle of the eighteenth century the merchant-princes of Manchester were putting out work to the households of "half-starved, half-clothed poor weavers" in upland villages like Old-ham.[127] In the last quarter of the eighteenth century the course of industrial growth changed radically. Old centres of woollen production were caught up in the wholesale switchover to cottons. We can see the shape of the growth-curve quite clearly by looking at the millions of pounds of cotton imported at several different dates:

1700 =	1,000,000
1750 =	3,000,000
1771 =	4,700,000
1781 =	5,300,000
1789 =	32,500,000
1802 =	60,500,000
1820 =	141,000,000
1840 =	452,000,000
1860 =	1,050,000,000.[128]

Prior to the advent of machine spinning, the agricultural enthusiast Arthur Young wrote that "they reckon twenty spinners and two or three other hands [i.e. carders, bleachers, dyers and so on] to every weaver".[129] The invention of the flying shuttle in the 1750s had created this pro-nounced imbalance between the two sides of the trade; in the following decades it was more than rectified. First, Hargreaves' spinning jenny and Arkwright's water-frame were developed at the end of the 1760s; then, Crompton's 'mule' in the 1770s improved the quality of mechanically spun thread; and, finally, the application of steam power, using the reciprocating engines developed by Boulton and Watt, had completely revolutionized the spinning branch by the 1780s. Most of the original output from the very first factories, driven by water power and located in neighbouring Derbyshire, was destined for the Nottingham stocking industry. The switchover to steam power was not immediate, however; water-powered mills continued to play an important role in machine spinning well into the nineteenth century. Manchester's hinterland of domestic industrial villages, its infrastructural linkages with the great port of Liverpool, its existent commercial bourgeoisie and, in particular, its proximity to the Duke of Bridgewater's collieries – just six miles away at Worsley – gave the town a pronounced advantage in the transition from water- to steam-powered factories. The fact that the Duke's Worsley canal was required to provide coal at a fixed rate until 1799 must have proved to be an undeniable boon. The impact of these factors was rapid, dramatic and awe-inspiring. In 1786 Manchester's skyline boasted one factory chimney; thereafter, the rate of expansion was quite literally hell-bent. Manchester had just over 27,000 inhabitants in 1773; in 1801 it had 95,000.

The emergence of Cottonopolis completely changed the organic balance of the textile trade so that a shortage of work for weavers was briefly transformed into a shortage of weavers to work. Between 1795 and 1811 handloom weavers had trebled in number and south-east Lancashire became one continuous village.[130] The statistical dimension of growth in Manchester's hinterland before 1795 must be inferred from other sources. We can gain a perspective on the accelerating pace of growth after 1780 from the contemporary observations of John Aikin. In Tildesley, a dozen miles north-west of Manchester there were 162 houses and 976 inhabitants in 1795, "employing 325 looms in the cotton manufactories". In 1780 the sleepy hamlet of Tildesley had boasted two farms and eight or nine cottages. In Middleton, some five miles from the centre of Manchester, the number of houses increased from "scarcely more than twenty" to "between four and five hundred" in ten years. Middleton in the 1790s was the home of Samuel Bamford's uncle, not surprisingly a weaver. His cottage "consisted of one principal room called 'the house'; on the same floor with this was the loomshop capable of containing four looms, and in the rear of the house on the same floor were a small kitchen and buttery. Over the house and loomshop were chambers [i.e. bedrooms)."[131] With four handlooms in the cottage it is apparent that the money earned by Bamford's uncle, the head of the household, would have given little indication of the family/household income.

The later eighteenth-century demand for weavers was thus met by an expanding supply as local cottagers, and their children, quickly moved into this high wage/low skill trade: in the 1790s farmers complained that servants-in-husbandry were impossible to hire, at reasonable wages. "The advance of wages and the preference given to manufacturing employment by labourers in general, where they may work by the piece and under cover, have many to forsake the spade for the shuttle, and have embarrassed the farmers by the scarcity of workmen, and of course advanced the price of labour." In this context it might be apposite to point out that Cobbett, in *Cottage Economy*, recognized the revolutionary consequences issuing from the hegemony of the "Lords of the Loom" who took away "The spinning, the carding, the reeling, the knitting [which] have been all taken away . . . from the agricultural women and children" and which had before his time been "so necessary to the well-being of the agricultural labourer."[132] The proletarianization of the industrialized *cottage economy* was mirrored by the pauperization of the family economy of agricultural labourers in southern and eastern regions. To feed the industrial population in the northern and western parts of the country, agricultural labour was tied to the land in the cereal belt. When Prometheus was unbound, Hodge was being shackled by the "parish law of England". It was in this way that the first stage of industrialization was revolutionary – it turned things upside down, reversed the natural order of society, and reconstructed it in fundamentally new ways. Only with the greatest dissociation of historical sensibility can one look at the *Industrial Revolution* apart from the agricultural revolution, or vice versa. What was happening in Lancashire cannot be understood apart from what was happening in Bedfordshire; similarly, what was happening in Bedfordshire cannot be understood outside a framework which includes the changes in production and reproduction in Lancashire. The Malthusian moment was a national event – a thunder-clap which shook English society down to its very foundations.

The rural-industrial population mushroomed in south-east Lancashire: migration was one source of labour, the fertility of the cottagers was another. It seems not unlikely that the rise of the cotton trade had stimulated growth rates among the cottagers in the surrounding belt of counties. Extensive labour migration had been a feature of the pastoral economies in these upland areas where servants-in-husbandry often changed employers and "settlements" on an annual basis. The industrialization of the *cottage economy* in south-east Lancashire offered these uplanders a window of opportunity. It attracted surplus members of the *cottage economy* from the adjacent, pastoral counties of Cumberland, Derbyshire, the North Riding of Yorkshire, Staffordshire and Westmorland, all of which seem to have experienced high levels of generational replacement yet suffered enormous "net" losses during the eighteenth century. Many others came from industrializing regions in Cheshire and Yorkshire and, of course, a veritable horde of Irish men and women arrived on Merseyside and made their way to Manchester and its belt of satellites. At the same time, pro-active interpretations of the "prudential check" unleashed the full powers of human reproduction among the members of the industrialized *cottage economy*.

The mechanization of spinning created a looking-glass through which the industrialized *cottage economy* passed into complete proletarianization. Initially, it knocked the props out from under the integrated cottage production unit: "Carding, roving and spinning were now given up in the cottages" but the loss of work in one branch was compensated by the vigorous demand in the other as "the women and children formerly employed in those operations applied themselves to the loom. The invention of the mule, by enabling the spinners to make finer yarn than any the jenny or water-frame could produce, gave birth to the muslin manufacture and found employment for this additional number of weavers."[133] For the next two generations after 1780 the handloom weavers rode the roller-coaster of *Industrial Revolution* and *involution*, expansion and recomposition. The mechanization of spinning drew some erstwhile cottage industrialists into the dark Satanic mills but in the main the pioneering factories were staffed by orphaned and abandoned "parish apprentices" and other young children who were sent to work there, often very much against their will. They had no choice; the lot of children was hard. Among the remnants of splintered families – perhaps a third of all families were broken by death and desertion – children's room for manoeuvre was strictly limited. Quite simply, they were objects of social policy who had little or no say in their own futures. They were expected to do what they were told and to face their lot stoically. In addition, vagabonds, tramp labourers, convicts and single women – often single mothers – were drafted into this work. The original factory proletariat was thus composed of people who were notoriously dependent on the powers of others. Adult males, especially, were reluctant to swap their birthright for "a mess of pottage". Georgian social policy had made its workhouses the model for the factory; independent adults thus hated it as much for what it symbolized as for what it entailed – disciplining oneself to the pace and rhythm of a machine, losing one's personality and skill and craft-pride in exchange for money. The early factories, therefore, usually had a complement of casual adult males but the labour force was dominated by children and women: in 1816, for example, forty-eight Manchester mills were surveyed and it was found that 6,687 adults (two-thirds of them women) and 6,253 children were employed there. The colonization of children's and women's labour gave the factory operatives a distinctive age- and gender-specificity which was retained after the initial resistance to mill work was overcome and a "mature" proletariat had been created. Even as late as 1907 adult men (over eighteen) made up only 28.3 per cent of the labour force; almost all the rest were "women and girls".[134]

In 1800 there were several million spindles at work in steam-powered factories but only a few hundred power looms. The generation of handloom weavers living between 1780 and 1815 enjoyed the best of times; their children reaped the whirlwind. Technical change resolved the "imbalance" between the mechanization of the trade's spinning and weaving branches in the 1820s with the introduction of new model power looms. But, meanwhile, the phenomenal levels of population growth obtaining in the Malthusian period had created a momentum which proved to be impossible to stop. The creation of a wide-based age-pyramid meant that the marriageable population in the succeeding generations proliferated at speed. In a period of social free-fall following the end of the Napoleonic Wars, the children of the first generation were plunged into a crowded labour market in which they not only competed with each other but also with new machines. Writing in 1835 Edward Baines commented "it is by iron fingers, teeth and wheels moving with exhaustless energy and devouring speed that the cotton is opened, cleaned, spread, carded, drawn, roved, spun, wound, warped, dressed and woven".[135] Against such competition the handicraft family could only offer its product at a lower and lower price. Such a downward spiral of self-exploitation could not last indefinitely but for those caught up in it the consequences were ghastly. So, the rise and decline of the handloom weavers can be understood within the framework of technical innovation and their own prolific power. The first shift in technology had underwritten the massive expansion of the *cottage industry* of handloom weaving; the equilibration of the technical imbalance signalled its demise. During the second quarter of the nineteenth century competition with the factory drove the *proto-industrialists'* children into an urban labour market, swarming with the overflow from the declining *cottage industries* – in Lancashire and Ireland – and, of course, its own self-generated proletariat. Sucked in by good times, the "industrial reserve army" was spewed out on to the streets during the inevitable and recurrent cyclical downturns.[136]

Badlands: darkness on the edge of town

Greeting Engels on his arrival "there were everywhere crowds of unemployed still standing at street corners, and many factories were still standing idle. Between then and the middle of 1843 those who had been lounging at street corners through no fault of their own gradually disappeared, as the factories came once again into activity."[137] Immediately, then, he was brought face-to-face with the twin characteristics of the early industrial economy – urbanization, even of peripheral towns, and the roller-coaster ride of boom and slump. It was the wonder and horror of the age. For Engels' conservative contemporary, Benjamin Disraeli, this "Lancashire village ... expanded into a mighty region of factories and warehouses ... [which] is as great a human exploit as Athens".[138] For Alexis de Tocqueville, who visited Manchester in 1835, the Parthenon of the cotton trade was a more contradictory place: "From this foul drain the greatest stream of human industry flows to fertilize the whole world. From this filthy sewer pure gold flows. Here humanity attains its most complete development and its most brutish; here civilization works its miracles, and civilized man is turned back almost into a savage."[139] Engels, too, shared de Tocqueville's contradictory appreciation of this new moral world.

Between his arrival and the winter of 1844–5, when he was writing his masterpiece *The Condition of the Working Class in England* Engels walked through the foul streets of Cottonopolis "getting to know the city from the ground – and from below the ground – up". His walks were taken at all hours of the day and night; he flung himself into his exploration of working-class Manchester with the reckless abandon of a latter-day Columbus. He, too, was literally going over the edge of the civilized world. He married his politics and was accompanied on these expeditions by Mary Burns, his common-law wife for the next eighteen years, "who inducted him into certain working-class circles and into the domestic lives of the Manchester proletariat. Thus Engels learned how to read a city in the company – or through the mediation – of an illiterate Irish factory girl. He learned to read it with his eyes, ears, nose and feet."[140] Working-class habitation in the mushrooming urban regions can only be described in terms more fitting the Augean stable than the manger: "Twelve insanitary houses on a hillside may be a picturesque village, but twelve hundred are a grave nuisance and twelve thousand a pest and a horror."[141] De Tocqueville's insight that the working class was quite literally living in shit is amply borne out in Engels' account of his experience.

The overpowering impression one comes away with from reading *The Condition of the Working Class in England* is of indescribable filth, segregated and confined, out of sight and out of the "public" mind.

If we must briefly formulate the result of our wanderings, we must admit that 350,000 working-people of Manchester and its environs live, almost all of them, in wretched, damp, filthy cottages, that the streets which surround them are usually in the most miserable and filthy condition, laid out without the slightest reference to ventilation, with reference solely to the profit secured by the contractor. In a word, we must confess that in the working-men's dwellings of Manchester, no cleanliness, no convenience, and consequently no family life is possible; that in such dwellings only a physically degenerate race, robbed of all humanity degraded, reduced morally and physically to bestiality, could feel comfortable and at home. And I am not alone in making this assertion.[142]

It should be noted that in this passage Engels is describing conditions in Manchester; he makes the point that the satellite towns – Ashton, Bolton, Bury, Middleton, Oldham, Preston, Rochdale, Stalybridge, Stockport and Wigan – each had "its own peculiarities, but in general, the working-people live in them just as in Manchester".[143]

The birth-trauma of a new order

Engels was not alone in his views; they were shared by concerned contemporaries and resonated throughout the Parliamentary Blue Books which compiled mountains of evidence on social conditions in the second quarter of the century. Engels' text is chock-full of references to these official investigations and they give his account an analytical rigour which is lacking in the more traditionally humane discussions of de Tocqueville, Dickens, Disraeli and the others. It needs to be emphasized that the central thrust of his description has not been shaken one jot by historical revisionists. E. J. Hobsbawm is at pains to point out that the "footling" attempts to contradict Engels have simply missed the point that one cannot compress the transformation of a way of life into a cost-benefit equation. Such an exercise might reveal the price of everything; it understands the value of nothing.[144]

Living in shit and reduced to bestiality. That is the gist of Engels' indictment of the social changes of the *Industrial Revolution*. One might well ask whether it really mattered that wage-rates in the city were higher, no matter what the costs. One might also ask if this choice was a decision made in the full light of reason – i.e. were the workers in these conurbations living there after having made a free choice or out of dire necessity. Living in shit and reduced to bestiality – how does one incorporate these factors into a neo-classical cost-benefit analysis?

Engels described the birth-trauma of a new order. Having lost control of their way of life, the urban proletariat were subjected to a brutal discipline as both producers and consumers. Their work became the subject of intensive controls and their lives subjected to a quasi-military supervision. During Wellington's Peninsular Campaign there were more soldiers barracked in the industrial counties than fighting with the Iron Duke against Napoleon's armies.[145] Within the urban areas they were ghettoized "with systematic thoroughness and consistency, although the ghetto is itself the largest part of the town".[146] Their food was adulterated and their houses were jerry-built. Their living conditions meant that their children died in great numbers; those who survived were forced into repetitive labour from an early age. For the most part, they had neither a formal, secular education nor much in the way of traditional, religious instruction. Conditions of life were subject to no law except that of the market, which was itself out of control. The state apparatus of social administration was guided by principles of unreconstructed political-economy so that there was no organizational infrastructure to clean up water supplies, sanitary conditions and air-borne pollution. Workers were unprotected from machinery while their conditions of labour were under no control save that of their masters' discretion. Not surprisingly, the parliamentary inquiries uncovered levels of mortality in the urban cores which were double that obtaining in the countryside. In addition, the very experience of work meant that "Besides the deformed persons, a great number of maimed ones may be seen going about in Manchester; this one lost an arm or a part of one, that one a foot, the third half a leg; it is like living in the midst of an army just returned from a campaign."[147] Women of the operative class suffered an array of poverty-induced gynaecological problems: prolapsed uteruses and deformed pelvises, a result of rickets, were associated with bone-crushing toil and inadequate diet. Childbirth was a fearsome experience.[148] Even those who survived the ultimate sanctions of this harrowing death-in-life were not left untouched. "There are few vigorous, well-built, healthy persons among the workers, i.e. among the factory operatives, who are employed in confined rooms, and we are discussing these only. They are almost all weakly, of angular but not powerful build, lean, pale, and of relaxed fibre, with the exception of the muscles especially exercised in their work."[149] Similarly, among non-factory operatives, this generation was ground down by their poverty. Domestic workers were thought to be completely useless for military recruitment. Of the handloom weavers it was said "They are decayed in their bodies; the whole race of them is rapidly descending to the size of Lilliputians. You could not raise a grenadier company amongst them all."[150] Similarly, it was a widely held belief that the framework knitters were simply not strong enough to be employed as manual labourers and "no one would employ them as farm labourers".[151] Furthermore, "The cleanliness, providence and attention to cooking and mending, must be inevitably neglected when the mother and any daughters capable of working are compelled to toil for bread at a trade." This situation was said to be so common that "the female population must certainly to some extent be brought up ignorant of the thrifty management of a household".[152]

The forcing-house of historical change

The involution of the first phase of industrialization and the contemporaneous urbanization of the proletariat caught working people between the Scylla of absolute want and the Charybdis of secondary poverty. One response to their brutalization and alienation was, as Steven Marcus suggests, consonant with the "Culture of Poverty" thesis. Its salient characteristics are drunkenness, unpredictable and violent behaviour, impulsive and promiscuous sexuality, improvidence and a lack of foresight most marked by an inability to plan for the future, a failure to internalize discipline, regularities and normative controls.[153] Indeed, this very point is made forcefully by Engels

The failings of the workers in general may be traced to an unbridled thirst for pleasure, to want of providence, and of flexibility in fitting into the social order, to the general inability to sacrifice the pleasure of the moment to a remoter advantage. But is that to be wondered at? When a class can purchase few and only the most sensual pleasures by its wearying toil, must it not give itself over blindly and madly to these pleasures?[154]

Engels was as much a social philosopher as he was a social observer. His Hegelianism had taught him to look for "negations". Thus, he recognized that the proletariat was capable of pro-active behaviour, too. In what is perhaps the single most important statement of his analysis the Hegelian dialectic is quite clearly operative:

If the centralization of population stimulates and develops the property-holding class, it forces the development of the workers yet more rapidly. The workers begin to feel as a class, as a whole; they begin to perceive that, though feeble as individuals, they form a power united; their separation from the bourgeoisie, the development of views peculiar to the workers and corresponding to their position in life, is fostered, the consciousness of oppression awakens, and the workers attain social and political importance. The great cities are the birthplaces of labour movements; in them the workers first began to reflect upon their own condition, and to struggle against it; in them the opposition between proletariat and bourgeoisie first made itself manifest; from them proceeded Trades Unions, Chartism, and Socialism. The great cities have transformed the disease of the social body, which appears in a chronic form in the country, into an acute one, and so made manifest its real nature and the means of curing it. Without the great cities and their forcing influence upon the popular intelligence, the working class would be far less advanced than it is. Moreover, they have destroyed the last remnant of the patriarchal relation between working-men and employers, a result to which manufacture on a large scale has contributed by multiplying the employees dependent upon a single employer. The bourgeoisie deplores all this, it is true, and has good reason to do so; for, under the old conditions, the bourgeois was comparatively secure against a revolt on the part of his hands. He could tyrannize over them and plunder them to his heart's content, and yet receive obedience, gratitude, and assent from these stupid people by bestowing a trifle of patronizing friendliness which cost him nothing, and perhaps some paltry present, all apparently out of pure, uncalled-for goodness of heart, but really not one-tenth part of his duty. As an individual bourgeois, placed under conditions which he had not himself created, he might do his duty at least in part; but, as a member of the ruling class, which, by the mere fact of its ruling, is responsible for the condition of the whole nation, he did nothing of what his position involved. On the contrary, he plundered the whole nation for his own individual advantage. In the patriarchal relation that hypocritically concealed the slavery of the worker, the latter must have remained an intellectual zero, totally ignorant of his own interest, a mere private individual. Only when estranged from his employer, when convinced that the sole bond between employer and employee is the bond of pecuniary profit, when the sentimental bond between them, which stood not the slightest test, had wholly fallen away, then only did the worker begin to recognize his own interests and develop independently; then only did he cease to be the slave of the bourgeoisie in his thoughts, feelings, and the expression of his will. And to this end manufacture on a grand scale and in the great cities has most largely contributed.[155]

As events would fall out, Engels captured an historical moment, and a ripely contingent one at that; yet his account is blind to the future. In one of those bitter ironies, with which history is replete, the master has had the final say:

One more word about giving instruction as to what the world ought to be. Philosophy in any case always comes on the scene too late to give it. As the thought of the world it appears only when actuality is already there cut and dried after its process of formation has been complete ... When philosophy paints it gray in gray, then has a shape of life grown old. By philosophy's gray in gray it cannot be rejuvenated but only understood. The owl of Minerva spreads its wings only with the falling dusk.[156]

The owl of Minerva meets the stork

Engels wrote at the moment of transformation when the entire political economy was in the process of shedding its early modern chrysalis and was incorrect in ascribing the course of the future to the track by which the past had led to the present. In focussing our attention on the public political struggle as the main arena in which working-class pro-activity suggested the likelihood of a dramatic break with the past, Engels (and Marx) were profoundly mistaken. Their assessment of that moment's historical potential was misunderstood not least because of their complete disregard for, and disdain of, the private dimension of struggle. The enormous implications of this inwardness is evident from a consideration of recent historical demographic research which has made it clear that there was also a pro-active approach to reproduction within the pro-letarian family's redefined prudential marriage. Michael Anderson's study of household structure in mid-century Preston, Lancashire, suggests that co-residence in the early years of marriage and quite deliberate attempts to establish residential clusters were strategies employed to break down the anonymity of the urban world. Although he considers that kin relations had a large element of "instrumentality", nevertheless his account makes the importance of family networks evident.[157] Further evidence detailing this pro-active reproductive strategy is derived from a study of the framework knitters of Shepshed, Leicestershire.

The framework knitting industry, on which about two-thirds of the villagers were dependent, entered its involutionary phase after 1815. Real wages fell by 40 per cent. Emigration became a popular response to these conditions and many young people left Shepshed, forced out by the terrible conditions at home at least as much as they were attracted by the magnetism of urban labour markets. A simple index of this phenomenon is provided by the number of marriages celebrated in the village. In both relative and absolute terms 1815–16 marked the high point in the marriage curve during the first half of the century. Since the village population contained an increasingly large number of children of marrying age, as a result of the broadening base of its age-pyramid in conditions of very rapid growth, it seems likely that considerable emigration occurred among those of marrying age. Moreover, movement appears to have been largely one-way; first, the proportion of marriages involving partners who were both residents of Shepshed went up; and, second, in comparison with the agricultural areas of Leicestershire, the framework knitting villages had far higher rates of nativity at the time of the 1851 census. There was, then, substantial emigration from industrial villages like Shepshed, but little immigration. Moreover, the few immigrants were almost all from neighbouring industrial villages.

By the mid-century the framework knitters, like the factory operatives in Preston, had responded to their adverse circumstances by making adjustments in their household structures. Far from displaying the irrational behaviour contemporaries frequently ascribed to them, these proletarians were apparently well aware of the disastrous consequences that would occur if a family was dependent on just one wage-earner – in only 18 per cent of their households was this the case. In contrast to the agricultural labourers and village craftsmen and artisans, the framework knitters not only had the largest proportion of working wives but also children most likely to work from an early age. It was quite common for two, three, four, five or even more household members to be employed in some branch of the hosiery trade. Living with relatives and lodgers was another way they could increase the number of co-resident wage-earners. Sharing houses was significantly higher among the framework knitters, among whom more than one household in eight headed by a married man contained a co-resident family. Among the non-industrial villagers such sharing was unusual – just one in twenty such complex households were found to have existed. The framework knitters' preference for living in large domestic units was part of their conscious effort to protect themselves from precarious economic conditions.

The most revealing evidence of pro-active reproduction is derived from the family reconstitution study of Shepshed, Leicestershire. Among industrialists, married after 1825, women deliberately restricted their fertility as they grew older. Furthermore, this control was sufficient to distinguish their rates of replacement from those of other villagers. But no evidence was forthcoming that they throttled back their ages at first marriage towards the levels which were discovered among their ancestors in the seventeenth century. Why did these villagers continue to follow the high-pressure reproductive strategy which had been unveiled in the late eighteenth century? An answer to this question must, I think, be framed in terms of the peculiar demo-economic conditions of **industrial involution**. Of prime importance, therefore, is the economics of the family life-cycle.

For the framework knitter there appears to have been a *positive* incentive to marry early and, in particular, to concentrate marital fertility into the early years of marriages. These were the years when co-residence was greatest and the nature of the labour process made it inefficient for a machine operator to work alone – he needed help at a number of stages in his work. To do everything by himself meant that the stockinger had to pay for this supplementary work in the currency of his own labour even though such work could be performed cheaply by members of the framework knitter's own family. It might be pointed out that employing wives and children in a *family work unit* was a way of supplementing the wages of the head of the unit in such a way that wage-rates alone would be a misleading indicator of the economic health (or illness) of the head. In an essentially family mode of production, family wages were far more important than the individual earning capacity of the household head even if that measure could be determined in a single, uncomplicated statistic. Moreover, the alternative – seeking employment in a workshop – was notoriously unattractive because of the confiscatory charges demanded from individual knitters by the small masters. Thus, there was a positive incentive to set up an independent family unit of production. This factor was of no small importance in shaping the **proto-industrialists'** family formation strategies and may account for their persistently low age at first marriage (for both men and women) in the face of deteriorating conditions. Their fertility strategy seems to have been determined by the consideration that once one married there was a positive incentive to concentrate fertility in the early years of marriage during which time the dependency ratio within the family was the most disadvantageous. In these first years the babies and infants, of course, contributed nothing to production and consumed the cost of their own support and, in addition, distracted their mothers so that their contribution was reduced. The sooner children could contribute to the family economy by helping their parents with the simple supplementary operations, the sooner the family could emerge from its state of semi-dependency which seemed to characterize the first years of marriage. Lastly, the cost of having an additional child was not commensurate with that of having the previous one. That is to say, having another child created a marginal cost, not equal to the cost of the previous child and, thus, less than the average cost. However, it seems that this last factor was re-considered in the conditions of *industrial involution* because, no matter the cost of additional children, the desperation of the time made cost-cutting a pre-eminent consideration.

Beyond these short-term economics of fertility, the question of security in old age might have played a role in the perpetuation of still-high rates of replacement. So, too, did the increasing level of infant mortality: whereas 16 per cent of children born to framework knitters died in their first year before 1825, thereafter the comparable statistic was 22 per cent. Bearing in mind that proletarianized workers had nothing of value except their innate physical skills and that these tended to decline as they reached later middle age, we can infer that the sudden rise in infant mortality upset a reproductive strategy based on pre-1825 life expectancy. Parents found that beyond the necessity of getting over the "dependency hump", which fostered high levels of fertility in the early years of marriage, the rising infant mortality rate decreed that at the *presumed* end of this stage, say after six or seven years, there was now less likelihood of a child surviving. Thus, the state of dependency was attenuated because mortality among first, and to a lesser extent, second children, was above the average. Even if a couple wanted to limit their family, they had to make sure that their first children survived the early years during which time the risk of death was so great. A contradiction therefore developed because, given the increased uncertainty of each child's survival, a couple was liable to the great hardship of repeating the whole dependency stage by "investing" too heavily in the survival of any one child. It appears that this contradiction was resolved by maintaining high fertility until at least one child was old enough to contribute his or her labour to the family economy. At this point conscious family limitation began.[158]

By the second quarter of the nineteenth century workshops were becoming a common feature of the East Midlands stocking knitting industry, particularly in the urban entrepots of Leicester, Loughborough and Nottingham. The stabilization of the market for standardized, low-priced knitted goods, especially hosiery, forced merchants into a corner – small masters, the so-called "bag hosiers", brought as many as fifty machines together into a "frame shop". Within such frame shops it became common for the knitted products to be produced in sections rather than "fully-fashioned" in the traditional manner. These "cutups" were cheaper to produce although there was no improvement in technology, merely a subdivided process of labour.[159] In the industrial villages like Shepshed this process of subdivided production was not so well developed and the village's stockingers complained that the prevalence of these cheap, shoddy "cutups" undermined the reputation of local manufacturers. Such a response was common among *proto-industrialists* whose way of life was threatened by the advent of mass production. In this sense the labour process in Shepshed was representative of a whole range of domestic industries in which these semi-skilled workers had first multiplied and then slowly starved.

Their crafts and traditions may have been dying. Their hostility to the new industrialism may have been backward-looking. Their communitarian ideals may have been fantasies. Their insurrectionary conspiracies may have been foolhardy. But they lived through these times of acute social disturbance, and we did not. Their aspirations were valid in terms of their own experience; and, if they were casualties of history, they remain, condemned in their own lives, as casualties.[160]

The strength of Luddism, "physical force" Chartism and non-conformity suggests that the stockingers of Shepshed were neither passive sufferers nor were they hopelessly anomic victims of a culture of poverty. By dint of emigration, co-residence, family labour and a prudential demographic strategy these villagers had created a system of family formation that enabled them to survive in a situation of *proto-industrial involution*. But survival merely intensified the pressures. Living in a demographic hothouse supercharged the contradictions in the household mode of production and made its confrontation with more intensive forms of subdivided labour one of the human tragedies of the *Industrial Revolution*. In seeking to rescue these people from "the enormous condescension of posterity" it is as necessary to consider their private struggles as their public ones. Living in the wake of the Malthusian moment, the personal was political.

The Malthusian moment in perspective

For most of the early modern period of English history there was a rough homeostatic balance in which population growth was not allowed to overwhelm a finely tuned social and economic system of family production and its attendant strategies of reproduction. The period of the classic *Industrial Revolution* thus stands out starkly. Its peculiarity has been explained by reference to the demise of the *cottage economy* of the peasantry, with its inherently self-stabilizing controls. By relating English social and economic history with contemporaneous demographic events, and vice versa, we have seen how family formation strategies subtly metamorphosed while still retaining allegiance to the triadic axiom of economic independence before marriage, nuclear family households after marriage and relatively late ages at first marriage for women. The burgeoning *proto-industrial* proletariat, freed from magisterial supervision, swarmed across the countryside and built over the very land on which the *cottage economy* had been predicated. A not insignificant part of their impoverishment was directly related to their "prolific power", resulting from their proletarianization and the disintegration of their traditional way of life during the Malthusian period. A vivid testament to the unparalleled agonies of this bleak age is that in the wake of a couple of generations of the *proletarian demography model*, millions of English men, women and children were impoverished in fundamentally new ways – quite literally, they lost control of everything but their ability to reproduce. Thereafter, they struggled desperately to regain control of their labour power. As we shall discuss in the next chapter, one cannot understand the specific history of the fertility decline in England without placing it in the much longer perspective of population explosion and social disintegration which accompanied the death-bed agonies of the *cottage economy*.

4

The decline of working-class fertility

The revolution in the family

The decline of fertility is arguably the most important social-historical development of the past century.[1] It is also quite clearly near the head of the political agenda of our own world. Whereas childbearing and child-rearing had been the usual experience of most adults throughout most of their married lives, it has now become simply one of many life-cycle stages. The very quality of family life was dramatically reconfigured in the space of two generations. Most analysts of this revolution in family life concentrate on the middle-class experience and seem to believe implicitly that the working-class fertility decline represented a kind of "trickle-down demography". Thus, J. A. Banks, in his classic work *Prosperity and Parenthood*, related the advent of family limitation to the contradiction between the middle-class family's goals for its children and its pinched resources in the "Great Depression" of the 1870s. In these straightened circumstances, so Banks argues, middle-class parents began to choose quality instead of quantity; they traded-off large families for smaller ones in which more resources were devoted to each child.[2] Working-class participation in the classic fertility decline is given little attention in the scholarly literature, almost all of which is directed towards middle- and lower-middle class responses to consumerism, status and prestige. Since four-fifths of the population lived in social groups below this level such factors are only of value if we hold with a diffusionist argument.

Strangely, this "trickle-down" theory has been largely unchallenged until the recent incursions of J. C. Caldwell. His writings represent a major attempt to refocus the discussion away from elite sensibilities to popular behaviour. Caldwell's ambitious reconceptualization of the problem has been undertaken from the perspective of a contemporary demographer who has sought to vitalize present-day studies of population processes by adding an historical component. In so doing he has tried to draw attention away from the so-called "modernization" of mentalities and towards the

160

organization of family life in conditions of rapid change. At the heart of his analysis is the "fundamental" belief that "fertility behaviour is economically rational within the context of socially determined economic goals and within bounds largely set by biological and psychological factors".[3] In order to explain the advent of new reproductive strategies Caldwell has seen the change occurring as a result of exogenous changes, thrust upon the family, and fundamentally redefined its "socially determined economic goals". This redefinition has occurred, so Caldwell's theory maintains and as modernization theorists would suggest, because the traditional family morality has disintegrated in the face of coherent and more powerful competition. Caldwell indentifies the turning-point with the advent of mass education: "The direction of the wealth flow between generations is changed with the introduction of mass education, at least partly because the relationships between members of the family [i.e. parents and children] are transformed as the morality governing those relationships changes."[4]

Caldwell's quinpartite argument is that production and reproduction, the double helix of family life, have been recomposed by the impact of mass schooling: first, schooling alienates children from traditional chores and responsibilities which are seen to be at odds with the child's new-found status; second, education increases the cost of children not only because they remain dependent longer but also because they develop new wants and expectations; third, schooling increases state intervention in family matters, through the expansion of the "helping professions" and, in effect, arbitrates between the demands of the family and the needs of the child on the side of its investment in the future generation thus pitting traditional morality against individualism; fourth, schooling accelerates cultural change and creates entirely new cultural expectations which, again, pit the patriarchal morality of the parents against the self-interest of their children; and fifth, the school promotes essentially foreign values, more appropriate to a bourgeois society than one in which the family is the *locus classicus* of social life.[5]

Where I part ways with Caldwell is in his ascription, in common with those who hold to a "trickle-down" theory of demographic change, of primacy to the institution of schooling. His theorizing is, it seems to me, half-right in its focus on the logic of the family's domestic economy and its changing configuration, but his theorizing is half-wrong in not following through with this logic and relating the changing configuration of the family economy to the shifting organization of production and consumption itself. In essence, it is my opinion that Caldwell has misunderstood the essential character of the two-phased process of English industrialization and, in so doing, has wrenched his historical analysis out of its specific context.[6] Nevertheless, Caldwell's revised theory of fertility decline is of *immense* importance and if in the following pages I disagree with its particular application to English history I have still learned an enormous amount from it. In large part this book has been written in response to his provocative incursion into the debate concerning the revolution in family life which is transforming the world in which we are all living. He has made me think and I can offer no other tribute than to contest his ideas in the crucible of historical argument.

In my argument, Caldwell's interpretation is turned upside-down: the popular demand for schooling is considered to be of far less significance than the supply of scholars. Schooling and education, which Caldwell considers to be the primary independent variables creating a new family morality, are relegated to a secondary role as variables dependent upon the changing value of children in the proletarian family economy. Moreover, the transformation of popular mentalities by the homogenizing agencies of a supposedly dominant culture are countered by an insistence on the continuities of older traditions which have proved to be surprisingly resilient. My purpose is not to reject totally an interpretation of "ideological integration" but rather to revise it by addressing its vast silences. One can point to the middle-class supply of birth control information and techniques but that tells us nothing about the working-class demand for them. Another line of explanation is possible even if little considered; it fits the dynamics of proletarian family formation strategies with social and economic change which were, to be sure, mediated by ideological forces. This was a materially conditioned seed-bed within which ideological novelties were implanted. It is thus my contention that one can only begin to make sense of the working-class participation in the fertility decline by paying heed to *their* primary concerns and *their* own mentalities – especially their attitude to ***respectability*** and their overarching concern for self-control and independence. Let us turn to a discursive consideration of the second phase of English industrialization, reading it in the context of Caldwell's theories of fertility decline. We will therefore pay particular attention to the impact of changing forms of production on inter-generational wealth flows and the perdurance of popular mentalities, especially insofar as they informed the formation of new families and their subsequent reproductive strategies.

An economic imperium

The later 1840s marked a turning-point in the economy of working-class life, at work and at home. From these years the very character of the society began to change. In short, "History from now on became world history." This change was uneven but, nonetheless, cumulatively very important. At its heart was the iron horse, prancing across its ribbons of metal rails – in 1840 there were some 4,500 miles of track, mostly in England and the north-eastern United States; in 1880 there were 228,400 miles stretching over all five continents. Together with ancillary developments in telegraphy and steamships, it meant that the world became smaller and more inter-connected than before. At least one contemporary thought that the unification of the nineteenth-century world was of an order of historical magnitude comparable to the age of discovery, the age of Columbus, Vasco Da Gama, Cortez and Pizarro. In the event, English manufacturing and commerce were reconfigured. Many of the infra-structural advantages, built up in the first stage of industrialization when English coal and steam power had joined forces to break free from the dominance of agrarian organization, now proved to be decisive in the establishment of an economic imperium.

It was in direct response to these changes that there was an orgy of profits. The fears of an asymptotic "stable state", so common in the early 1840s, were laid to rest and "politics went into hibernation".[7] The lateral expansion of the capitalist economy, and its world-wide integration, was overseen by English capital and in return contributed towards restructuring the operation of its financial operations. The formation of a railway economy precipitated one of the two great moments in the history of English finance.[8] Just as the formation of the Bank of England had played no small role in stabilizing the Hanoverian state by floating a national debt from which Britannia could find the ready cash to rule the waves, the capitalization of the railways similarly won acceptance for the general limited liability company.[9] With the emergence of this kind of securities, the whole nature of the stock market began to change and money soon began to flow into profitable undertakings which could, and did, flourish and multiply. There were two features of this development which should be elaborated. Both were of the greatest importance in structuring the Victorian economy and configuring the English upper classes who consumed so many products from the world's workshop. First, the preference share, debenture and later the overseas public utility stocks provided a conduit for English capital to flow abroad in its search for steady, secured income. By 1875 £1,000 million had been invested abroad; three-quarters since 1850. In the next generation this figure quadrupled so that in 1913 "Britain owned perhaps £4,000 million worth [of investments] abroad."[10] Second, the remission of profits from these investments created a quite disproportionate number of English men and women who were rentiers, pure and simple. They, together with their agents in the rest of the world, provided an enormously well-defined yet highly articulated market, completely unlike the mass-consumption base on which American industrial capitalism was then being built. Having this stable, conservative and, most of all, highly articulated demand for its products meant that the handicraft mode of production was further entrenched. And, as we shall see presently, this concatenation of forces was absolutely central to the marketing strategies of English industrial capitalists.

England is a small country well-endowed with navigable rivers – a characteristic of real importance in the first stage of industrialization – but the railways represented a quantum leap forward in transportation and communication. The mid-Victorian railway boom had a more profound effect on English social and economic life than the emergence of the cotton factories in south-east Lancashire. Its tentacles reached into the smallest village – soon, most were no more than a few miles from a station – and broke down the remnants of rural isolation. One can grasp some measure of this advantage in the comparative statistic that in the middle 1850s, by the test of territorial area compared with railway mileage, England was three times better serviced than its closest competitors, Belgium and the states of New York and Pennsylvania, and more than seven times ahead of France and Germany. The mid-Victorian railway boom reconstructed markets, forced down transport costs and, in the process, tore local economies apart. Transport costs plummeted and food prices, so vital to an industrial economy seeking to maintain its head start and dependent for its lead on abundant supplies of relatively cheap labour, quickly became a reflection of world not local arrangements. At the height of the railway "mania", in the quinquennium 1846–51, it was thought that as many people were dependent upon domestic railway construction, 600,000, as were engaged in factories.[11] When the domestic network had been largely put in place, early in the 1850s, the skills and advantages enjoyed by English labour and capital made it possible, perhaps even imperative, to build railways abroad. The well-known "multiplier effect" worked itself out with greater intensity in England than abroad. English workshops worked furiously to meet foreign orders for locomotives and rolling stock, as well as the iron rails; engineering activity at home was revolutionized. Machinery exports grew ten-fold between 1846–50 and 1870–5.[12] These exports, together with those of capital and labour, laid the basis for an economic imperium by creating many of the "traditional" markets whose demand was first engendered by and then slowly came to define the marketing and manufacturing strategies of English capitalism. This is a most important point and one which will be a recurrent sub-theme in our consideration of the character of English industrial organization during the second phase of industrialization. Indeed, it must be stated with some emphasis that the magnitude of English *forwardness* laid the foundations of an industrial economy which was admirably suited to its own time but basically unable to change with the times. In effect, the mid-Victorian solution was the source of the present-day problem.

The Janus-face of English industrial capitalism

The relative unimportance of automatic machinery in mid-nineteenth-century England meant that the proletariat exercised a very significant degree of leverage over the rate and pace of production. In the orgy of profit-making there was a general recognition that an ordered labour supply was necessary for the smooth functioning of the engine of economic growth – there was little desire to put this gravy train off the rails. Such a situation did not develop in a vacuum nor was it without its reverberations in the social relations of production. In cotton-textile and coal mining communities it was both the condition of and response to the symbiotic relations between incomplete mechanization and proletarian job-control, relatively low wages and more or less peaceful social conditions, on the one hand, *but*, on the other hand, it resulted in two quite different forms of reproduction. Indeed, one of the main themes of this essay is that the contingency of context did much to set the historical stage on to which actors strutted and showed their stuff. For this reason we shall also discuss those other workers who were able to control their work and their reproduction in markedly different conditions – more rapid growth being a convenient short-hand for their market position and that of their "trades". And, finally, those workers who had no leverage, and whose lives and whose labour were out of control, will be brought into the analysis in order further to specify the contextual contingency of relations between production and reproduction. For many, their present was conditioned by their parents' pasts; their present, in turn, conditioned their children's future. In framing an account of shifting strategies of reproduction it is necessary to see the private lives of the proletariat through a prism refracting the changes and continuities of the labour process. In this way we can locate the impact of social relations of production within the grid of private relations of reproduction.

In the mid-Victorian world of small workshops, technological conservatism, sub-contracting and relatively steady profit-margins it did not behoove the employer to be "offensive". The very conditions of English *forwardness* meant that the economy had enormous infrastructural advantages over its competitors so that profit *optimization* did not necessarily demand the immediate switchover to state-of-the-art techniques of production, management or sales. In fact, there was a sort of *quid pro quo* which, in Lancashire at least, found its expression in a deferential dialectic. The "natural exchange for paternalism" was that "paternalism had to deliver the economic goods", the most important of which was regular employment. As Patrick Joyce remarks of the mid-Victorian equipoise in the Lancashire textile towns, "The need for security was elevated into the beginning and the end of life ... Dependence therefore bred the need for certainty and coherence that the acceptance of caste and hierarchy met."[13] The helplessness of the working class, adrift in chaos, is nowhere better recounted than in the bitter-sweet remonstrances of Allen Clarke, a cotton factory operative and socialist militant:

> They have no true idea of life. They believe they are born to work; they do not see that work is but a means to life ... They have no rational grasp of politics, or political economy ... They think that the masters build factories and workshops not to make a living by trading but in order to find the people employment. They honestly believe that if there were no mills or workshops the poor people would all perish.[14]

There was another side to this relationship; that which played itself out in the workplace and centred upon struggles to define and re-define the "rules of the game". In Oldham between 1883 and 1890, for example, there were some 3,000 industrial disputes suggesting the tension between public deference and workplace struggle. Thus, the same workers who proudly celebrated their boss's party politics and their boss's son's coming-of-age also militantly defended their labour power. The Lancashire cotton factory was in some senses atypical but in it we find the mid-Victorian crystallization of politics, industrial organization and unionization; frozen, as it were, in a marriage of convenience between profit-optimizing capitalists and job-controlling workers. Around this social centre of gravity in which a core labour market of factory workers set the "rules of the game", marginal workers were defined by their relation to the paradigmatic structure. In cotton spinning, the crown-jewel of the factory system, the triumph of machinofacture was halting. Although self-acting mules, which reduced labourers to mere machine attendants, were introduced in the 1830s, as late at 1851 according to the Secretary of the Oldham Master Spinners "on account of their excessive cost very few firms were able to purchase the self-actor ... and therefore hand mules were the rule and self-actor mules the exception".[15] The global impact of the self-acting machinery was further circumscribed by the social relations of production within the factory and the industry. Spinners were at the base of one work-hierarchy within the larger command-structure of the factory, but within the work-room itself cotton spinners maintained substantial control over their labour and that of their work-team thereby disordering the managerial thrust towards switching over to full-scale automation. In the 1850s boom the demand for "minders" meant that the operatives were able to establish a precarious, privileged perch for themselves which was rendered more stable because of the fierce internal feuds and rivalries between competing capitalists, a great many of whom were small-fry. It was this set of circumstances which made it possible for the workers to form a united bargaining association fully two decades before their employers began to organize themselves. The minders were able to upgrade their position from that approximating common street labourers in the 1840s to that of "labour aristocrats" in the space of a generation. Their victory and social mobility, as a group, was achieved at the expense of their assistants (called "piecers"), often members of their own family, who were consigned to the lower-paid tasks with little opportunity to advance unless the chief spinner died. Moreover, the cornerstone of their victory derived from their control over job-entrance so that even though there was an over-supply of qualified, adult male minders the demand was rigidly regulated.[16] In the weaving sector similar conditions seem to have blunted the movement towards unrestrained machinofacture: as late as 1914 there were only 15,000 fully automatic looms in British mills while in the smaller American industry there were 400,000.[17] In the cotton industry there was a tendency towards concentration, yet the average size of firms seems not to have doubled between 1850 and 1890. In fact, a good deal of this growth was due to the combination of businesses as industrial organizations became monolithic "limiteds" rather than because of any significant increases in the factories themselves. A very good many firms must have found it unprofitable to embark on capital-intensive technological upgrading and instead remained true to the course of "inner colonization" of intensive exploitation which had been set in the second quarter of the nineteenth century.

The cotton industry was atypical mainly because it was able to change so little for such a very long time whereas by the 1880s there was a movement towards large-scale, vertically integrated enterprises in some other sectors of the economy. This development provided the backdrop to the contemporaneous assault on the artisan's precariously poised privilege and custodial craft control. Workplace struggle was especially concentrated in engineering works, and then in those more traditional sectors which were feeling the forced-draughts of international competition in which the opportunities for mass production were most pressing. Sir John Clapham has written that we should regard the Black Country, around Birmingham, "even more truly than . . . Lancashire" as "the strength of the new age".[18] In this locality steam power was introduced relatively late so that "By the 1890s the city of Birmingham was poised between the town of a thousand workshops and the home of the great industries of the 20th century."[19] The real triumph of machinofacture in Birmingham at the end of the Victorian period was accompanied by a spatial transformation of the city and its region as "manufactory-based industries were established on the edge of the growing city" while "the industries of inner Birmingham and its vicinity were declining, stagnant or expanding only very slowly".[20] The politics of the time teetered between the conception of class struggle proposed by Marx and the older tradition of "the producer ideology" incarnated and brought up to date by Birmingham's own Joseph Chamberlain. What E. J. Hobsbawm has called "Sheer bloody-minded shop-floor resistance" was contemporaneous with the Liberal programme of social reform, engendered as much by fears of incipient revolution as by imperialist concerns for military preparedness. The very narrowness of support offered to the offensive employers is a vivid testament to the way in which not only work but also the social relations of work had got under "the skin of everyday life" in Victorian England. In the result, the late nineteenth-century employers' offensives were beaten back and the English kept their peculiarities.[21] Yet again, the past inflected the course of historical change in decisive ways so that the Coventry Toolroom Agreement of 1941 mixed a measure of de-skilling, open access and piece-rates, so-called "payment by results", with shop-steward power. This compromise resulted in the persistence of shop-floor conflicts, most of which concerned the definition (and re-definition) of a renovated and redefined "custom of the trade".[22] In steel making, too, attempts at "scientific management" were thwarted and workers maintained a very significant measure of control over the pace of work and even manning levels. Indeed, general practice seems to have been that job-control and job-security were of more significance to workers than maximization of short-term wage rises with the possibility of de-skilling and downward mobility. The diversity and fragmentation of the manufacturing sector, like that in cottons, meant that the men were more organized than their masters. Individual firms, therefore, negotiated on terms largely dictated by the unions, which combined mass membership with the characteristic stance of craftsmen.[23]

The workshop of the world: an ambivalent hegemony

It is in the *relatively* relaxed atmosphere which pervaded English manufacturing in the second phase of industrialization that most analysts have rooted the subsequent decline. In analysing the relationship between the deployment of new technologies and labour relations it is important to situate this so-called "retardation" in its historical context. C. K. Harley has argued that the resilience of unmechanized production controlled by human energy and dependent upon human skill was a significant element in the "industrial retardation" which seemed to characterize the second phase of industrialization in England. "So long as factor prices left 'handicraft' methods the low cost technique in Britain there was little incentive to specialize."[24] In cotton textiles, the nation's largest industrial employer providing a quarter of its export earnings in 1914, industrial organization fell back on an inherited division of labour and did not re-order it to keep pace with either the technological or the organizational state-of-the-art. This situation had been precipitated when the moral, social and political economies of the industrial north congealed in the immediate post-Chartist period. The long-term implications were "a considerable reliance on the skill, initiative and authority of workers, so that in the course of change skill was re-defined and re-negotiated, carrying with it a marked degree of control over the immediate work situation". Thus, in conditions of abundant labour, it was "economically rational" for employers to adopt paternalistic methods of control.[25]

In point of fact, the English made the first **Industrial Revolution** but they were reluctant to adopt the new system of production. Inventions were applied relatively slowly in England, as compared to her rivals. In part, as Habakkuk argues, the *relative* "Abundance of labour favoured accumulation with existing techniques – widening rather than deepening capital – even though the supply of capital might have permitted a technologically more advanced development."[26] The triumph of the factory system and the mechanization of manufacturing processes proceeded unevenly; even after 1850 its first steps were tentative. Given the low fixed-capital commitments, allied with the cheapness of human labour and the complexity of replacing human skill with inanimate machines, it is not altogether surprising that steam-powered machinery made comparatively little impact in the period before 1851. Raphael Samuel has remainded us that many of the new industries which were thrown up in the course of the nineteenth century were organized on the basis of human skill: "The industrial revolution, so far from abridging human labour, created a whole new world of labour-intensive jobs." Steam-powered machinofacture had by no means obliterated conservative production routines for the perfectly sensible reason that

Human beings ... were a great deal cheaper to install than a power house, and much more adaptable in their action than a self-acting stamp or press. When they broke down, the master did not have to pay for repairs; when they made a mistake, he could fine them; when there was no work for them to do he could give them the sack. Skills too were cheaper than machinery to come by.[27]

The economic development of the period fostered a symbiotic growth of both steam technology and handicraft skill, often in different parts of the same manufacturing process. The second phase of English industrialization was predicated on "technological change ... [which featured] the recomposition of skills rather than a unilinear process of downgrading".[28]

Institutional factors, as much as economic ones, have been used to describe the *comparatively* lackadaisical efforts of English entrepreneurs. Industrial capitalists seem to have embraced a "counterrevolution of values" looking back to an ordered, rural "English way of life" which led them to de-value industrialism and scientific education as opposed to imperialism and classical education.[29] By the 1860s "the demon of gentility" drew the leading industrialists in Lancashire's smaller industrial communities towards increasing incorporation into the currents of national political and, particularly, cultural life. By the last quarter of the century the "southern" mentality had clearly triumphed and nowhere was this triumph more clearly apparent than in the ideological ramparts that were erected upon "the articulation of notions of social responsibility, drawn from feudal, or pseudo-feudal, ideals".[30] The Lancashire patriarchs opted for stability and social harmony at the expense of break-neck growth and technological innovation thereby retarding economic expansion in such a way that "the social and intellectual revolution implicit in industrialism was muted, perhaps even aborted".[31]

British capitalists frequently found it profitable to stick with "outmoded" technologies because many were motivated by profit *optimization* rather than its maximization.[32] The character of the second phase of industrialization in England was thus profoundly influenced by the social relations of production which had been worked out in the course of its first phase. Charles Sabel's comparison of gung-ho, American mass production with English "half-hearted support" makes this point; it also suggests that the English developed an alternative system of industrial development amounting to the "mechanization of handicraft production". By concentrating on as wide a market as possible, English industrialists "customized" production using general purpose machines which "were often a sophisticated version of the artisan's original tools, which could be quickly shifted from the manufacture of one thing to another. Instead of unskilled labor he employed craftsmen, whose skill was required to make full use of the machines' potential." Thus, in Sabel's view the Victorian industrial system resembled Adam Smith's pin factory as much as, if not more than, Henry Ford's assembly line. The genius of this system was that it could respond to shifts in demand by reorganizing the skills of the machine-assisted artisans and by rearranging sub-contracts so that when "demand shifted, the workshops could be recombined in new ways to make new goods".[33] Most entrepreneurs were reluctant and/or unable to invest heavily in state-of-the-art machinery so that steam power made very little impression in a great many industrial processes until the last quarter of the nineteenth century. Slow growth and piecemeal innovation brings the reproduction of the labour force into the centre of the stage from where it cannot be removed without seriously distorting our appreciation of not only the social relations of production but also the peculiarities of the English experience.

The negation of the Malthusian proletariat

The lessons learned from the involution of the **proto-industrial** mode of production were well learned. The population explosion after 1780 gave the balance of power to capitalists who had used their advantage to intensify the division of labour and to segment the labour process. The over-supply of labour was self-destructive. The bad odour in which Malthus was held by almost all radicals meant that the interplay between production and reproduction was largely ignored on a public level. Indeed, the attack upon Francis Place, Richard Carlile and Robert Dale Owen, who all suggested that birth control could ameliorate the exploitation borne of competition, was vitriolic. "The hub of the anti-Malthusian argument was that population pressure did not cause poverty; poverty caused population pressure."[34] But if the reactionary radical William Cobbett, the primitive socialist Thomas Hodgskin, the unionist John Gast and then Karl Marx won the rhetorical battle it is not altogether clear that they successfully routed the radical adaptation of Malthusian logic. In the previous chapter I discussed the post-1815 downturn in the rate of reproduction. I also showed how (in the village of Shepshed, at least) the involution of the **proto-industrial** mode of production led to a new strategy of early marriage *and* controlled fertility. In essence, the strategy unveiled in Shepshed, and apparently practised in many other places undergoing the similar process of **industrial involution**, was built upon a much older tradition of spacing births across the woman's fertile period. This method of "birth control" was employed both to avoid a rapid succession of pregnancies and to afford some protection to women and their newborn infants. Such a practice of fertility control optimized family size arising from "a concern of not only how many children were born but of who had them, when, how far apart, and up to what age". The ingredients for a systematic programme of fertility control were neither original nor, it should be added, was their application unprecedented. In fact, approximately one woman in five born in the second quarter of the nineteenth century controlled her fertility within marriage.[35] The most important methods for controlling fertility were either abstinence or withdrawal; they were well known in the early nineteenth century, and earlier, and were effective enough to account for almost all contraceptive practice throughout the fertility decline.

The real issue confronting birth controllers was not technical; rather it was attitudinal and, even more importantly, strategic. People controlled their fertility because they found it in their interest to do so. Yet any such motivation must have been mediated by the social relations of reproduction and for many proletarians the necessity of maintaining a *family economy* meant that there was a profound contradiction between the politics of reproduction and the household economics of family formation. Nevertheless, it would be mistaken to ignore or downplay the shards of evidence which have survived on this subject. Barbara Taylor argues for a persistent "feminist tradition within plebian [*sic*] circles which ran counter to the increasing sexual conservatism of mainstream labour organizations, and also the pronounced anti-feminist bias of some later Marxist socialist associations". And while "None of these women ever openly raised the issue of contraception . . . lack of control over reproduction was obviously a crucial factor shaping their views on sexuality."[36] The importance of these straws-in-the-wind is thrown into relief by Angus McLaren's analysis of the "commercial exploitation" of contraception. Reading meaning into an active underground interest in traditional curing practices and folk medicine, he argues that "What all of this suggests is that [in the second half of the nineteenth century] the idea of birth control already had a place in the working classes' own scientific sub-culture and therefore the adoption of family limitation did not signify a capitulation to the teachings of neo-Malthusians or eugenists."[37] Moreover, we have seen from the example of the framework knitting village of Shepshed, Leicestershire, that such a strategy of fertility control was, in fact, being applied. Neither Malthus nor Cobbett nor Marx had the final word, however.

After Owenism and then Chartism had failed to secure an alternative future, the primary objective of labour politics focussed upon exercising control over the labour supply. Job security and wages became the flash-points of contention. Richard Price writes that "The conception of property rights in a certain job was, of course, common to nineteenth-century craftsmen, and amongst workers in general the desire to spread and share the work provided much of the rationale for hours agitation, demarcation rules and restriction of output."[38] Thus, in a curious way, the world-view of the industrial breadwinner came to resemble that of the peasantry, who also considered that wealth was a "limited good", rather more than the *proto-industrialist* for whom the "prolifick power" of reproduction meant the addition of hands and the extension of the unit of production.[39] The distinctions between the stages in capitalist development were internalized and shaped the outlook, politics and family lives of the working class.

The conditions of bargaining changed dramatically in the mid-century period. First, population growth slowed, wages rose and well-paid workers took advantage of this breathing space to withdraw their wives and children from the labour force, thus further restricting the scope of self-defeating competition. Second, the nature of technological change was frequently such that it actually increased the number of semi-skilled operatives and its capital-intensiveness made employers less able to engage in wholesale recruitment so that they, too, had an interest in maintaining regular crews. In addition, the extension of the workshop at the expense of the cottage meant that there was a significant separation between the workplace and the home. Thus the withdrawal of women and children from the labour force also reflected the trajectory of the production process. The sorts of jobs which women and particularly children had usually performed were slowly being superseded by mechanization so that their withdrawal from the labour force was only partly a matter of choice, it was also a matter of fact. Nevertheless, the salient point is that the participation of women and children was declining; very young children were being freed from the working world and most mid-century census enumerations make it clear that the older tradition of child labour was in the process of disintegration. Only in the outwork, domestic industries was it possible to retain the family mode of production and "by 1900 cottage industries had ceased to be significant contributors to the income of labouring families in the way that they had once been".[40] Child labour had been an integral component of the first phase of industrialization, it was a marginal one in the second phase. Third, most businesses were profitable so that the imperatives to cut labour costs were less than pressing. Fourth, the culture of paternalism permeated the upper class, particularly those who had been educated in public schools. It mediated between the maximization of profits and the public reproduction of "neo-feudal" labour relations. Fifth, even though it was usually on the side of capitalist status quo, the intervention of the state nevertheless signified an important development. Moreover, the state was not simply the hand-maiden of the industrial capitalists. It had a life of its own and an inner logic which often set it against the very class which "controlled" it. In point of fact, the spread of the franchise and Disraeli's end-run to make the Conservatives into the successful "natural" governing party changed the orientation of the political culture in important ways. Because the working day was shortened, because the labour of women and children was restricted, because workers' rights to organize were recognized, and because employers were held to be liable for injuries sustained by their employees, the entrepreneurial choice of extensive exploitation was less accessible.[41]

Despite the *relative* slowness of change, in comparison to her rivals, one cannot but be impressed by the *absolute* speed of change compared with what had gone before. "In fact there are good grounds for regarding the period 1850–1914 as that in which the Industrial Revolution really occurred, on a massive scale, transforming the whole economy and society much more widely and deeply than the earlier changes had done."[42] History happened faster. Many, many, many more innovations and products were available in 1914 than in 1850. The speed-up of the historical process is hardly surprising since, in a material sense, HISTORY bears eloquent witness to our mastery of the physical world.

One would not, however, want to suggest that these changes in the reproduction of the social order were technologically determined. Far from it. In fact, the particular historical evolution of the second phase of English industrialization and the way it interacted with the family lives of the proletarian majority of the population can only be understood if, and only if, attention is given to continuities as well as the changes inherent in the process. Indeed, it is the tension between enormous transformations and perdurant traditions which is at the heart of the matter. Change proceeded unevenly and its impact was felt selectively. In a most funda-mental sense, only when the working-class family freed itself from the fetters of the family economy did it "modernize" itself. The family mode of production was part of the problem; its supersession was part of the solution. The act of liberation was not a free choice, independent of material forces. This "modern" solution was not without its costs – the segregation and compartmentalization of men and women, parents and children being foremost – but it was a necessary step in emancipating the family from the self-exploitation inherent in the involutionary mode of reproduction accompanying the involutionary mode of production of the first phase of industrialization.

Respectable, private pro-activity

The material recomposition of the labour process was mirrored in the privatized pro-activity of the working class in the wake of the disastrous failure of public politics in the Chartist period. There are, I think, several aspects to this privatization which are integrally related to the reconfigur-ation of reproduction. First, sectional activity flourished as energy was devoted to the narrow demands for wages and job-control instead of the much wider demands for social restructuring. Learning the "rules of the game" was an acknowledgement that "the game" was here to stay. Amelioration took the place of revolution. The "chiliasm of despair" gave way to the bureaucratization of spiritual life. The decline of expressive spontaneity can be related to the final fragmentation and splintering of an older struggle for moral authority. Radical working-class educational efforts became more privatized, too; they switched from their suspicion of "provided" education of the churches to agitation for state intervention. Second, material well-being and improvements in living standards really took root. One finds evidence of this improvement in wage-rate evidence but, in the usual way, this sort of evidence misses the main point since a very large part of the improvement was environmental, not just narrowly economic. The cities were cleansed, streets lit, water supplies were freed from contamination, and the waste of humans, horses and industry became a matter of social concern. Enormous differentials in height between the upper and working classes, evident in the early stages of industrialization, narrowed.[43] To be sure, proletarians' homes were smaller and damper, their neighbourhoods were more crowded, and improvements were put in place with less alacrity than in the wealthier parts of town but these *relative* differences almost pale into insignificance when placed next to the *absolute* horrors of Engels' Manchester and Mayhew's London. The "aristocracy of labour" enjoyed these improvements before the "residuum" but inexorably they had begun to make their way felt in the lives of all who lived and worked in urban England by the first decades of the twentieth century. Third, and of paramount importance, the family became the focus for self-definition. Working-class *respectability* signified self-control. The rise of *respectability* to a place in the pantheon of Victorian virtues – domesticity and self-help, above all – cannot be overestimated. Working-class concerns with *respectability* had little to do with cultural mimesis but quite a lot to do with a conception of self-*respect* founded upon a notion of independence. As Geoffrey Crossick has argued, "What divided middle-class conceptions of achievement from those of working men was the role of collective strength." This kind of collective strength was actualized in family ties, neighbourliness and the formation of mutual-aid societies. At the end of the nineteenth century nearly four in five male industrial workers were members of friendly societies. Working-class egalitarian independence found its expression in the internalization of the habits of sobriety, thrift and self-discipline. The *respectable* working-class man and his family looked after themselves and were beholden to no one else for their social and economic position. *Respectability* meant avoiding the workhouse and the shame of a pauper funeral.[44] Culturally, then, the working class made itself in its rejection of both the patronage and paternalism of an older moral world and the subordination of the new one growing up around them. "The will to seek this independence and the moral qualities needed to achieve it, were proof of respectability."[45] If this *respectability* was something which all could not achieve, it was nonetheless the goal to which almost all aspired.

In contrast to the family economy of the early industrialists in which men's labour might contribute as little as a quarter of the total income, by the later decades of the nineteenth century the chief breadwinners generally brought home more than two-thirds of the cash.[46] These changing terms of trade between husbands and fathers on the one hand and wives and children on the other had far-reaching implications for family formation strategies. The age at first marriage for women began to rise, the incidence of permanent celibacy for women crept up too. The cost of children soared. "Wealth flows" within the family changed direction not only because of new attitudes engendered by schooling, not only because of factory acts or philanthropic legislation, not only because of the embourgeoisement of the workers, but primarily because the second phase of industrialization led to the dissolution of the family wage economy and the compartmentalization of sex-roles. The nuclear family's material base was being revolutionized. Stripped bare of its productive functions, the working class family became the locus of reproduction and consumption. Although we can discern the lineage of these revolutionary forces in the mid-century period of equipoise, and even earlier, they only became generalized later. These new circumstances made fertility control a rational response for the working-class family. It might not be too far short of the truth to suggest that the restrictive reproductive regime was the correlative of the restrictive social discipline and workplace control exercised against the worst nightmares of their fathers' reproductive economy. The working class was thus "re-made", at work and at home. Within this evolving material context the value of adult men's labour – relative to that of women and children – began to rise dramatically. This differentiation was most marked in those sections of the economy in which women and children were almost completely excluded – engineering and heavy industry, the myriad of skilled trades which were thrown up by the workshop and, to a lesser extent, the factory mode of production. However, in textiles the perdurance of an older family wage economy meant that even skilled male workers within the factory found their bargaining power rather more limited than in other sectors.

Demographic involution: a perduring peculiarity

In the 1840s the cotton operatives of Oldham and Preston had a distinctive pattern of inter-marriage and residential segregation. In this way the mill workers were distinguished from the rest of the community in these Lancashire towns.[47] Engels noted that among the first factory proletariat

every improvement in machinery throws the real work, the expenditure of force, more and more upon the machine, and transforms the work of full-grown men into mere supervision, which a feeble woman or even a child can do quite as well, and does for half or even one-third the wages . . . In many cases the family is not wholly dissolved by the employment of the wife, but turned upside down. The wife supports the family, the husband sits at home, tends the children, sweeps the room and cooks.[48]

As we discussed in the previous chapter, the involution of the final phase of *proto-industrialization* interacted with the recruitment of the first factory proletariat. The perduring peculiarities of the cotton towns' social milieu can be explained by reference to the character of their labour markets and its interaction with the family economy of cotton-factory workers.

The family system of multiple wage-earners and co-residence, made possible by the availability of family-work in the mills, meant that life-cycle poverty was less pressing in Oldham. Though still particularly likely during the period of the "dependency hump", poverty was less intense among the cotton factory operatives than was the case in other industrial communities because family wages in cotton factory employment were near the top of the table. There was a marked tendency for men and women operatives to marry within their own occupational group – perhaps two-thirds of all married women workers had husbands working in the same industry – and "employers expected and received the child labour of their adult workers".[49] In this way the workers in mid-century cotton mills enjoyed a relatively favourable standard of living compared with workers in the heavy industries and shipping who lived in South Shields. The garret-cobblers of Northampton, Foster's third group, can be likened to the framework knitters of Shepshed in that they were struggling to maintain their independence in a dying trade in which subdivided labour and cost-cutting became the established system of sweating a profit out of the workers.[50]

Mid-century advantages favouring the cotton operatives had a boomerang effect in the later part of the century since it had by then become customary for wages to be set for men *on the assumption* that they were part of a family wage economy. Elizabeth Roberts' study of three Lancashire towns – Barrow, Lancaster and Preston, 1890–1940 – makes the distinctive family economy of the cotton town apparent. The Preston textile factories had maintained their employment of women and youths which had had significant implications for the character of social life.[51] In a word, the social structure of the late Victorian cotton towns was involutionary. We might back-track a bit in order to follow through with this point so as to highlight its importance for the family formations of the mill-hands.

John Lyons' work on the family strategies employed by displaced handloom weavers during the crisis of the second quarter of the nineteenth century starts from the observation that the family remained the nexus of income-generation in urban areas even when it had ceased to be an integrated unit of production. The cotton towns of Lancashire were thus characterized by a superfluity of labour, almost constant real wages and life-cycle poverty amongst the operatives, dense urbanization and very high levels of co-residence and "income pooling". Factories employed boys and girls and women, in preference to men, in the unskilled machine-minding tasks. Some boys could move up the ladder within the factory to skilled jobs; most could not. The age- and gender-specificity of the factories made them an attractive proposition for *families*, not breadwinners. Indeed, the wages of and demand for adult males in the cotton industry followed a quite different curve from that of women and children. Irish immigrants and displaced handloom weavers crowded about and pushed down their own wages to a dishonourable level. The repercussions of this particular conjuncture were contradictory: first, movement to the city by handloom weavers made sense in terms of their *family economy* because their wives and children could and did find factory work there; but, second, the glut of unskilled male workers forced down their wages and meant that the *family wage* could not be replaced by the earnings of a single breadwinner.[52]

Unlike many other mid-century male workers, most of those in textile factories were unable to control job-access and so their domestic conditions more nearly approximated those in the declining outwork industries than the skilled artisan in a workshop. For this reason, their demographic and residential configuration resembled that of the Shepshed framework knitters discussed earlier. Low male wage-rates, high levels of female employment, co-residence, the perdurance of an income-generating family unit and restrictive fertility were distinguishing characteristics of the textile towns. Even in the 1930s the investigators from The Pilgrim Trust found that "Wages have always been fixed in Blackburn on the assumption that several members of the family will be working" so that "the wages in most of the Lancashire cotton towns assume the double earnings of man and wife. The husband's wage alone would reduce many families into poverty and it was consequently necessary for the wife to earn all the time."[53] Later in her essay Roberts argues that the usual ascription of controlled fertility among textile workers is wrong because their legitimate fertility *ratios* were similar to those in non-textile towns; however, she seems to ignore the interaction between total fertility and infant mortality which is important because infant mortality levels were very substantially higher in Preston than Barrow so that it would seem likely that *completed* family sizes were most probably lower among the textile families. Since they married earlier, too, the fertility *ratios* of the textile workers would have necessarily been higher even though their fertility *rates* would have been lower because Preston women were "at risk" for a longer period of time. The point is not that they were absolutely successful in bringing down their family size but that they were trying to do so in conjunction with other strategies. The data and methods employed by Roberts cannot answer this question because they do not permit her to observe the sequential stages in the organization of family formation and fertility. Nevertheless, her study admirably succeeds in its main goal of providing a textured account of the family lives of these working men. One might venture that the pattern found in Shepshed of low wages and family wage economies, early marriage and co-residence, together with life-cycle fertility control in association with high levels of infant mortality created a very particular kind of *demographic involution*. The cotton-factory operatives in the Lancashire textile towns seem to have conformed to this paradigm in the later Victorian and Edwardian period. The labour market, defined by the *proto-industrial* family's reproductive regime, thus played havoc with the lives of both the children and grandchildren of these early industrial proletarians.

Breadwinners: the recomposition of the proletarian family

E. J. Hobsbawm remarks that during the second phase of industrialization there was "a remarkable improvement of employment all round, and a large-scale transfer from worse- to better-paid jobs".[54] This transfer was as much between older sectors of the industrial economy and newer ones as it was from family work to men's work. As we have seen, this differentiation was explicitly integrated into the political agenda of the *respectable* working man who demanded that his labours be recompensed with a "living wage". The quest for *respectability* was not confined to an aristocracy of labourers but was a vital element cementing working people together. Moreover, it is best understood in terms of aspirations and states of mind rather than as an expression, *tout court*, of an underlying concrete reality. If it was not pursued with equal success by all proletarians, nevertheless *respectability* was the cornerstone of their self-definition. The material foundation of this ideology can be traced in the emergent factories, the sexual division and age-gradation of labour and, crucially, the mid-Victorian boom in adult male wage-rates and living standards. Together, these factors made the breadwinner-family a practical reality and attainable goal for a very substantial minority among the working class. A new material base was emerging: fixed-capital costs rose and precision engineering enabled "the mechanics of standardization ... to penetrate old industries which had hitherto withstood the impact of the machine".[55] Robert Gray has written that "Economic structure and ideology were mutually reinforcing, in perpetuating the sexual division of labour. The exclusion of women, and the demand for a breadwinner's wage for men was an industrial bargaining strategy, enabling men to make sectional gains while women provided employers with a pool of below-subsistence wages."[56] When such breadwinners' wives worked it was frequently "casual, episodic and irregular ... and they covered only a small range of occupations, charring, washing, baby-minding, sewing, taking lodgers and trading, but it is impossible to quantify them further. They were carried out for a varying number of hours in the week and for very variable rates of pay."[57]

In considering the recomposition of the working-class family in the second half of the nineteenth century it is also important to recognize that the deflationary forces of the Great Depression (1873–96) led to a major shift in consumption patterns. Lower prices were, for many, equivalent to a major rise in their real incomes which could not be spent on "an entire new world of cheap, imported, foodstuffs [which] opened before the British people".[58] These years also witnessed the rise of the specialist shop and factory production for a working-class public. From the 1880s popular culture itself was transformed and

In a word, between 1870 and 1900 the pattern of British working-class life which the writers, dramatists and TV producers of the 1950s thought of as 'traditional', came into being. It was not traditional then, but new. It came to be thought of as age-old and unchanging, because it ceased in fact to change very much until the major transformation of British life in the affluent 1950s, and because its most complete expression was to be found in the characteristic centres of late-nineteenth century working class life, the industrial North or the proletarian areas of large non-industrial cities like Liverpool and south and east London, which did not change very much, except for the worse in the first half of the twentieth century.[59]

The flight from the countryside

After 1850 England became an urban society; it ceased being a rural one. Nineteenth-century England first saw rural communities reach their peak before dissolving in the face of urbanization. George Sturt's eye for the totality of this change was keen: "in the slow transition from village or provincial industry to city or cosmopolitan industry, one sees a change comparable to the geologic changes that are still altering the face of the earth; a change like them unnoticed, yet like them irresistible and cumulatively immense."[60] The vestiges of a way of life, undermined by the demise of the *cottage economy*, was now definitely laid to rest. The sense of loss was profound and it is from these years that William Cobbett's reputation grew by leaps and bounds. Thereafter, "the dream of an Elysian England of patriarchs, well-fed peasants, contented, if illiterate, craftsmen, and compassionate profit-sharing landowners, has haunted English radicalism" and become a staple of the mainstream cultural inheritance.[61]

The second phase of industrialization largely centralized manufacturing in specialized locations and in so doing it pastoralized the English countryside thereby reconfiguring the rural population. The flight from the countryside meant that whereas one in two people had lived in urban areas in the mid-century period, by the end of Victoria's reign about four in five did so. The rural areas experienced a net loss of 4.06 million people.[62] From the mid-century droves of agricultural labourers in the prime of life began to leave the land, its abysmal working conditions and its tied cottages, when the railways broke down the isolation of local labour markets thereby destroying the rural fabric woven by the Poor Laws. Between 1851 and 1911 the number of farmers remained stable but they had progressively fewer labourers at their disposal; moreover, the age-structure of the residual workforce was unusual, being mostly under twenty and over fifty-five. The de-industrialization of the countryside was accompanied by the mechanization of agriculture and "It is a rough token of the additional power given to agriculture by the instruments of urban industry that the product of [its] adolescent and senescent workforce was improved."[63] Although it would, on the surface, seem likely that ruralists should have made up a large component of the overseas migrants, this was not their usual destination. W. A. Armstrong summarizes research on this subject commenting that "In the round, despite a well-marked preference for countrymen on the part of receiving countries, it seems probable that the majority of the labourers who left the land were destined to fill the places of townsmen who at most times showed a greater propensity to emigrate."[64] In fact, until the 1880s the demand for urban labour in England was buoyant enough to soak up the rural exodus so that agricultural labourers and displaced cottage industrialists took over the places of departing artisans, craftsmen and industrial workers.

An enormous volume of people moved into and out of urban England in these years. Alongside the flood of rural labourers, immigrants from the "Celtic Fringe" flowed into London and the industrial conurbations; some became permanent settlers, many others merely stopped over on their way to the New World. The English *Industrial Revolution* had had disastrous consequences for the rural Irish. Irish industrial development in the eighteenth century was narrowly based, but spectacular. Vast sections of the countryside were pitted with households growing flax, spinning the yarn and weaving linen cloth. In response to their diminishing chances of maintaining a family income without the prop of industrial wages, many Irish *proto-industrialists* left their green land. Not a few ended up in British textile centres – Dundee and Paisley in Scotland, as well as Lancashire – because of the opportunities of their wives and female children finding work in the mills. Some men, like those in Lyons' Lancashire sample, continued to work in handloom weaving in its declining phase because, in the crowded urban labour markets work for unskilled men was in shorter supply than elsewhere, as we have already seen.[65] Irish industrial growth and disintegration provide the essential backdrop to much of the country's spectacular population movements. Even before the potato famine, between 1781 and 1841, an estimated 1,750,000 left Ireland.[66] Immediately after the Famine, in the seven-year period 1849–56, another 1,480,000 were driven out by either destitution or physical violence; usually both.

The naked exploitation and physical misery of these Irishmen during the first phase of industrialization was extraordinary, so too was their crucial role in providing raw muscle and undertaking the dirtiest of jobs. Whole classes of work had passed to the Irish navvy by the 1830s because "the English either refused the menial, unpleasant tasks or could not keep up with the pace".[67] These Irish proletarians were the "mobile shock troops of the industrial revolution". Their presence smoothed out the labour market while depressing the marginal return to labour because they could, so to speak, be called forth when required, "particularly at the top of booms", and dispensed with when not needed.[68] In 1841 there were 386,588 Irish-born adults, men and women, in addition to many, many more who were second- or third-generation immigrants. These people were the bottom of the heap. They did the heaviest jobs and showed "willingness, alacrity and perseverance in the severest, the most irksome and most disagreeable kinds of coarse labour, such as attending on masons, bricklayers and plasterers, excavating earth for harbours, docks, canals and roads, carrying heavy goods, loading and unloading vessels".[69] Industrialization cannot be divorced from the growth of England's empire. Britannia ruled more than just the waves – her subjects' labour power was just one form of tribute which was to be presented to the "Mother Country", with alacrity, when that great imperial mistress called.

Even during the second phase of industrialization the Irish continued to play a disproportionate role in British overseas migrations although from the middle years of the century Celtic in-migration more or less balanced English out-migration. The outflow from England was enormous. It has been estimated that between 1851 and 1910 American officals registered 2,156,531 English immigrants. Since some two-thirds of the English migrants in these years went to the United States, either directly or else through the Canadian back-door, it would not be far short of the mark to suggest that rather more than 3 million English men and women crossed the Atlantic, never to return.[70] Who were these migrants?

American ship-lists suggest that four out of every five Englishmen landing in New York gave a principal town as place of last residence.[71] A very substantial proportion had been employed in skilled trades – in the 1890 American census "fully 48 per cent of the men and 42 per cent of the women were in industrial occupations", half-again as many as among others who were foreign-born. Even after their arrival and settlement the English continued to practise their original occupations. Indeed, their specialized skills and industrial experience were a primary reason for their recruitment by labour-hungry American industrialists. American industrialization advanced in Seven League Boots, as Marx wrote, and "In the early days of such industries in the United States, British immigrants won wages and responsibilities unattainable at home. Thus they immigrated even when their trades were also flourishing in Britain, but *especially if foreign – largely American – competition undermined them.*"[72]

The pastoralization of the countryside

These "pull" factors are obvious; rather less so were the "push" factors. The pastoralization of the countryside was an important but too often forgotten side-effect of industrialization. In the trans-Atlantic migrations we have a distant mirror reflecting an image of social dislocation and personal adjustments. It is an image whose resolution distinguishes the nooks from the crannies of English life revealing, once again, the quantum shift which occurred during the second phase of industrialization. The native could not return to a world that was now irrevocably lost, "the process, humorously designated by statisticians as 'the tendency of the rural population towards the large towns' being really the tendency of water to flow uphill when forced by machinery."[73] We can locate some of the migrants' motivations in the disruption caused by industrialization. Let us therefore consider the way in which such huge numbers were displaced by the exhalation of the social respiratory system which had first inhaled so many millions out of the countryside and the Celtic Fringe into the urban-industrial crisis of the mid-century.

Industrialization inexorably destroyed many traditional rural crafts. The process of pastoralization has been studied by John Saville who has described how the specialization of function, so characteristic of the early modern countryside, was expunged in a couple of generations in the tiny county of Rutland. Its population fell by 11 per cent between 1851 and 1911, yet the number of millers dropped by 70 per cent, brick-makers by 65 per cent, sawyers by 70 per cent, cabinet makers by 65 per cent, coopers and turners by 87 per cent, wheelwrights by 43 per cent, blacksmiths by 28 per cent, building-trades workers by 19 per cent, saddlers by 23 per cent, tailors by 64 per cent and shoemakers by 42 per cent.[74] The second phase of industrialization also decimated rural industries. By the middle of the nineteenth century the older dual economy, with its complementarity of agriculture and industry, was in sharp decline. Its persistence in some outlying districts on the fringes of the conurbations was vestigial. By the end of the century it was largely gone from these places, too. For example, as late as 1843 one industrialist still delivered wool to villagers in the Yorkshire dales who lived up to 10 miles distant (from the town of Hawes): "they work it up at home, and bring back the articles when finished to the mill. A clever knitter might perhaps earn 3s. in any given week by incessant toil ...; a child, according to its age and proficiency earns 6d., 9d., up to 1s. 3d. in the same time." Although the earnings were small this was "in some degree compensated by the cheapness of provisions and the low rent of their cottages".[75] In many parts of rural England during the first half of the nineteenth century the sorts of by-employments, rural industries and specialized sub-crafts, which Joan Thirsk describes springing up in the countryside three centuries earlier, were still in evidence: "Pillow lacemaking in the south Midlands and Devon; straw plaiting for the hat and bonnet trade around Luton and Dunstable; glovemaking in Somerset, Devon, Dorset, Worcestershire and Herefordshire; buttonmaking in east Dorset; hosiery work in the east Midlands; and netmaking or 'braiding' on the East Anglian, Dorset and Cornish coasts."[76] Such forms of specialized women's and children's work could double the family income of an agricultural labourer, an important consideration when agricultural wages were usually less than 50 per cent of those paid to industrial workers. The imperatives of the family economy, and particularly the atrocious wages of the head of the household, meant that even though this income was gained at the cost of condemning their offspring to childhoods of toil, they had little real choice. Indeed, the self-exploitation so characteristic of the ***proto-industrial*** mode of production lasted longest in some of these ***cottage industries***, employing women and children in rural areas. The loss of this component in the family income must have been the deciding factor pushing many agricultural labourers to seek the higher wages and terrible costs of urban employment. In David J. Jeremy's study of the early diffusion of industrial technologies it was found that many of the English immigrants were young, single males, usually displaced handloom weavers, who possessed a "preponderance of preindustrial skills".[77] While by no means all emigrants were similar to Jeremy's displaced handloom weavers, his is still an instructive example. It corresponds to Lyons' finding that migration from the countryside was high on the list of adjustment strategies deployed in response to the spasmodic reconfiguration of the industrial economy. Migration to America in the nineteenth century, then, is the most revealing sort of indicator delineating the reverberations of English industrial recomposition at one remove, as it were. Of the British migrants to America, 60 per cent were males; two-thirds were between the ages of fifteen and thirty-nine. This age- and gender-specificity strikingly paralleled the early modern trans-Atlantic migrations and had similar repercussions on the marriage market back home: once again, the sex-ratio became imbalanced, the age at first marriage for women rose, permanent celibacy rates increased and illegitimacy dropped.

The loss of women's employment opportunities in cottage industries created a flood out of the countryside. The vast expansion of domestic service in the Orwellian "lower-upper-middle-class" household can, and should, be seen as a massive form of "disguised underemployment".[78] Domestic service should also be seen as a carceral regime whose "no followers" edicts rigidly circumscribed the sexual freedom and personal liberty of millions of young women.[79] Their bonnies were over the ocean, their bonnies were over the sea.

The logic of restraint

In the Edwardian period the average age at marriage for men (twenty-seven) and women (twenty-five) was roughly similar to what it had been in 1700. The later Victorian re-equilibration of this marriage-driven family system cannot be understood apart from the historical forces which dramatically changed the operation of the marriage market. Mirroring this resurgent prudence, the ratio of illegitimate births fell from 6.68 per cent in 1851 to 3.94 per cent in 1901. Bridal pregnancy rates dropped, too; but among agricultural and cottage-industrial labourers around 1900 it would seem that "It was accounted no shame for a child to be begotten out of wedlock – the shame was when there was no wedding to follow."[80] Marriage deferred; not promiscuity rampant. Since the marriage age was also rising at this time it is likely that the decline in the illegitimacy *rate* was even steeper than in its ratio.[81] The proportion of women, aged twenty to twenty-four who were ever-married was 34.8 per cent in 1871 and just 24.3 per cent in 1911. The proportion of permanently celibate women (defined as those who were never-married at forty-five to fifty-four) rose from 12.2 per cent in 1871 to 16.0 per cent in 1911. Wrigley and Schofield argue that "The combined effect of a rising marriage age and a rising proportion never marrying in the later nineteenth century would have sufficed [by 1911] to reduce the GRR by between 10 and 15 per cent from its 1871 peak, quite apart from fall in [*sic*] marital fertility occurring in the same period."[82]

The intensive work regime of the factories and the larger, more specialized workshops began to divorce production from leisure. It differentiated the adolescent experience of boys and girls and rendered young women more passive. Courtship became less public because "matchmaking was confined to the workers' free time and located in those commercialized places, first the pub, later the music hall, and finally the cinema, which became the locus of urban working-class culture".[83] The darkened cinema left the young couple quite alone but, of course, together. Such privacy was a very far cry from the "publicity" of village courtship. One can gain an appreciation of its popularity from the statistic that *every week* in the 1930s 20 million tickets were being sold. In Liverpool, for example, it was thought that 40 per cent of the total population went once a week, and 25 per cent twice or more.[84]

The need to save in order to finance the creation of a new household necessarily meant that the courtships of the urban proletariat were much more attenuated affairs than those of the *proto-industrialists* who were, as we have seen, greatly assisted in this task by their family, friends and neighbours. In contrast to the big weddings of the *proto-industrialists*, the proletarian wedding was a private affair. Marriage itself became the object of strategic planning of a new kind. Or, perhaps more correctly, old strategies were re-deployed in an altogether new environment. The decline of the family work unit meant that once more economic indepen-dence had to be predicated on the property a couple had at its disposal. As in the peasant family system where such property was unambivalently connected with land so, too, among the industrial proletariat the acqui-sition of, or control over, property became a central consideration for those couples contemplating marriage. However, there was a crucial difference. Among the proletariat such "property" was more attenuated; it was equated with the achievement of a financial sufficiency which could underwrite the creation of a new household. And, of course, such "property" was predicated upon and sustained by the wage-labour of adult males. Autobiographical evidence suggests that at least some people were able to save prodigious sums from their meagre wages: Mary Hollinrake's father, an "extremely" *respectable* cotton-mill supervisor in Todmorden, Yorkshire, not only furnished his new home with custom-built furniture but also "was able to begin his married life with a hundred golden sovereigns in hand"; Frank Marling insured his life for £100 "to use for the future education of his children" and made monthly payments of £1 to his building society; while Louise Jermy, who worked as a seam-stress, was able somehow to accumulate an astonishing £100 from her wages in that notoriously sweated trade before she married in 1911.[85] While there is no way of knowing the representativeness of these examples, they underscore the prudential character of the marriage process among *respectable* proletarians.[86] The fact that marriages could be started with some sort of reserve must have made the "dependency hump" far less stressful among those who had had the foresight and strength of will to put money aside for their most important enterprise. Mex Weber would have been proud of such people. The fact that Hollinrake, Marling and Jermy invested in their families, not in business enterprises, is not really germane; they exemplified the spirit of thrift and the internalization of self-discipline which he thought was so crucial to the growth of modern society. Yet, the very fact that their prodigious efforts were directed towards private reproduction looks backwards to an earlier mentality at least as much as towards the modern one which Weber championed. So, too, must we understand the investment in consumer durables which were so much a part of their *respectability* – the "parlour" reserved for "best occasions" and the household equipment which was purchased to upgrade the astonishingly primitive basic services (cooking, washing and sanitation) of the Victorian working class.[87] Commercial thrift may have replaced peasant thrift but the focus of it remained with the maintenance of, and incremental improvements in, the domestic economy.

The workplace had been removed from the home to become an essentially male preserve. Correlatively, the home became a haven from the heartless world. The Victorian cult of virginity and femininity ideal-ized the lady who presided over the king's castle. Here, again, we see no simplified relationship but rather that ambivalence which characterizes a hegemonic duality – the man, husband and father, delegated responsi-bility to the woman, wife and mother, and kept himself above domestic affairs.[88] The obverse of this "benign neglect", of course, is that the woman had a substantial arena over which she exercised a limited but real authority. This segregation of activities meant that women usually saw themselves in prescribed roles and, indeed, it was a hallmark of the *respectable* family to be able to present a suitable public face. The necessity to appear "seemly" and "keep up appearances" were merely the outward manifestations of a deeper reconstruction of women's social identity. It is obvious that such a reconstruction could not proceed evenly if only because it needed to be financed – at a cost. While women's work has always been undervalued, it has never been free. The demands of *respectable* social reproduction had greatly intensified the social import-ance of housework to the extent that it became an *obsessive occupation* for many, many Victorian women. The *respectable* housewife appears to have been quite neurotic about "cleanliness and polish, order and tidiness" in her "preoccupation with the conquest of dirt". One cannot understand the advice-cum-prescriptive literature of the period in any other way. But to have to control over the home with only half of one's time and energy was an almost super-human task. For those women who had to work outside the home, life was a double-bind. It is in this light that we might interpret George Orwell's observation that in Wigan "The best-kept interiors were always childless houses or houses where there were only one or two children; with, say, six children in a three-roomed house it is quite impossible to keep anything decent."[89] One wants to ask if these families were *respectable* because they were small, or small because they were *respectable*. In all likelihood, the causal arrows flowed in both directions. What is not so uncertain, however, is the fact that this new cultural constellation had its roots in the separation of home and work, especially in the demise of women's active role in production.

"Street arabs": the casualties of involution

The cost of children rose as a result of their falling industrial participation. Not only did children begin work later as the kinds of jobs they had traditionally done were being phased out by technological change but the remaining forms of work were marginal, low-paid and utterly dis-*respectable*. In the course of English industrialization children were a crucially elastic component of the labour supply; as such they, perhaps more than any group, were ravaged by the conjuncture of high rates of reproduction – and hence a flooded job-market – and technological obsolescence. More and more kids crowded into a job-market which had less and less children's work. Nowhere was the problem more acute than in London. The unique concatenation of sweated labour in the "slop trades", seasonality and a huge demand for casual labour of all kinds contributed to the social crisis in the capital. The dominant characteristic of London's industrialization was that "skilled work was subdivided within the shell of small-scale production".[90] The later nineteenth century, then, saw the persistence of sub-contracting masters whose success was predicated on their access to a supply of labour which could be hired and fired according to the mini-cycles of the finishing trades which they dominated. In most of London's industries, the small workshop was the usual site of production, the garret-master its organizer, and fixed capital was an inconsequential feature. A vast supply of casual and sweated labour was the *sine qua non* of this involuted system of production; the immiseration of the proletariat, especially children, was its social correlate.

The horrors of child labour and its savage exploitation were recognized as outrages. In the middle of the nineteenth century a new sensitivity, born of a shocked social conscience, began to be mobilized. However, between the recognition of the problem and its resolution at least five decades of Victorian reformers – who believed in compulsory schooling, industrial and "ragged schools", forced emigration to the colonies, private charity, public intervention in the home, and state planning – battled with the proponents of *laissez-faire*. The contrast with Romantic notions of an economically useless but emotionally priceless child motivated the "child savers". Yet the economically useful child was valued even as its economic contribution became more and more problematic precisely because the persistence of a family-wage economy made it impossible for a great many working-class parents to put into practice the Victorian sentimentalization of the innocent child. In the long run the sentimentalization of childhood triumphed but in the short run – unredeemed time through which generations of children suffered without much in the way of material satisfaction – child destitution was urban, industrial England's crying shame.

Powerful forces inhibited the progressives' realization of a sentimental childhood for all children. The sheer poverty of their families made it absolutely necessary for many children, so-called "street arabs", to begin cadging for pennies at an early age. Usually headed by unskilled labourers, such families were the cruel victims of the demographic conjuncture of this Malthusian period. The transformed demographic hermeneutic of the short period created an age-pyramid, so thick at its base that its effects resonated throughout the century. New generations – much larger than their predecessors – came to maturity. In the absence of a wholesale reconfiguration of fertility within marriage, these people inevitably had children. These children flooded into the capital's job-market from the fast-pastoralizing rural – agricultural and industrial – world; many others came from famine-stricken Ireland. Gangs of children "personified, in a particularly dirty and rebellious form, the wider social dislocations which the Victorians identified with the city. These children dominate the evidence just as they dominated the streets. They were to be seen in knots and bands, in streets and alleyways, and dotting contemporary photographs." Many had homes and parents, yet spent their lives on the streets. This fact tells us in no uncertain terms that they, and those who had no home at all, "shared a culture which was characterized by ill-health, vermin, dirt and crime".[91]

The changing configuration of the urban market for casual labour provides a revealing look into the post-Malthusian conjuncture of demography and economy. In Victorian London there were separate job-markets for juvenile and unskilled adult labour. Moreover, much of this "boy labour" had crowded out even younger children who had been in no position to gain a foothold into the world of paid work until they had achieved at least some semblance of strength and responsibility. The dead-end nature of this job-market – the competition from the next cohort meant that many youngsters were thrown on the scrap-heap when they reached young adulthood – alarmed contemporaries and sparked much investigation. Gareth Stedman-Jones has written that

casual labour virtually necessitated family work in order to attain a bearable level of subsistence. But, on the other hand family work, which was normally of an unskilled kind, redoubled the immobility of the casual labourer. For the uncertain gamble of obtaining more regular work elsewhere entailed not only risking his own livelihood [and the local connections which made such a network of jobs add up to a single employment experience] but also that of his wife. Moreover, it was precisely in areas dominated by casual labour that suitable female employment [in "slop work"] was most likely to be found. Thus the growing under-employment of male casual workers forced more and more of their wives and daughters into a falling labour market. The immobility of the family unit was reinforced, and this in turn worsened the problem of casual surplus.[92]

Casual work for men, "slop work" for their wives and daughters, "boy labour" for their older sons, and foraging for their youngest children – the rolling thunder of the Malthusian age-pyramid echoed in the lives of the grandchildren of pro-active proletarians.

Just as a working wife was *déclassé*, so too was a gang of kids sent out to forage as "street arabs". Without education or specialized training graduates from the school of "boy labour" crowded into a pool of unskilled labourers, keeping adult wages low and thereby perpetuating the vicious cycle of primary poverty engendered by the casual nature of employment. But education and specialized training were impossible without the economic wherewithal to forego "boy labour". This involuted constellation of forces militated against **respectability** in both public demeanour and private behaviour.

The policing of families

The logic of reproduction started to change as very young children lost contact with the working world to be confined to a special age-graded sphere of their own. Schooling took up some of the slack and it is obvious from school attendance figures that for many families child-minding was of at least as much importance as the opportunity to learn. Moreover, scholars ate up resources while providing no income in return so that the period of dependency was greatly prolonged – whereas the **proto-industrialists** could count on their children beginning to pay their way at six or seven and becoming a real contributor by ten, the proletarians had to wait much longer. In addition, the emergence of a distinctive youth culture among proletarians created tensions between the generations. Teenaged and young-adult children bridled at the demands of the family particularly because their fathers' inevitably declining incomes meant that children's contributions were prized. A tussle between the centripetal forces of the family and the centrifugal forces of individualism must have been a common experience. One can well imagine the contest between generations in the Hollinrake, Marling and Jermy households. It is a tribute to the resilient solidarity of the working-class family that the age at first marriage rose until the first decade of the twentieth century.

The social welfare legislation of the Liberal government, 1906–11, began to counteract the private insecurity of the family economy. A safety-net of social benefits was placed between those living in primary poverty and the mean streets. These reforms were promoted by Churchill and Lloyd George in an attempt to play Disraeli's trump-card and turn the Liberals into the natural governing party. They were enacted in an atmosphere of social confrontation and national military preparedness; they seem to have been little influenced by a militant social conscience but rather as a managerial solution. Winston Churchill, for example, called for "a sort of Germanized network of state intervention and regulation". The English Bismarck believed that no matter what England expected, the English ruling class should not expect to get much from its citizens if it gave them little in return.

However willing the working classes may to be to remain in passive opposition to the existing social system, they will not continue to bear, they cannot, the awful uncertainties of their lives. Minimum standards of wages and comfort, insurance in some effective form or another against sickness, unemployment, old age – these are the questions by which parties are going to live in the future.

The massive intervention of the state – its policing of families – dates from these years. The working classes became identified as those for whom the possession of insurance cards, for health and unemployment, were essential. As A. J. P. Taylor has written, it was in the war years that "The state established a hold over its citizens which, though relaxed in peacetime, was never to be removed ... [so that] The history of the English state and of the English people merged for the first time."[93]

Wealth flows: the cost of the sentimental family

In no small way the loss of a family economy meant that the logic of a high-fertility regime ran smack-up against the restrictive demands of **respectability**, the centrifugal forces of the life-cycle and the new-found security of the social welfare safety-net. Of course I am telescoping a process which took place over two generations but in so doing we can see the ways in which the second phase of industrialization and the independent interventions of the state began dramatically to reorder the private lives of men, women and children.

From 1876 until after World War I crude birth rates declined at an annual rate of 1.2 per cent, followed by fourteen more years at twice that pace.[94] The marriage cohort of 1861–9 had an average of 6.16 children; the 1890–9 cohort had 4.13 children; and the 1920–4 cohort had 2.31 children.[95] Statistics derived from the 1911 census, based on completed family sizes, describe a high degree of differentiation in fertility rates between social classes. Of even more interest to our present discussion is the fact that within the proletariat those families headed by a textile worker, a skilled worker or a semi-skilled worker experienced a very substantially faster rate of marital fertility decline in the 1871/81 to 1881/91 period than did other members of the working population, whose families were headed by miners, agricultural labourers and unskilled workers.[96] Thus, the working class was generally split along income lines.[97] Those at the bottom of the heap, whose low wages demanded the perpetuation of a family-wage economy, maintained an earlier demographic profile whereas those who were not able to finance the trappings of a *respectable* lifestyle with their rising wages began to restrict fertility within marriage.

It was a hallmark of the *respectable* working class that *their* kids were sent to school and kept off the streets. These *respectable* workers could invest in their children but others required the contributions of their children's income. While it is true that in the early years of compulsory schooling the state did begin to involve itself in the operation of the labour market and that factory legislation did stipulate minimum ages for child workers and did limit their working hours, *legislation was one thing and enforcement was quite another*. The 1867 Workshops Regulation Act decreed that no child under eight was to be employed in any handicraft and that for older workers a minimal attendance at school was required. But, together with another fifteen similar acts on the statute books in the 1870s, it proved difficult to implement. Large numbers of very young children were still employed in the outwork and sweated industries right into the last years of Victoria's reign. In point of fact child employment disappeared as a result of technological supersession of handicraft production, not legislation.[98] While the demand for child labour slowly dried up, its supply was dominated by the exigencies of the family economy. In the mid-1880s a Royal Commission on education and the working class found that parental poverty proved to be one of the most significant obstacles to regular attendance.[99] Although few parents were summoned before the magistrates for their children's non-attendance, many were willing to keep them out of school and risked paying fines out of their wages while others – more impressed by the letter than the spirit of the laws – made them attend regularly so as to insure that they could quickly meet the minimum demands for entering the labour force. The 1880 Act stipulating "compulsory attendance" therefore remained a fiction until the turn of the century, or even later in some areas. Yet it is important to acknowledge that the working-class family's self-exploitation and the working-class child's non-attendance at school diminished in tandem. The motor-force was provided by the reorganized labour process during the second phase of industrialization, not primarily by the intervention of the state. Seen in a longer perspective, one which considers both the traditions of working-class self-help and auto-didacticism as well as the exigencies of the family economy, it seems clear that the issue is not the supply of educational facilities but rather the demand for them on the part of working-class parents and their children. We will return to the ambivalence of working-class "demand" for schooling presently but let us briefly detour *en route* by considering other aspects of the wealth flows within the family economy.

The patriarchal politics of the working-class family operated in such a way that the breadwinner's demands were considered first. Working-class family budgets reveal that there was an unequal allocation of food within the family and that "fathers got by far the largest share of meat, and sometimes were given all of it when the amount bought was small. In order to keep up their strength and morale, fathers were given chops and sausages, while children and sometimes wives ate bread and drippings."[100] Laura Oren has explained the operation of this "patriarchy of the table" in terms of the "rational" allocation of resources in which women had little real choice in the matter so that they "deferred to the breadwinner because without him . . . [their] situation would have been even worse". Male demands for special physical and psychological consideration meant that the needs of the rest of the family took second place.[101] Evidence presented before a 1904 Parliamentary Inquiry into "Physical Deterioration", hastily called after so many working-class recruits were rejected by the military during the Boer War, tended to show that in the early period of the fertility decline in England the very poor maintained a high fertility rate and an upward flow of wealth – to the father.[102]

Existing evidence suggests that while the cost of children may have risen there was little sentimentalization of either children or childhood among the working class. I am purposely distinguishing "sentiment" from "sentimentalization" because I mean that working-class parents may have loved their children, they may have sacrificed for them – and many did both love and sacrifice for them in ways that are almost unimaginable to those of us for whom decisions rarely if ever have a life-or-death quality – but they do not seem to have regarded their children's childhood as something special and magical to be treasured and valued as a good in itself. In this sense, their children had to grow up fast; they had to face serious responsibilities and be ready to acquit themselves as if their little lives depended on it. Frequently they did. Such maturity was, in fact, a critical prop on which others depended. "Brought into the world by no will of their own, children had a right to be fed, clothed, sheltered and, to some degree, educated, but in return they were expected to contribute to the maintenance of the household as soon as they were old enough to be useful."[103] Many proletarians had little alternative but to consign their children to a life of labour at an early age, no matter what they may have thought, wished and prayed for for them. Indeed, loving care and selfless sacrifice seem to have been provided unstintingly by many parents, especially mothers, yet the complete and utter lack of material prospects for sentimentalization was, perhaps, the single most striking feature of the working-class family's experience. David Vincent has remarked that among early nineteenth-century working-class autobiographers "The most striking characteristic of the treatment of this topic is the general recognition of the subordination of education to the demands of the family economy."[104] Furthermore, there is a great deal of evidence which suggests that the advent of compulsory education, in the 1876 and 1880 Acts, was not in any way conterminous with a dramatic reordering of what Caldwell calls the "family system of morality". Burnett's auto-biographers, mainly from the later nineteenth and early twentieth centuries tell a story similar to Vincent's. For them, too, childhood was experienced in relation to the family's economic resources. "This concept of the child as an integral part of the domestic economy was a distinguishing feature of the working-class family, rural and urban, but was not normally found at higher social levels where servants released both mother and children from most domestic chores."[105] Putting sentimental ideas about childhood and education into practice costs money. Most people were quite literally penniless.

"Tidy platonism", "actual history"

"Minds which thirst after a tidy platonism very soon become impatient with actual history."[106] E. P. Thompson wrote this about the ambiguities in, and protracted character of, the historical formation of the English nation-state; he was not referring to the nineteenth-century educational system, yet his words are apposite in this context. The educational system was a hodge-podge. It was quite evidently not the product of a systematic programme of social control. The key point here is not that education was not part of a system of social control but that that system was not itself systematic. Like so many other aspects of English history, mass education was the product of competing and often contradictory forces.

The Georgian and Victorian "political nation" was deeply divided over the question of mass schooling. The public discussion within the political nation took place in the context of a conservative reaction to the French Revolution, urbanization and industrialization. Fears of disrespect, insubordination, moral corruption, sedition, atheism and the general subversion of authority were pervasive. Conservatives saw that nothing good could come from disturbing the ordered universe prescribed by the moral economy of patriarchalism and elaborated in the deferential dialectic of master and man. Political divisions were further complicated by the denominational battles taking place between Anglicans and Dissenters. Fear of sectarian education cemented a Tory–High Church alliance on educational policy, frustrating legislation promoted by Whitbread in 1807 and Brougham in 1820. Hopes of an omnibus bill were thus quite completely thwarted by the conservative majority in the unreformed Parliament.

It was not until the second quarter of the nineteenth century that liberal reformers gained any significant credibility for their views on education within the political nation. By then, the fear of revolution was not so much resolved as sublimated into more immediate concerns about poverty and moral vice. Reform-minded liberals, joined together in an ideological alliance of "philosophic radicals", wanted to free men from the dead hand of the past and to release their intellects to the pure air of prudential rationality. We have already mentioned Malthus' belief that education could counteract the "vice" and "immorality" he detected in the actions of those who had lost their independence. When Edwin Chadwick and Nassau Senior wrote their concluding remarks in the 1834 Poor Law Report they, too, were concerned to construct social actors who were rationally prudent. "We are perfectly aware that for the general diffusion of right principles and habits we are to look, not so much for any economic arrangements and regulations as to the influence of a moral and religious education." A dozen years later their comrade Kay-Shuttleworth echoed this concern and suggested that "There are certain objects too vast, or too complicated, or too important to be intrusted in voluntary associations; they need the assertion of [state] power."[107] These philosophic radicals were radical in the sense that they wanted to change men's and women's hearts and minds and they were quite willing to take advantage of the coercive powers of the state, if need be. But, in a very real sense, the terms of debate had subtly shifted. Historical contingencies had changed. New forms of institutionalized education had emerged. Sectional initiatives had created a crazy-quilt of schools. In 1851 two-thirds of all full-time students attended day-schools affiliated with either the Church of England or the non-conformists' British and Foreign School Society. Most of the rest were enrolled in the so-called "dame schools" which were organized locally, often by an elderly woman (i.e. a "dame") or a self-taught worker. These "dame schools" looked after young children, rather like nursery schools. Their teachers were usually able to teach their charges rudimentary literacy and numeracy skills. Working-class parents were willing to pay for this service, partly because it was local but frequently because it was not "provided" nor was it associated with alienating demands for a "moral education" which had few resonances among many members of the proletariat. When, from 1870, the state threw its full weight into education it found two competing systems, neither of which was interested in yielding. In a straightforward act of compromise the state absorbed both systems while letting each maintain a fair degree of independence within its capacious umbrella. Far from creating a unified system of social control, mass education in England entrenched historic divisions and froze them in time. Until well into the twentieth century a very great deal of the primary education supplied by the state was overlain with religious teachings. In this way, at the very least, the hopes of Chadwick and Senior for "a moral and religious education" were fulfilled; but this type of schooling was profoundly conservative and hardly likely to have met their stringent demands for independence of mind.

Upper-class attitudes towards compulsory education remained ambivalent. What was problematic was not the issue of social control – since the seventeenth-century revolutions the political nation had been in agreement that "men of property" were the natural ruling class – rather, the question of strategy split the controllers. Conservatives found safety in the ignorance of the masses; the old elixir of magic, mystery and authority had had a long and successful life and was not dead yet. Moreover, the very issue of strategy called into question just what schooling was to be for – was it for education or was it for socialization? The heart of the strategic issue is neatly captured in the following remark from the 1861 Newcastle Report on Education:

Independence is of more importance than education; and if the wages of the child's labour are necessary, either to keep the parents from the poor rates, or to relieve the pressure of severe and bitter poverty, it is far better that it [i.e. the child] should go to work at the earliest age at which it can bear the physical exertion than that it should remain at school.[108]

Bureaucratic intrusions into working-class family life were not, then, necessarily a good thing in the eyes of many who remained in a position of authority. Inasmuch as the magistrates' benches retained a Tory flavour, this reluctance to punish parents who kept their children away from school persisted until the end of the nineteenth century. There were strict limits placed on the state's intrusiveness by those very people who made up the ruling class. Such ambiguity in the strategy of social control both reflected and constituted the peculiar historical conjuncture in the equilibration of social, economic and political forces. The nineteenth-century state was quite simply not the reflexive strong-arm of the body politic. It is, therefore, one thing to quote demands for state-intervention but quite another to explicate its practice at ground-level.

The rhythm of work dictated the rhythm of schooling for proletarian children. School registration statistics tell us nothing about attendance. Truant children proved to be difficult targets for social controllers who wanted to use the schools to effect a cultural revolution. Thus a profound gulf existed between the appearance of an educational "system" and the social reality experienced by the boys and girls of working-class families. Finally, when the state was able to fill its classrooms there was no guarantee that its will would be done in quite the way its promoters envisaged. There can be little denying the expectations which educationalists placed upon schooling but the problem they faced was that "actual history" did not often square with their "tidy platonism".

Forming the minds of reasoning animals; or "Stick to Facts, Sir!"

The Victorian political economists looked to the schools to inculcate discipline, what Malthus would have called prudence. The internalization of "rationality" by pupils would thereby promote industrial efficiency, public peace and political order. However, a consideration of the method and content of their schooling makes it readily apparent why Victorian education filled so few students with enthusiasm for learning or enabled them to see it as a viable avenue for individual social mobility. In the very best utilitarian fashion the shaping of young minds was dominated by a penny-pinching, cost-accounting – "the division of labour applied to educational purposes". Students were taught by rote in enormous classes presided over by school-masters and -mistresses who delegated the real teaching, first, to "monitors" and then, later, to student assistants. In its full-bloom, this utilitarian system focussed on "payment by results" so that the financial health of a school depended upon the ability of its scholars to exhibit rudimentary knowledge, regurgitated in a mechanical form. Basic literacy was thus drilled into the students by a combination of repetition and brutality. Corporal punishment was commonplace and most autobiographers seem to remember being in fear of their teachers who "caned almost automatically, without special vindictiveness".[109] In a functional sense, this monstrous curriculum had a simple rationale – most scholars were put into school to prepare them for submission to a life of labour and the cheapest methods involved bullying them into submissive acceptance.

Discipline, order and obedience were the chief goals of this pedagogy. One graduate of the Chillingham Road Elementary School in Newcastle-on-Tyne, born in 1899, remembered that "The main idea was to get us out to earn money ... Reading, writing and arithmetic were essential, and children were clobbered until they mastered them."[110] When Charles Dickens described the Gradgrind model day school in *Hard Times* he was not relying on his imagination. For J. G. Tait and innumerable others, this description was drawn from life. Facts. Facts. Facts. "Now, what I want is Facts. Teach these boys and girls nothing but Facts. Facts alone are wanted in life. Plant nothing else, and root out everything else. You can only form the minds of reasoning animals upon Facts: nothing else will ever be of any service to them. Stick to Facts, sir!" Children were taught facts, common sense and conformity; not the exercise of their imaginations and most assuredly not curiosity. Such a perspective leads one to question whether the hard-won attainment of basic literacy opened minds to new experiences and implanted a "modern" attitude dividing the student's loyalties. It is hard to believe that such schooling could lead to anything except discipline, order and obedience. Even within this narrow utilitarian set of expectations it is not clear that such pedagogy did much to oppose the "counter-school" morality of the street and the community and, above all, the family.

To be sure, some highly motivated people did succeed and improved themselves right out of the working class. They, however, were the exceptions; for most, schooling was not much more than a phase preparatory to real life – a holding operation which was an "interlude between babyhood and the world of work". Not infrequently, income and family size were inversely related to educational opportunity, much to the detriment of children from poorer, larger families. And while no single attribute can be used to explain the adherence to the constellation of virtues associated with *respectability* and family morality, it nonetheless appears that in almost all cases an adequate breadwinner's wage was a necessary, if not a sufficient, correlate to modernization, family limitation and the belief that social security via education was possible. Yet, even then, one does not see much evidence of this transformation of personal identity until the 1920s. Most had no illusions that theirs was to be anything but a life of labour. Most simply did not envisage any realistic alternatives to following in their parents' footsteps.[111] When the odds against any child obtaining a free education after the age of eleven were forty to one in 1914, and the odds for those from the working class even higher still, it is not surprising that elementary and secondary education were dichotomized, hardly thought to be connected stages in a coherent process.[112] The social centre of gravity in proletarian life was definitely not the school.

From John Burnett's account of working-class autobiographers' experiences it is hard not to be more impressed by the continuities in schooling and society, even after the advent of compulsory attendance in 1880, than by the changes in response to the systematic streaming of children through the schools. Working-class attitudes to education appear to have remained as profoundly ambivalent in the later nineteenth century as they had been earlier. On the one hand, a smattering of learning was prized and the ability to read and write appears to have been a hallmark of *respectability*, evincing one's mastery over the world; yet, most autobiographers imply that there was little contact between their parents and their school; their parents took little *active* interest in their education. In the crunch, parents were almost always more likely to send their sons and daughters out to work than to struggle to keep them at school. One sees the latter set of characteristics at work even after the turn of the century.

They bore down with particular force among those few children who did succeed in winning entrance and/or a scholarship to secondary education. In fact, the experience of working-class children in secondary school is a far better acid-test for the competition between family and school than their perfunctory attendance at elementary school because, progressively throughout the second phase of industrialization, child labour was being superseded and phased out so that it was only when they were in their teens that children (and their parents) were faced with something like a real choice between work and school.[113] Bearing this point in mind it is surely of the greatest importance that those few working-class children who were successful in school often found themselves "socially ostracized" by the contempt of their new school mates and ostracized by their less successful fellows who had failed to pass the bar. In fact, for many "Successful [scholars] integration often involved the rejection of former values and former friends, even a distancing from parents and kin who were not capable of sharing the experience."[114] It is only in relation to these very few successful scholars that one can see a connection between schooling and the adoption of "modern" mentalities stressing individualism. Most proletarians came to terms with their educational segregation with passive acceptance. There is almost no evidence that the experience of schooling and education did anything to transform the profoundly resilient and perdurant family morality of the *respectable* working class. Their attendance at elementary school may have relieved them from childhoods of labour, but in return they were shackled by a utilitarian pedagogy which imprisoned their bodies and constricted their minds' development.

Schools were carceral institutions – they were frequently justified as the best source of crime prevention, designed like prisons with high walls, and organized along the principles of subdivided labour found in the proto-typical industrial establishment. This strategy of social reproduction drew its inspiration from the struggle between classes, not from the tidy platonism of educational reformers. In fact, there was no educational reform in Victorian England but rather an elaboration of older systems of control which had their roots in the charity schools and Sunday schools of the eighteenth century. The major accomplishment of Victorian education was the extension of this method of social policing so that by the end of the century all children were nominally under its authority. The educational system was never much more than a bureaucratic nightmare but its aims were remarkably fixed in their intent and hardly challenged in theory, if resisted in practice. One can understand the Victorian notion of education within the same paradigmatic framework as the period's missionary activities – just like their religious brethren, teachers and administrators were primarily concerned to pacify lesser breeds without the law. The blackboard jungle was the site of this inner colonization. Schools were the social police designed especially for children; the New Poor Law policed their parents. Both institutions reproduced the social system.

The fabric of working-class life

In contrast to the privatization of middle-class family life, among pro-letarians the family and the community were permeable institutions which inter-penetrated each other: " 'home' therefore extended into the street beyond the front door". Local support networks drew people together in an age when there was no system of public assistance except the repulsive workhouse. It was in response to the dis-*respectable* alternatives proposed by the state that working-class families developed extended ties, both with other kin, "fictive kin" (such lodgers who were not infrequently dubbed "uncles" and "aunts" and were found in some 23 per cent of mid-century Preston households), and neighbours. In cockney London at the end of the nineteenth century, the neighbours often functioned as "auxiliary parents" while "informal adoptions by neigh-bours were not unusual".[115] For most crucial situations – sickness and death, unemployment and old age, marriage, childbirth and childmind-ing – the state was the court of last resort and, indeed, was quite explicitly intended to be so by those who framed the New Poor Law. The workhouse was required to be more unpleasant than the conditions endured by the poorest, most dis-*respectable* worker. In this way, it was thought, the excesses of the Old Poor Law and its bureaucratized hand-outs would be avoided. Labour's preference for a backwards-bending supply curve would be thwarted and its cost thereby reduced. Reciprocity, both between family and neighbours, became a hallmark of the working-class community in contrast to the social darwinist indi-vidualism sanctioned by Victorian ideology. Working-class life was built upon a quite different vision; a communalism in which mutual-aid complemented self-help.

The localism of this community life was intense: "the sense of place, and of identity with the place, is very powerful" in the recollections of autobiographers. Large families and small houses meant that, in our terms, privacy was unexpected; even working-class readers had to learn to be solitary in a crowd. Working-class children played in the street, not in their gardens; indeed, terraced housing in the large conurbations rarely afforded much in the way of "green space". And yet there is little to suggest that many of these people recalled that their childhood had been impoverished by the lack of access to the material comforts of the middle class. Most children seem to have made the best of what they had and no one could prevent them from exercising their imaginations so that much of their play was "to a large extent classless and timeless". The stuff of their games bore the imprint of an earlier, rural tradition which "required little beyond improvised equipment and a good deal of imagination". Working-class children played together; that is, they played with only the loosest of supervision from their parents because the street "offered the protection of a known community and was virtually free from traffic dangers". Parents usually only concerned themselves with their children's play when it threatened their status as *respectable* householders. For more than one little boy or girl the known world – "at once a terrible, exciting place . . . in the labyrinth of mean, intricate streets" – ended at the street-corner. Edna Bold was born in 1904 not far from the centre of Manchester where "Not a blade of grass, not a tree grew anywhere in the district", yet she recalled "no sense of deprivation". For this little girl, and her twin brother, the sounds, smells and sights of the urban street-scape were "as evocative as Thomas Hood's sun, roses, lilies, for they touched our tiny hearts and minds to life".[116]

The centre of the child's universe was his or her family, usually set in motion by Mum. The working-class mother is a figure of mythic proportions; judging from some of the autobiographical material, no doubt clouded over by the mist of time and the memories of an uncomplicated primal bond, the strength of character of these women was extraordinary. Their children do not seem to have been unduly nostalgic in romanticising their mothers' achievements. Material impediments gave an air of quiet desperation to their struggles; a not inconsiderable number were married to brutes or drunkards and the level of family violence – wife battering and child abuse – was appallingly high. Yet even in the face of these odds, enormous numbers triumphed through an exercise of will and sheer moral courage. Over and over the autobiographers repeat the same message: "one long life of loving sacrifice".[117] A huge number of working-class husbands paid their wives "wages" so that

At all times, wives' skill and energy provided the only real barrier between mere survival and a decent level of comfort. A mother's aptitude for bargaining with the pawnshop assistant, the shopkeepers, and the school board visitors; her domestic arts; her friendship with the landlady – all were worth solid cash, and provided wives with some leverage against their husbands. When children went to work, they viewed themselves as "working for" their mothers; their earnings entered the female part of the family exchequer.

When the working-class mother died early or was not able to withstand the pressures and demands of life, her children suffered greatly. If their father died they would certainly be poor; if their mother died they would likely be anomic.[118] Men may have "often played king at home" but this monarch governed a circumscribed realm. While he played at being the lord and master in his own house this was more usually a matter of style than substance.[119] Mothers were their children's primary role models; they taught by example. Insofar as women, especially in *respectable* working-class families, had a circumscribed experience of the world it is difficult to imagine that their precepts gave children anything but a traditional view of morality. One would hardly expect the working-class mother to have been a vehicle of psycho-social modernization, much less the bearer of new cultural standards.

Autobiographies and oral-history materials provide a phenomenological dimension which other forms of historical evidence simply cannot match. They tell us what people thought and how they felt, albeit at some remove from the period in question. As we have seen from the foregoing discussion of the documents collected by David Vincent and John Burnett, even at the distance of a life-time there is little suggestion that anything but a tiny minority of working-class men and women were significantly influenced by their schooling.[120] Moreover, it seems far-fetched to suggest that it instilled individualism in the terrorized scholars. Schools processed, packaged and then passed along these children to the labour market.

Material imperatives and the timing of the English fertility decline

Working-class education was meant to reproduce the social system, not replace it. Victorian and Edwardian education was not meant to do anything else for the masses. If they learned to love poetry or question authority then one can only attribute such behaviour to their indomitable wills. The voices of those exceptional proletarians who have told us of their sufferings and satisfactions give no support whatsoever to an argument which sees their church- and, later, state-sponsored education providing a serious alternative to the centripetal forces of family and community. For as long as individual welfare was a matter of no concern to the state, which operated on the principle of "less eligibility" and demeaned its recipients by stripping them of whatever vestigial form of *respectability* they possessed, working-class people saw their survival and protection as being quite clearly linked to their immediate family, kin and neighbours. Only in exceptional instances do we glimpse a contending view, suggesting possible alternatives. In fact, it was only when the English state became the father of all the English people that it penetrated the lives of those who lived in "Our Street, Darkest England". The hard-heartedness of the Victorian Poor Law and workhouse system stood in direct opposition to the cultural values which gave meaning to the lives of the respectable working class. For most people, compulsory schooling was viewed as being part of this nexus of domination and was, ultimately, foreign to the fabric of working-class life.

The full force of the fertility decline among the lower-paid sections of the working class did not really take hold until after World War I, suggesting that although the working-class family may have wanted to participate in the Victorian sentimentalization of the home and the family, it was only in the second quarter of the twentieth century that this redefined *respectability* could be completely worked out in practice. The sentimentalization of childhood in the working-class family was only realized when it became possible to finance such cultural trappings. To be sure, the process had its roots in the last quarter of the nineteenth century but until the 1920s the imperatives of the family economy took precedence over the realization of sentiment. It was only in these new circumstances that wealth flows were reversed so that they could now flow from parents to children. The flow of wealth within the working-class family had been reversed because its recomposition, its privatization and the quest for a redefined *respectability* combined to render its "prolifick power" a thing of the past. Furthermore, public health campaigns, improved nutrition, better sanitation and higher living standards all meant that even though the impact of falling infant mortality was experienced last by the poorest members, one cannot but be struck by the enormous *absolute* decline in levels for all groups in society in the first quarter of this century. The highest recorded infant mortality rate in the nineteenth century occurred in 1899: 156 per 1,000. In that year in Liverpool, families living in the upper-class neighbourhoods lost 136 infants, in the working-class sections the infant mortality rate was 274, while in the very poorest places it was a staggering 509 per 1,000.[121] Quite obviously, the implications of family formation strategies would be crucially determined by the survival of children; high levels of fertility among the poorest in conditions of appalling mortality did not necessarily mean high rates of survival. Within a generation, in 1930, the overall rate of infant mortality had plummeted to 67 per 1,000; in addition, the differences between classes became smaller in both absolute and relative terms.

The records of school attendance, the attitudes of the masses to schooling itself, the persistence of a patriarchal distribution of family resources and the slow fall in marital fertility among lowest-paid members of the English working class make the immediate effects of compulsory education seem rather less dramatic than Caldwell claims.

Changing wealth flows

The changing direction of wealth flows within the family transformed the morality governing family relationships, and not vice versa. These social changes occurred within the English family during the second phase of industrialization. Even then it was a protracted and uneven process, taking several decades to gain a hold among the poorest families in which the breadwinners' wages were insufficient to underwrite the new morality. It was only in the period after World War I, when the extension of Edwardian social welfare legislation finally ended the unpredictability inherent in the lives of the poorest strata of the working classes, that their fertility began to fall. By the third decade of the twentieth century economic, social and institutional changes guaranteed "shelter for nearly all, satisfactory wage-rises for most and the certainty of relief in old age and time of trouble".[122] Government expenditure on social services, in constant prices, rose eight-fold between 1890 and 1930. Of course much of this money was merely recycled from the pockets of the working class back into the pockets of the working class through the agency of regressive taxation.[123] Yet these social welfare benefits must clearly be added to the rising real wages of the previous two generations. The very poor, living in a cycle of poverty, were becoming an ever-smaller part of the population. Destitution, described by Seebohm Rowntree as "primary poverty" was halved in the first three decades of the twentieth century; falling from 15.46 per cent to 6.8 per cent of the working population of York.[124] Moreover, "primary poverty" in the twentieth-century was different: just 5 per cent of such destitution in 1899 was caused by unemployment, the rest was presumably the result of low wages; whereas in 1936 irregular work accounted for fully half of all such cases of destitution.[125] Indeed, Clapham suggests that in this period the gains made by those at the very bottom were the greatest largely because the most dreaded features of living below the poverty line had been largely removed.[126]

What may partly explain the sluggishness of response among the poorest groups within the working class during the initial stage of the fertility decline, through the first decades of the twentieth century, is the perpetuation of child labour in their homes and in the sweatshops of the large urban centres in spite of the best efforts of factory legislators and School Board bye-laws. Even as late as 1907 children were employed in virtually every branch of home work in London, including matchbox production, fetching and carrying, boot finishing and glass-making. Child labour seems to have been a major impediment to school attendance. Among the sizeable minority of working-class families in London caught up in the world of casual labour and sweatshops, "pitifully low wages of children might be needed to avoid destitution" so that "education must have seemed utterly irrelevant in the struggle to exist". Rubinstein further states that "It is clear that the very poor section of the community had little sympathy with the aims of the London School Board which used its visitors [inspectors] to spy on them and attempted to prevent children from working to support their families." "Like the workhouse, the Board School must have seemed a symbol of oppression." Moreover, attempts by School Boards to prosecute derelict parents very often met with little sympathy from magistrates. As we have already seen there was a considerable paternalist sentiment within the upper classes which generally opposed compulsory education on principle and tended to side with recalcitrant parents against truant officers and other interventionist bureaucrats. Rubinstein states that in 1880 almost 30 per cent of the population of England and Wales was still untouched by compulsory education. Half-time attendance continued to be legally sanctioned until 1900; it was especially common in the textile areas.[127]

Miners: a special case

As we saw in our earlier mention of the intra-class differentials in marital fertility, miners were exceptional in that they combined comparatively high wages with high levels of fertility. In many senses, the north-eastern coal miners were the quintessential breadwinners and we might consider them as a counterpoint to the symmetrical family of the cottage industrialists. In the north-east, for example, colliers were almost exclusively males who had been bred to their station.[128] Boys served an apprenticeship underground during which time they acted as hauliers and assistants. With the development of substantial underground ventilation systems in the second half of the eighteenth century another sphere of employment for young boys opened up and the age of first employment seemed to drop accordingly. Women played almost no role in the underground activity of hacking and hauling the black stuff. If they worked at all it was because they were widowed and only then did they find employment above the ground sorting the coal into various grades. For most women there was a strict division of tasks and their primary concern was with the social reproduction of their men's labour. In 1842 rather less than 3,000 women worked underground in all of England.[129]

The wages of adult males "hewers" in the prime of their working lives were about double those of other workers. In the words of one Lancashire miners' song which dates from the early nineteenth century

> Collier lads get gold and silver,
> Factory lads get nowt but brass.
> Who'd be bother'd with a spindle bobber
> When there are plenty of collier lads?

The collier's lifestyle, according to J. D. Leifchild (Inspector of North Durham and Northumberland for the Commission on Children's Employments), placed a premium on the heavy consumption of meat and other so-called luxuries. Of course, the danger of underground work and the physical reality of working oneself to death made the earnings of the chief breadwinner a thin reed on which to poise the welfare of the whole family. Obviously, the employment of sons could both enhance the family's total earnings and spread its risks. For this reason miners were thought to have been reluctant to take their boys from early employment to send them to school.[130] After the advent of compulsory education and, more particularly, once the question of school attendance had been taken out of parental control, the day a lad reached the state-designated school-leaving age was the day he went down the pit with dad.[131] Sometimes, the "bairn's" first day of work was marked by a small family celebration to mark his coming-of-age.

The contributions which sons made to the mining family's income could be substantial and in some circumstances crucial. Co-residing sons were likely to be contributing during the years when the father's earning capacity declined from its peak – i.e. around the age of thirty-five or forty. For a further twenty years the father's strength and earnings might have declined in tandem but his diminishing piece-rate wages would have been supplemented by the money his son or, if he was prolific, his sons brought home. Daughters, too, provided valued labour although it was not monetized. They served an "informal apprenticeship" as "handmaidens to their fathers and brothers who worked underground". Adeline Hodges, born in the Country Durham pit village of Dawdon in 1899, recalled that "Daughters had to work very hard in a family of pit workers. Woe betide you if you ever forgot to fill up the boiler [for the men's baths] at the side of the fireplace."[132] The logic of a high level of reproduction was thus built into the mode of production and it was not surprising that miners were always at the top of the table in their fertility into the twentieth century.[133] This was especially the case because coal mining was essentially non-mechanized and can, with some licence, be considered as a kind of underground "putting-out" in the sense that production was increased by multiplying units of production (i.e. miners) not through increased efficiencies of scale. For all the technological development associated with mining during the **Industrial Revolution**, the labour of the miner was little changed except for the fact that he might have worked in larger, deeper pits. Until the early twentieth century, most of the steam power employed in mining was *not* related to hewing at all, but rather to the ancillary tasks of haulage and ventilation and drainage. In 1914 only 7 per cent of all British coal was cut by machine; in the United States the comparable figure was over 50 per cent. In addition, the miners' fecundity seems to have created a labour market not dissimilar to the involutionary **proto-industrial** regime described earlier. At the beginning of the twentieth century their ranks grew by leaps and bounds in tandem with absolute levels of production yet statistics reveal *declining productivity* per man-shift – from 4.23 tons in 1879 to 3.30 in 1911– and wages seem to have peaked in relative terms at the beginning of the last quarter of the nineteenth century; thereafter miners lost ground and status to other workers. Their weakening bargaining power was evinced in the "sliding scale" they were forced to accept which made them bear part of the costs, in the form of wage-cuts, when the industry was in a bad way. Behind the statistics of awesome growth there were disturbing signs of overmanning and technological stagnation.[134] In mining, as in so many other sectors of English capitalism the "rational" response for entrepreneurs was a form of profit optimization, which meant the perpetuation of low-wage, primitive technologies made possible by the superfluity of workers. Truly, the causal arrows flowed in both directions and the problems twentieth-century miners have experienced in their labour bargaining can be traced back to the ways in which production and reproduction were organized during the protean phase of industrialization.

It is against this background that we can see George Orwell's description of his visit to Wigan in 1936 in an historical perspective. The assembly-line down the pit reflected the perdurance of a handicraft mode of extraction.

It is impossible to watch the "fillers" at work without feeling a pang of envy for their toughness. It is a dreadful job they do, an almost superhuman job by the standards of an ordinary person. For they are not only shifting monstrous quantities of coal, they are also doing it in a [kneeling] position that doubles or trebles the work ... the fillers look and work as though they were made of iron. They really do look like iron – hammered iron statues – under the smooth coat of coal dust which clings to them head to foot. You can never forget that spectacle once you have seen it – the line of bowed, kneeling figures, sooty black all over, driving their huge shovels under the coal with stupendous force and speed.[135]

Orwell later notes that not one miner's boy in a thousand does not pine for the day when he will be doing "real work" because "The idea of a great big boy of eighteen, who ought to be bringing a pound a week home to his parents, going to school in a ridiculous uniform ... seems contemptible and unmanly."[136] Orwell's reference to the remission of wages from child to parent within the Wigan miners' families is perversely illuminating. What he took to be the typical working-class family pattern was then fast-receding and it was only in northern mining and textile communities that he could have found it. For others, in either new industries or more buoyant ones, the reconfiguration of the economy had meant a liberation from the exigencies of an earlier system in which the chief breadwinner was able to earn enough to start a family but not enough to maintain it without supplementary income from his older children. Orwell, like

Engels a century before him, misunderstood what he saw. He took the death throes of the family wage economy to be the reality of proletarian life in the twentieth century. He, too, little understood the dialectic of production and reproduction.

Cultural perdurance/traditional morality

Well into the twentieth century the working-class family withstood the onslaught of cultural homogenization which supposedly accompanied mass education. Caldwell's claim that family morality was fairly rapidly superseded by a community-wide consensus engendered by the schools and the media, which rarely gave priority to family interests and rarely competed with the schools, is therefore dubious. The advent of compulsory education may even have served to intensify sexual differentiation by relegating children to the supervision of women, both at home and at school. Brian Jackson and Dennis Marsden observe that in contrast to middle-class families in which the father usually plays the important decision-making role with reference to the children's future education, among the working class it is the mother: "Its roots seem to push much deeper into the basic rhythms and expectations of working-class life, belonging to that whole pattern of living in which the mother rather than the father was the organic centre."[137] In the working-class community of Bethnal Green in East London in the 1950s, Michael Young and Peter Willmott observed a social system in which mother/daughter ties were the keystone in the arch of family relationships.[138] This aspect of working-class life in which women's influence in the private sphere was paramount had its roots in the separation of workplace and home that took place after the middle years of the nineteenth century.

This cultural world was, until recently, thought of as being "traditional" because it changed so little between its crystallization in the later nineteenth century and the immediate past.[139] Growing up in the Hunslet district of Leeds, between the wars, it was mother who was the "pivot of the home". She was responsible for most aspects of domestic life while the breadwinner served primarily as the "chief contact with the outer world which puts money into the house".[140] In fact, wives frequently attended to important family business. Contraception, therefore, was a woman's responsibility although without her husband's active involvement fertility limitation would be impossible to realize. "The husband's shyness and an assumption that this is really her affair often ensure that he expects her to take care of it, that he 'can't be bothered with it.' "[141]

Dr Marie Stopes' vigorous campaigns for family planning and a "rational" approach to fertility made her, in A. J. P. Taylor's words, "among the great benefactors of the age".[142] This is an accolade which at least one Birmingham woman would have warmly seconded in writing:

We women of the working classes only know how the horrible servitude, poverty and constitutional undermining excess of child bearing means, with the consequent lack of means to educate those surplus children and to equip them with knowledge with which to secure posts and positions of the sciences, letters and art of this land, relieving them of the nightmare of serfdom and slavery the mass of the lower orders are condemned to. I am the mother of two children and desire no more. My ambition is satisfied, but with the recent knowledge of my sufferings with them, another would drive me mad. I am asking you to forward the names of your books and prices that I may be one of the fortunate ones who have the superior knowledge of contraception.[143]

This mother's letter neatly captures a concern for her children and their futures, her concern for herself and her understanding that such knowledge can liberate them all from the tyranny of a reproductive regime which was now obviously outdated and irrelevant. It was written in 1923, fully two generations after the fertility decline had commenced and represents a reproductive strategy which is a 180 degree compass-swing from that which her grandmother most likely possessed.

Far from destroying family and neighbourhood morality among the working classes, compulsory education seems to have strengthened them. The Victorian autobiographers make it clearly evident that the social centre of gravity in the working-class world was "an inner, secret life which perpetuated traditional values and patterns of behaviour". In particular, they "for long rejected this unpalatable and alien notion" that work was to be the centre of human existence, taking precedence over other values. The working class thus created its "own exclusive world" in opposition to the ideology and public institutions of the eminent Victorians.[144] For working-class children, the Board School resonated of the earlier institutions which had been erected to discipline recalcitrants. Stephen Humphries, in his study of oral testimony of working-class scholars, suggests that when his informants had been pupils they were disobedient, disorderly, reluctant, apathetic, un-cooperative and sometimes openly hostile in resisting this carceral regime. In Humphries' account, the relationship of working-class scholars to the state schools evokes a memory of the first factory proletarians who had been forced to forego their cultural attachment to the rhythms of the *cottage economy* and to submit to an alien notion of time and work. For these children, as for their great-grandparents, the key issue was one of independence: control over one's own way of life. Enforced confinement, a curriculum based on rote learning, rigid and often brutal punishments took place in a setting which was alien and seemed meaningless. The truth of this point was brought home to George Orwell in the 1930s during his experience of living with proletarians and observing their lives. "Working people often have a vague reverence for learning in others, but where 'education' touches their own lives they see through it and reject it by a healthy instinct."[145] Because housing and health were seen as more pressing items on the working-class agenda than education, it is probably the case that the majority of the working class in work, and during the Depression fully 75 per cent of all workers were working, were impressed by their rising real wages, the 4 million houses which had been built, the precipitous decline in infant mortality, the foundation of a welfare state and the abolition of the hated workhouses all of which occurred in the second quarter of the twentieth century. While one can hardly be sanguine about the persistence of inequalities and injustices, nevertheless it is quite clearly the case that for most working-class families things got better, even in the midst of the Depression. Some suffered terribly; most did not. As with so many other historical events, much depends on which way you look at the problem.

School daze

What Orwell did not misunderstand was the total lack of resonance of anything approaching a "trickle-down" attitude to schooling on the part of the poorest sections in the proletariat before World War II. Indeed, the working-class "kids" of "Hammertown" studied by Paul Willis in the 1970s also experienced alienation from and rebellion against the school. It is Willis' contention that working-class resistance to the cultural neutering propagated by the schools is a crucial component in its reproduction as a social class-fragment. "The counter-school culture, however, responds in its own way to the special nature of labour power. As if by instinct it limits it. In its own immediate logic this is to maintain the pre-condition for the sensuous physical and mental involvement of its members in its own activities."[146] In the most penetrating and original sections of his book Willis explains how the working-class lads who are learning to labour do so as an expression of their masculinity "by a huge detour into the symbolic sexual realm". He notes that among the kids he knew "The male wage packet is held to be central, not simply because of its size, but because it is won in a masculine mode of confrontation with the 'real' world which is too tough for the woman. Thus the man in the domestic household is held to be the breadwinner, the worker, whilst the wife works for 'the extras'."[147] It should be mentioned that Willis' "kids" were a self-selected group who represented only one group among many in their school; in the segmented working class created by late twentieth-century capitalism one witnesses the fragmentation of the older cultural tradition. But one should not push this line of analysis too far back into the

210

past since most evidence accrued by educational sociologists and "participant observations" emphasizes the perdurance of this "inner, secret life" which took place within its "own secret world". Secret secrets.

When we come to consider working-class children's lack of success in the state school system the persistence of their self-contained, counter-school culture is readily apparent. English state schools in the first half of this century have continued to provide "a different and mainly inferior, education for those who had previously received none". The dividing line between the elite system and the state system was, in A. J. P. Taylor's words, "as hard as that between Hindu castes". He is only slightly rhetorical in claiming that "No child ever crossed it."[148] This gloomy picture is borne out in Jackson and Marsden's study of secondary education in Huddersfield where it was unusual for the minority of working-class children in secondary schools to complete their education and continue on to college or university. In the same grammar schools, the middle-class child was usually much more successful because "the prevailing grammar school tone was a natural extension of his home life".[149] When the successful scholars from working-class families were carefully analysed it was found that many of them came from small families, a third were only-children, and that they often were members of what was termed the "sunken middle-class". Furthermore, there was a price to pay for their success. Just as was the case among the upwardly mobile individuals in the nineteenth century, only a minority of them maintained their earlier codes of judgement and behaviour or persisted in counter-school cultural attachments. For successful working-class children from Huddersfield, grammar school represented an important break with their former neighbourhood and family world.[150] Almost all found that they could not go home again; for some this was a relief, but for others such individualism created emotional havoc.

When we consider that Jackson and Marsden's study focusses on a cohort of students from the 1950s it is readily apparent that the result of several generations of mass education seems to have been quite contrary to that posited in Caldwell's thesis of national incorporation. A small minority of the working class has been torn away from its family and community, rendered socially mobile and embourgeoised. For the vast majority of the working class mass education seems to have had the effect of reinforcing their separateness while preparing them for industrial labour.

The irony of mass education is that the uses of literacy have served not to assimilate the working classes but to expunge their cultural inheritance. Or, rather, they have been served a flimsy, counterfeit freight of sensationalism "full of a corrupt brightness, of improper appeals and moral evasions" to take its place.[151] Orwell makes much the same point in arguing that material advances and benefits have been achieved at a cost which strongly offended his puritanical, elite sensibilities. "Whole sections of the working class who have been plundered of all they really need are being compensated, in part, by cheap luxuries which mitigate the surface of life."[152] Yet though the lower-upper-middle-class moralist may find the proletarian's response to a commercialized and often tasteless popular culture offensive, almost tragic and certainly demeaning, Hoggart is enough of a realist to note that it "is not simply a power of passive resistance, but something which, though not articulate, is positive. The working-classes have a strong natural ability to survive change by adapting or assimilating what they want in the new and ignoring the rest."[153] Much of their attitude to the education provided by the Sunday schools, the contending churches and now the state can be subsumed within this framework of analysis.

Is it any wonder that an educational system which has for so long been so tightly meshed with the reproduction of a patently unequal social system should be looked upon with suspicion? The hidden injuries of class have quite naturally created *ressentimente* on the part of the injured. There is thus little evidence that the English educational system has had any role in creating a new system of morality which confronted and ultimately obliterated the traditional family arrangements of the working class. Only for the last forty years could such an argument be advanced, and then only for those areas of the country in which there is "comprehensive" system of state education. But such an argument would be after the fact – the fertility decline was substantially completed before comprehensive schools admitted their first students

Respectable reproduction

Reflecting upon the changes in family life which had taken place since the end of World War I a middle-aged Lancashire housewife told interviewers in 1945

My own opinion is that people wish to have a small family on account of public opinion which has now hardened into custom. It is customary – and has been so during the last twenty-five years or so – to have two children and no more if you can avoid it. A family of five or six children loses in prestige and, some think, in respectability. It is on behalf of their children that parents feel this most keenly.[154]

Here, in a nutshell, we have evidence of the internalized application of community morality which was at the heart of the fertility decline. Yet it is surely worth noting that such behaviour was, in the opinion of our respondent, new and of recent origin. It took place some two generations *after* the advent of compulsory education. **Respectability** in early twentieth-century Lancashire had been metamorphosed into concern for children's welfare and actualized in the form of a prudent reproductive profile. Losing prestige in having a large family stands in stark contrast to the imperatives of an earlier age when children were valued *both* for themselves and as contributors to the family economy. The loss of their economic functions meant that working-class children could only be considered as "consumer durables". When this change took place it quickly became "natural" for working-class parents to lavish their available resources on them. "Modernization" and the sentimentalization of childhood were part-and-parcel of the reordering of family life and, in particular, the demographic transition which took place within the context of the second phase of industrialization.

In the years since the revolution in the family broke the age-old Gordian knot between production and reproduction England has undergone industrial disintegration. One sees evidence of this in the sites of the older centres – the wastelands of working-class London, the abandoned collieries and steelworks dotting the landscape in the north-east, the skeletal remains of the Lancashire cotton trade, and so on. In the past decade this state of free-fall has been aided and abetted by the nakedness of the British state in face of international forces. In the wake of the spiralling inflation provoked by the oil crisis of the mid-1970s and the monetary retrenchment of the present government – demanded by its creditors and eagerly implemented by the hard-faced "realists" – English industrial disintegration is proceeding at an ever-faster pace. The tax-base is thereby narrowed and so the welfare state is being eroded as the level of benefits is constantly downgraded. The inner cities are decaying as their housing stocks deteriorate and the urban infrastructure sags. Petty crime and urban violence provoke fears and a call to corporal punishment; not remedies. The alienation of the present government – elected by the smallest plurality in the twentieth century – manifests itself in deepening these contradictions as if by conscious policy. Within this devolutionary political economy there has grown up a peculiarly devolutionary system of reproduction. Perhaps, we might say, a culture of poverty dependent upon the state's welfare mechanisms to bridge a gap between youth and joblessness.

Beatrix Campbell returned to Wigan Pier in 1982 in a conscious effort to retrace Orwell's footsteps. Her focus on the plight of teenaged mothers provides a counterpoint to the recomposition of the working-class family which had taken place during the second phase of industrialization. In contrast to the breadwinners and patriarchs who characterized the traditional but new working class of the later nineteenth and early twentieth centuries, Campbell discovered a netherworld in which the social imperatives of *respectability* had been completely reinterpreted.

213

If [the Victorian and Edwardian notion of] respectability was undermined after the Second World War by married women refusing dependence and returning to waged work while also having children, it is being undermined again by the new wave of dole-queue mothers who find a measure of independence in motherhood. Both disrupt the rules and regulations of respectability, which was about nothing if it was not about controlling the social status of women. These single parents care about being mothers but they don't care so much about being married and they care even less for being rendered dependent. Unemployment steals from them the economic conditions which supported the new wave of feminism in the sixties and early seventies, but the welfare state, the provision of child benefit, minimal as it is, and supplementary benefit, mean they can survive in the absence of jobs and wages of their own. At least they can get out when the going gets rough, as their grandmothers couldn't ... Single mothers are disrupting the conservatism of Labourism, they confront the patriarchal principles of women's dependence which is embedded in the old labour movement's codes of behaviour, in housing policies and in the distribution of incomes. But their dissidence is cauterized by their isolation and poverty ... So their revolt is fraught with contradictions – resilient and yet pessimistic, they have the stamina to survive and not enough to spare.[155]

In an age of deliquescent capitalism, the reproductive family is being deconstructed.

Reprise

Family formations reproduce social formations; equally, social formations are reproduced by family formations. In England, shifting balances within the plebeian family led to historically specific demographic responses, and vice versa. For most of the nine centuries we have surveyed a rough equilibrium was maintained: population growth only rarely overwhelmed a finely tuned system of family production. Yet in the space of a couple of generations of revolutionary social change, during which time cottagers were irrevocably transformed into urban proletarians, this balancing act was quite completely destabilized. In the act of re-establishing control the English groped their way towards a revolution in the family, every bit as profound as the social revolution in material life.

The study of family history, like all branches of the subject, is a discipline of context. We have studied the transition from feudalism to capitalism in some detail in order to explain the complementary processes of production and reproduction without recourse to neo-classical theorizing. This struggle, at the heart of which was the protracted death rattle of the peasantry, provides the essential context for understanding the political economy of English population history. Within it we can resolve both traditional preferences for the independent *cottage economy* and novel proletarian family strategies in a single plane of focus. Upon the demise of the *cottage economy*, with its prudential system of late marriage, there was a brief period during which earlier ages at first marriage created a population explosion. The supersession of the homeostatic *peasant demography model* in the later eighteenth century thus led to the short-lived efflorescence of the *proletarian demography model*. In the ensuing population explosion, millions of English men, women and children were impoverished in fundamentally new ways. A very significant part of their impoverishment was directly related to, first, the disintegration of their traditional way of life and, second, their making of a new one. Throughout the nineteenth century they struggled desperately to regain control of their labour power and, in so doing, devised new

215

strategies of reproduction. We cannot understand the subsequent fertility decline in England without placing it in an historically contingent perspective – one which focusses attention on the vicious cycle of social dislocation, population explosion and cultural recomposition following on the disintegration of the *cottage economy*.

Over the long run the respiration of the social system inhaled peasants and exhaled proletarians. In the short run, it reproduced a series of family formations which differed only in detail from one another. By relating English social and economic history with demographic events we have seen how family formation strategies subtly metamorphosed, while still retaining allegiance to the triadic axiom of economic independence before marriage, nuclear family households after marriage and relatively late ages at first marriage for women. The retention of these homeostatic imperatives was a cultural characteristic of English society, deeply embedded in the lives and thoughts of individuals and social groups. Their modified transformation during the Malthusian period is a vivid testament to the unparalleled upheaval of that bleak age. It underscores the point made at the outset: humans are social animals; humankind is subject to biological laws.

Notes

Introduction: production and reproduction

1 J. C. Caldwell, "A Restatement of Demographic Transition Theory", *Population and Development Review*, 2 (1976), 345.
2 E. H. Carr, *What is History?*, Harmondsworth: 1964, 14–15 (my emphasis).
3 The only point where I diverge from this self-denying ordinance is in my reliance on the works of David Vincent and John Burnett who have analysed a vast number of working-class autobiographies in order to discover the *structured regularities* revealed by these documents. The use of this material is not, therefore, very different in its methodological approach from historical demographic analyses which use the experiences of individual events to construct a picture of similarly structured regularities in order to discover the social centre of gravity about which most reproductive life revolved. (David Vincent, *Bread, Knowledge and Freedom. A Study of Nineteenth-Century Autobiography*, London: 1981, and John Burnett, *Useful Toil*, Harmondsworth: 1974, and *Destiny Obscure*, Harmondsworth: 1982.)
4 Marshall Sahlins, *Stone Age Economics*, Chicago: 1972, 1.
5 "Questions from a Worker who Reads", *Bertholdt Brecht: Poems 1913–1956*, ed John Willett and Ralph Manheim, London: 1976, 252–3.
6 David Levine, *Family Formation in an Age of Nascent Capitalism*, New York: 1977. *Reproducing Families* takes the embryonic arguments regarding the contours of English population history from my earlier work and tries to build on them without seeing any real need to duplicate its close attention to standardized measurements. This present essay is a different sort of enterprise – it is a work of historical narrative rather more than a work of social-scientific analysis. It is also written for a different sort of audience, which probably goes without saying.

1 Feudalism and the peasant family

1 P. Boissonnade, *Life and Work in Medieval Europe* (trans. by Eileen Power), New York: 1964, 226, 230.
2 J. H. Plumb, "Farmers in Arms", *New York Review of Books*, 12, no. 12 (19 June 1969), 36.

3 E. P. Thompson, "The Grid of Inheritance, A Comment", in Jack Goody, Joan Thirsk and E. P. Thompson (eds.), *Family and Inheritance*, Cambridge: 1976, 341. Christopher Hill, "The Norman Yoke", in *Puritanism and Revolution*, London: 1958, 80.

4 Marc Bloch, *Feudal Society*, Chicago: 1961, 430.

5 W. G. Hoskins, *The Making of the English Landscape*, Harmondsworth: 1970, 90. Frank Barlow, *The Feudal Kingdom of England 1042–1216*, London: 1961, 123. While the royal forests were an obstacle to settlement, they did not prove to be an insurmountable one. Colonists often paid the monarch's administrators a licensing fee and could then farm their assarts (farms carved out of the forest) while still remaining subject to the forest laws. In many places the monarchy sold off certain of its feudal powers and the area was disafforested. Such land was not necessarily "de-feudalized" rather, it was freed from the discretionary excesses to which royal forests were subjected. The peasants who worked the disafforested land were not infrequently serfs; villeinage was a personal condition defined by law, irrespective of the land one worked.

6 Zvi Razi, *Life, Marriage and Death in a Medieval Parish*, Cambridge: 1980.

7 M. M. Postan, "Medieval Agrarian Society in Its Prime: England", in M. M. Postan (ed.), *The Cambridge Economic History of Europe*, Cambridge: 1966, Vol. I, 552–6.

8 Edward Britton, *The Community of the Vill*, Toronto: 1977, 161–2. H. C. Hallam, *Rural Society, 1066–1348*, London: 1981, esp. 65–7, 248–51. For an assessment of the contending points of view, see J. L. Bolton, *The Medieval English Economy, 1150–1500*, London: 1980, 33–6.

9 M. M. Postan *The Medieval Economy and Society*, London: 1972, 131 (my emphasis).

10 Postan, "Medieval Agrarian Society in Its Prime", 603 (my emphasis).

11 Postan, *The Medieval Economy and Society*, 128.

12 Bolton, *Medieval English Economy*, 114. R. H. Hilton has written that "in England, by the thirteenth century, there was a recognizable division between the peasants with holdings of twelve to fifteen arable acres (halfyardlanders) or more, and those with small holdings which in a large number of cases must have been under five acres", *The Decline of Serfdom in Medieval England* (second edn), London: 1983, 15.

13 Postan, *The Medieval Economy and Society*, 130, 132.

14 W. G. Hoskins, *The Age of Plunder*, London: 1976, 59 (emphasis in the original). I do not think that there is anything anachronistic about using Hoskins' quotation regarding the early sixteenth-century *cottage economy* in this context because the point is that this form of *cottage economy* persisted over time.

15 Karl Marx, *Capital: A Critique of Political Economy*, New York: 1967, Vol. I, 737. Max Weber, *The Protestant Ethic and the Spirit of Capitalism* (trans. by Talcott Parsons), New York: 1958, 62. Sahlins, *Stone Age Economics*, 86.

16 D. C. Coleman, "Labour in the English Economy of the Seventeenth Century", *Economic History Review*, second series, 8, (1956), 280–95. Postan, *The Medieval Economy and Society*, 133–4.

17 M. M. Postan, "The Charters of the Villeins", in *Essays on Medieval Agriculture and General Problems of the Medieval Economy*, Cambridge: 1973, 144.

18 Elinor Searle, "Rejoinder: Seigneurial Control of Women's Marriage", *Past and Present*, 99 (1983), 150. Searle goes on to note that "The poor, the landless . . . were disciplined by hunger" (151).

19 Searle, "Rejoinder: Seigneurial Control", 151.

20 R. H. Hilton, "The Crisis of Feudalism", *Past and Present*, 80 (1978), 9.

21 Rosamond Faith, "Debate: Seigneurial Control of Women's Marriage", *Past and Present*, 99 (1983), 140 (emphasis in the original).

22 Paul A. Brand and Paul R. Hyams, "Debate: Seigneurial Control of Women's Marriage", *Past and Present*, 99 (1983), 127.

23 Bolton, *Medieval English Economy*, 89.

24 Searle, "Rejoinder: Seigneurial Control", 153.

25 M. M. Postan, *The Famulus: The Estate Labourer in the Twelfth and Thirteenth Centuries* (*Economic History Review Supplement*, 2), Cambridge: 1954, 2.

26 Postan himself uses this phrase in his essay's penultimate sentence (*The Famulus*, 37).

27 Postan, *The Famulus*, 4–5.

28 Postan, *The Famulus*, 35 fn. 1.

29 Postan, *The Famulus*, 36.

30 Hilton, *Decline of Serfdom*, 25–6.

31 Hilton, *Decline of Serfdom*, 20, 21.

32 Bolton, *Medieval English Economy*, 58.

33 Postan, "Medieval Agrarian Society in Its Prime", 564.

34 Bolton, *Medieval English Economy*, 115.

35 I. Kershaw, "The Great Famine and Agrarian Crisis in England, 1315–1322", *Past and Present*, 59 (1973), 3–50.

36 M. M. Postan and J. Z. Titow, "Heriots and Prices on Winchester Manors", *Economic History Review*, second series, 11 (1958–9), 399, 407. I arrived at the "five times" figure by estimating that during normal years the mortality rate would have been 40 per 1,000 for the whole population and about a half of that for adult males (i.e. 20 per 1,000). Of course, this is the crudest form of guesstimation but we have nothing better.

37 Postan, *The Medieval Economy and Society*, 198–9.

38 R. H. Hilton, *Bond Men Made Free*, New York: 1973, 38.

39 Hilton, *Bond Men Made Free*, 35.

40 For a very interesting discussion of this dimension of the *cottage economy* see, Britton, *The Community of the Vill*, 161–2. For a detailed discussion of the adaptive strategies of landholding among medieval peasants see the essays by R. M. Smith, ("Families and Their Land in an Area of Partible Inheritance: Redgrave, Suffolk 1260–1320"), Bruce M. S. Campbell ("Population Pressure, Inheritance and the Land Market in a Fourteenth-Century Peasant Community"), Ian Blanchard ("Industrial Employment and the Rural Land Market 1380–1520") and Christopher Dyer ("Changes in the Size of Peasant Holdings in Some West Midland Villages 1400–1540"). These essays are published in R. M. Smith, (ed.), *Land, Kinship and Life-Cycle*, Cambridge: 1984.

41 Hilton, *Bond Men Made Free*, 38.

42 Even law cases tell us more about how people were *expected* to behave than about the representative experience.

43 Keith Thomas, *Religion and the Decline of Magic*, Harmondsworth: 1971, Chapters 2–6.

44 Brand and Hyams, "Debate: Seigneurial Control", 130–1.

45 H. S. Bennett, *Life on the English Manor*, Cambridge: 1937, 241.

46 George C. Homans, *English Villagers of the Thirteenth Century*, New York: 1941, 159. Although this book is now over forty years old it has the great merit of seeing manorial society as a whole, in contrast to the more recent research which has been analytically sophisticated but, too often, hopelessly literal-minded and all too forgetful of the basic fact of feudal power which set this manorial society in motion.

47 On the question of the "demographic lottery" see R. M. Smith, "Some Issues Concerning Families and Their Property in Rural England 1250–1800", in *Land, Kinship and Life-Cycle*, especially 38ff.

48 Bennett, *Life on the English Manor*, 251–2. Homans, *English Villagers of the Thirteenth Century*, 194.

49 Homans, *English Villagers of the Thirteenth Century*, 145. A similar argument regarding the cross-generational character of the peasant family in the later middle ages is made by R. H. Hilton (*The English Peasantry in the Later Middle Ages*, Oxford: 1975, 29–30).

50 Homans, *English Villagers of the Thirteenth Century*, 119–20. Hilton, too, concurs with this depiction of the domestic organization of the peasant household (*The English Peasantry in the Later Middle Ages*, 29–30).

51 H. E. Hallam, "Some Thirteenth-Century Censuses", *Economic History Review*, second series, 10 (1957–8), 340.

52 Britton, *The Community of the Vill*, 57–67. It should be noted that Britton is very circumspect on this matter and chides Homans for suggesting that there was an extended family system. Nevertheless, he does not think that the extended family was virtually insignificant as a domestic unit (65).

53 Bolton, *Medieval English Economy*, 53. For a similar point of view on the *situational* nature of peasants' household structures see, Hilton, *Bond Men Made Free*, 27.

54 C. Middleton, "The Sexual Division of Labour in Feudal England", *New Left Review*, 113–114 (1979), 160–1. On village bye-laws in the middle ages, specifically those regarding the harvest and agricultural work, see Keith Thomas, "Work and Leisure in Pre-Industrial Society", *Past and Present*, 26 (1964), 52–3. More generally, Doris Stenton, *The English Woman in History*, London: 1957, 75.

55 The best evidence regarding this difference relates to the parish register period, after 1538.

56 F. R. H. Du Boulay, *An Age of Ambition*, London: 1970, 89.

57 William Langland, *Piers The Ploughman* (trans. and ed. by J. F. Goodridge), Harmondsworth: 1966, 108.

58 Du Boulay, *Age of Ambition*, 99.

59 Homans, *English Villagers of the Thirteenth Century*, 177–8.

60 Homans, *English Villagers of the Thirteenth Century*, 166. He concedes, however, that there is no medieval evidence which specifically describes the hand-fasting ceremony and uses other material to infer its importance.

61 John Hatcher, "English Serfdom and Villeinage: Towards a Reassessment", *Past and Present*, 90 (1981), 37.

62 Quoted in E. Lipson, *The Economic History of England*, London: 1956, Vol. I, 114. From his study of village bye-laws before the Black Death, W. O. Ault has suggested that seigneurial control over the labour of the unmarried servants and adult agricultural labourers/dwarf-holders was not infrequently coincidental with the interests of those villagers who also employed labour – both wanted to inhibit the mobility of labour and fix it within a specified field of force, the manor in the case of the landlord and the family in the case of the substantial peasant (*Open-Field Husbandry and the Village Community*, Philadelphia: 1965 (Transactions of the American Philosophical Society, new series, no. 55)). For a recent assessment of the workings of the Statute see L. R. Poos, "The Social Context of Statute of Labourers' Enforcement", *Law and History Review*, 1 (1983), 27–52. Poos sees active intervention by wealthy villagers as a critical element in the prosecution of the law against their weaker and dependent fellows. He thus queries the solidarity of the peasantry in the face of the seigneurial reaction. While this point of view has an element of day-to-day truth, it seems striking to me that Essex (the county Poos has studied) was the leading site of the peasants' Revolt in 1381 and that their main target was the fiscal depradations of the seigneurial regime of the young King Richard II's "evil ministers".

63 Hilton, *Decline of Serfdom*, 40–1. This point is raised as a question and then answered affirmatively in the following pages. Indeed, several pages earlier (37) he specifically mentions "a general intensification of exploitation".

64 M. M. Postan, "Legal Status and Economic Conditions in Medieval Villages", in *Essays on Medieval Agriculture and General Problems of the Medieval Economy*, 283, 284.

65 Not all ruling classes had displayed the complete lack of solidarity which was evinced in England during the later middle ages. Faced with runaways, southern American slaveholders erected a complex system of rewards to ensure the immobility of their labour force and to protect their human property from the poaching of unscrupulous colleagues. In fact, in eastern Europe in the wake of the plummeting population of the later middle ages there was an intensification of feudal exactions.

66 R. Brenner, "The Agrarian Roots of European Capitalism", *Past and Present*, 97 (1982), 55.

67 K. B. McFarlane, "War and Society 1300–1600", in *England in the Fifteenth Century*, London: 1981, 143–9.

68 A. R. Bridbury, "The Hundred Years' War: Costs and Profits", in D. C. Coleman and A. H. John (eds.), *Trade, Government and Economy in Pre-Industrial England*, London: 1976, 85.

69 M. M. Postan, "The Costs of the Hundred Years War", in *Essays on Medieval Agriculture and General Problems of the Medieval Economy*, 66.

70 McFarlane, "War and Society 1300–1600", 140.

71 L. C. Latham, "The Manor and the Village", in G. Barraclough (ed.), *Social Life in Early England*, London: 1960, 49.

72 Christopher Dyer, "A Redistribution of Incomes in Fifteenth-Century England?", *Past and Present*, 39 (1968), 20.

73 Dyer, "A Redistribution of Incomes in Fifteenth-Century England?", 26.

74 Hilton, *Decline of Serfdom*, 33.

75 Searle, "Rejoinder: Seigneurial Control", 159. It should be understood that this juridical process of establishing ownership was second-best to maintaining feudal control over the tenants.

76 R. Brenner, "Agrarian Class Structure and Economic Development in Pre-Industrial Europe", *Past and Present*, 70 (1976), 62.

77 Brenner, "Agrarian Class Structure", 63.

78 M. M. Postan, "Some Agrarian Evidence of Declining Populations in the Later Middle Ages", in *Essays on Medieval Agriculture and General Problems of the Medieval Economy*, 211.

79 Postan, "Some Agrarian Evidence of Declining Populations", 191.

80 Thus, for example, Blanchard and Dyer have been able to explicate the demise of landlords' feudal powers, the retrenchment of an egalitarian peasant society and the breakdown of the social system of family recycling (see references in n. 40, above).

81 This point is made quite explicitly with reference to the organization of domestic life by Ian Blanchard although I am not impressed by the evidence he has brought to bear on his discussion ("Industrial Employment and the Rural Land Market 1380–1520", in Smith (ed.), *Land, Kinship and Life-Cycle*, esp. 254–64). Blanchard's argument might be plausible but it needs to be proven.

82 Quoted in Beatrice White, "Poet and Peasant", in F. R. H. Du Boulay and Caroline M. Barron, (eds.), *The Reign of Richard II*. London: 1971, 71.

83 Hilton, *Bond Men Made Free*, 40.

84 Postan, "Medieval Agrarian Society in Its Prime", 626.

85 Bolton, *Medieval English Economy*, 53 (quoted above).

2 Agrarian capitalism and rural proletarianization

1 It should be noted that not all land was "available" for peasant farming in the middle ages; many forests were kept in a primeval state because the feudal classes considered the hunt to be an integral part of their lifestyles, almost on a par with fighting. We shall return to the novel twists of fate to which these forests were subjected in the early modern period.

2 Postan, "Medieval Agrarian Society in Its Prime", 552.

3 Postan, "Medieval Agrarian Society in Its Prime", 554, 556.

4 M. W. Beresford, *The Lost Villages of England*, Gloucester, England: 1983, 28–9.

5 Hoskins, *The Age of Plunder*, 68.

6 K. B. McFarlane, "The Investment of Sir John Fastolf's Profits of War", in *England in the Fifteenth Century*, 196.

7 K. J. Allison, "Flock Management in the Sixteenth and Seventeenth Centuries", *Economic History Review*, second series, 11 (1958), 98–112.

8 Daniel Defoe *A Tour Through the Whole Island of Great Britain 1724–6* (abridged and ed. by Pat Rogers), Harmondsworth: 1972, 408.

9 Hoskins, *The Age of Plunder*, 81. Earlier in his book Hoskins suggests that there

might have been three or four sheep for every man, woman and child at the time of Henry VIII (ii).

10 Bolton, *Medieval English Economy*, 238.

11 Gordon Batho, "Noblemen, Gentlemen, and Yeomen", in Joan Thirsk, (ed.), *The Agrarian History of England and Wales, IV, 1500–1640*, Cambridge: 1967, 305.

12 This quotation is used to describe wet-rice agriculture in Indonesia; it seems to me equally applicable to cereal farming in medieval England. The source is Clifford Geertz, *Agricultural Involution. The Processes of Ecological Change in Indonesia*, Berkeley and Los Angeles: 1963, 32.

13 Of course, medieval peasants farmed for "the market"; the crucial point seems to be that they did so only in order to pay their rents in money as their landlords demanded. While there is some scattered evidence of medieval peasants accumulating capital, those who were able to do so could not buy their way into the feudal classes. Medieval society put a great premium on *the blood*; most peasants, by definition, had the wrong blood-type.

14 Mildred Campbell, *The English Yeoman under Elizabeth and the Early Stuarts*, New Haven: 1942, 220.

15 F. J. Furnivall (ed.), *Harrison's Description of England*, London: 1877, 105.

16 Alan Everitt, "Farm Labourers", in Thirsk (ed.), *The Agrarian History of England and Wales*, 397–8.

17 On servants-in-husbandry and their importance in family farming see, Ann Kussmaul, *Servants in Husbandry in Early Modern England*, Cambridge: 1981.

18 Everitt, "Farm Labourers", 400.

19 Peter Lindert, "English Occupations, 1670–1811", *Journal of Economic History*, 40 (1980), 685–712. For further reservations about the reliability of King's social reconstitution, see G. S. Holmes, "Gregory King and the Social Structure of Pre-Industrial England", *Transactions of the Royal Historical Society*, fifth series, 27 (1977), 41–68.

20 *Parliamentary Papers* (1852–3), LXXXVIII, Part 1, Table XXV.

21 It should be noted that both employers and potential employers of labour are lumped together in these statistics. Later in this chapter we will consider some finer distinctions among the employing class of agricultural capitalists in order to show how much more dramatic the divergence between labour and capital was in the countryside.

22 Christopher Hill, *Reformation to Industrial Revolution*, Harmondsworth: 1967, 47. For a recent assessment of the implications of the "Tudor Revolution in Government", see Philip Corrigan and Derek Sayer, *The Great Arch. English State Formation as Cultural Revolution*, Oxford: 1985, Chapters 2 and 3.

23 Quoted in Hoskins, *The Age of Plunder*, 232–3.

24 Hoskins, *The Age of Plunder*, 121, 136.

25 H. R. Trevor-Roper, "The Bishopric of Durham and the Capitalist Reformation", *Durham University Journal*, new series, 7 (1946), 45–58. For a more general account of these predatory policies of the Tudors and Stuarts, see Christopher Hill, *The Economic Problems of the Church*, Oxford: 1956.

26 This document is found in *Tudor Economic Documents*, ed. R. H. Tawney and E. Power, London: 1951, Vol. I, 1–11.

27 B. A. Holderness, "'Open' and 'Close' Parishes in England in the Eighteenth

and Nineteenth Centuries", *Agricultural History Review*, 20 (1972), 126–39. In this regard, the later medieval estate administrators' offensive to prove title to "property" is particularly apposite. They knew the difference between "ownership" and "occupation" and this knowledge was put to use in their own interest. In a society as legalistic as early modern England, many disputes were resolved on the basis of contracts between fifteenth-century peasants, clutching for freedom from feudal exactions, and estate administrators, anxious not to give too much away. History had a nasty way of repeating itself as tragedy for many of the descendants of these peasants whose bargain for freedom cost their children's children their land.

28 Joan Thirsk, "Enclosing and Engrossing", in Thirsk, (ed.), *The Agrarian History of England and Wales*, 255. Thirsk's emphasis on the irrevocable social change in the enclosed village makes the stakes of the game evident. However, I am not in complete agreement with this statement because Thirsk is, in my opinion, rather too much concerned with the "strong arguments" of the literate, political nation of landowners and their principal tenants. It is a pity that the voices of the dispossessed were neither as loud nor as insistently shrill as those who benefited from the "violence of the status quo". A little later in this chapter I will suggest that the losers' voices may have been faint but we can nevertheless recuperate their plaintiff cries. "Who paid the bill?" Indeed.

29 For some examples of intra-family social differentiation, see the three following books: W. G. Hoskins, *The Midland Peasant*, London: 1957, 199; David Hey, *An English Rural Community. Myddle under the Tudors and Stuarts*, Leicester: 1974, 204; and Margaret Spufford, *Contrasting Communities. English Villagers in the Sixteenth and Seventeenth Centuries*, Cambridge: 1974, 111.

30 Thorold Rogers, *Six Centuries of Work and Wages*, London: 1894, Vol. II, 479, quoted in N. H. Brailsford, *The Levellers and the English Revolution* (ed. Christopher Hill), London: 1976, 451.

31 On the public face of this debate in the 1650s, see Joyce Oldham Appleby, *Economic Thought and Ideology in Seventeenth Century England*, Princeton: 1978, esp. Chapter 3.

32 J. A. Yelling, "Common Land and Enclosure in East Worcestershire, 1540–1870", *Transactions of the Institute of British Geographers*, 43 (1967), 157–68, "The Combination and Rotation of Crops in East Worcestershire, 1540–1660", *Agricultural History Review*, 17 (1967), 24–43, and "Changes in Crop Production in East Worcestershire 1540–1867", *Agricultural History Review*, 21 (1973), 18–33. Erik Kerridge's discussion of the early modern "agricultural revolution" considers the national scene and draws a picture not dissimilar to the situation Yelling describes in one locality: see *The Agricultural Revolution*, London: 1967.

33 Beresford, *Lost Villages*, 216.

34 Andrew Appleby, "Epidemics and Famine in the Little Ice Age", *Journal of Interdisciplinary History*, 10 (1980), 643–63. See also D. M. Palliser, "Tawney's Century: Brave New World of Malthusian Trap?", *Economic History Review*, second series, 35 (1982), 339–53.

35 Christopher Hill, "'Pottage for Freeborn Englishmen': Attitudes to Wage-Labour in the Sixteenth and Seventeenth Centuries", in Charles Feinstein (ed.), *Socialism, Capitalism and Economic Growth*, Cambridge: 1964, 338–59.

36 Coleman, "Labour in the English Economy", 280–95; Appleby, *Economic Thought and Ideology*, Chapter 6; and E. J. Hundert, "The Conception of Work and the Worker in Early Industrial England" (Ph.D. dissertation, University of Rochester, 1969).

37 Hoskins, *The Age of Plunder*, 109.

38 Hoskins, *The Age of Plunder*, 108.

39 Hoskins, *The Age of Plunder*, 109–11.

40 Dudley, More and Starkey are quoted in C. Lis and H. Soly, "Policing the Early Modern Proletariat, 1450–1850", in David Levine (ed.), *Proletarianization and Family History*, Orlando, Florida: 1984, 167.

41 Lis and Soly, "Policing the Early Modern Proletariat", 169.

42 Peter Linebaugh, "All the Atlantic Mountains Shook", *Labour/Le Travailleur*, 10 (1982), 96, 98.

43 C. S. L. Davies, "Slavery and Protector Somerset", *Economic History Review*, second series, 19 (1966), 547.

44 For a discussion of the solidarity of late medieval countrymen, see R. B. Goheen, "Social ideals and Social Structure: Rural Gloucestershire, 1450–1500", *Social History/Histoire Sociale*, 12 (1979), 262–80.

45 Alan Macfarlane (ed.), *The Dairy of Ralph Josselin, 1616–1683*, London: 1976, 236, 252, 376, 424, 495–505.

46 Keith Wrightson and David Levine, *Poverty and Piety in an English Village. Terling, 1525–1700*, New York: 1979.

47 Keith Wrightson, *English Society 1580–1680*, London: 1982, 228.

48 On the continuing importance of deferential relationships in rural England in the nineteenth century see, Howard Newby, "The Deferential Dialectic", *Comparative Studies in Society and History*, 17 (1975), 139–64.

49 E. P. Thompson has written extensively on this point; see, esp. "The Free-Born Englishman" which is Chapter IV in his classic *The Making of the English Working Class*, London: 1963.

50 E. P. Thompson, "The Peculiarities of the English", in *The Poverty of Theory*, London: 1978, 86.

51 Charles Tilly, "Demographic Origins of the European Proletariat", in Levine (ed.), *Proletarianization and Family History*, 11.

52 On this point, see Gordon Schochet, "Patriarchalism, Politics and Mass Attitudes in Stuart England", *Historical Journal*, 12 (1969), 413–41, and Randolph Trumbach, *The Rise of the Egalitarian Family*, New York: 1978, 141–5.

53 Lawrence Stone, *The Family, Sex, and Marriage in England 1500–1800*, New York: 1977, 253–6. M. W. Barley, *The English Farmhouse and Cottage*, London: 1961, 159, 220, 248.

54 Douglas Hay, "Property, Authority and the Criminal Law", in Douglas Hay and E. P. Thompson (eds.), *Albion's Fatal Tree*, New York: 1975, 17–64. See also E. P. Thompson, "Patrician Society, Plebeian Culture", *Journal of Social History*, 7 (1974), 382–405

55 Robert W. Malcolmson, *Popular Recreations in English Society 1700–1850*, Cambridge: 1973 and Peter B. Munsche, *Gentlemen and Poachers: The English Game Laws 1671–1831*, Cambridge: 1981.

56 Appleby, *Economic Thought and Ideology*, 70–1.

57 Thomas, *Religion and the Decline of Magic*, esp. Chapter 17.

58 Evidence for this assertion regarding the class-specific nature of the decline of magical beliefs is scattered but, I think, overwhelming. Malcolmson provides a short discussion of this subject in Robert W. Malcolmson, *Life and Labour in England 1700–1780*, London: 1981, 87–91. Pamela Horn touches on it for the following period (*The Rural World 1780–1850*, London: 1980, 160–3). A rather fuller discussion of the nineteenth-century survival of "non-rational" aspects in popular mentalities is available in, James Obelkevich, *Religion and Rural Society: South Lindsey, 1825–1875*, Oxford: 1976, esp. Chapter 6. Seymour Tremenheere, the Victorian educational administrator, found in Norfolk, "here a wizard terrifying his neighbours by the power of inflicting injuries by his charms, there supernatural appearances, in another neighbourhood a quack curing all diseases by his knowledge of the stars" (quoted in Richard Johnson, "Educational Policy and Social Control in Early Victorian England", *Past and Present*, 49 (1976), 106). Richard Hoggart's all-too-brief description of the mental construction of social reality evinced by his grandmother, who had been born in rural Yorkshire in the middle of the nineteenth century and migrated to Leeds in the 1870s, lends a strikingly personal dimension to this point concerning the survival of popular mentalities (*The Uses of Literacy*, Harmondsworth: 1958, 24–6). See also, the references in John Burnett in his study of nineteenth-century autobiographies, *Destiny Obscure*, 31–2.

59 Richard Dunning quoted in Appleby, *Economic Thought and Ideology*, 131.

60 Linebaugh, "Atlantic Mountains", 101. See also, Marcus Rediker, "'Good Hands, Stout Hearts, and Fast Feet': The History and Culture of Working People in Early America", *Labour/Le Travailleur*, 10 (1982), 123–44. The reminder in these two works that "England" had become rather more than the Elizabethan "jewel set in an emerald sea" is important and directs our attention to the global significance of the processes of capital accumulation which were taking place on the land and on the waves, both of which were ruled by the same group of Britannia's loyal servants. We shall return to it later.

61 Appleby, *Economic Thought and Ideology*, 152, 153.

62 Sir Francis Brewster and John Houghton are quoted in Lis and Soly, "Policing the Early Modern Proletariat", 181.

63 Geoffrey W. Oxley, *Poor Relief in England and Wales 1601–1834*, Newton Abbot: 1974, 85. "No contrast could be greater than that between the [mercantilist] theorists' dreams and what we actually find, even in the best run workhouses" (92).

64 E. M. Hampson, *The Treatment of Poverty in Cambridgeshire 1597–1834*, Cambridge: 1934, 89, 96. See also, Oxley, *Poor Relief in England and Wales*, 91–2.

65 Dorothy Marshall, *The English Poor in the Eighteenth Century*, London: 1926, 151.

66 Dr Trotter, *Observations on the Poor Laws* (1775), 52, quoted in Marshall, *The English Poor in the Eighteenth Century*, 150.

67 R. North, *A Discourse of the Poor* (1753), 33, quoted in Marshall, *The English Poor in the Eighteenth Century*, 101.

68 Marshall, *The English Poor in the Eighteenth Century*, 151.

69 This following discussion is based on Kussmaul, *Servants in Husbandry in Early Modern England*.

70 Kussmaul, *Servants in Husbandry in Early Modern England*, 103, 101.

71 Later in this chapter we will analyse the nineteenth-century evidence of this reorganization of the national division of agricultural labour and its implications for the regional characteristics of rural life in the south and east as opposed to the north and west.

72 K. D. M. Snell, *Annals of the Labouring Poor*, Cambridge: 1985, 22, 52, 40, 49–51, 214ff; E. J. T. Collins, "Harvest Technology and Labour Supply in Britain, 1790–1870", *Economic History Review*, second series, 22 (1969); and M. Roberts, "Sickles and Scythes: Women's Work and Men's Work at Harvest Time", *History Workshop*, 7 (1979). My reading of the article by Collins leads me to a rather different explanation which has less to do with "neutral technology" and rather more to do with the over-supply of labour and the inherent patriarchalism of the village elders in giving priority to adult male breadwinners. Collins argues that the "majority adoption phase" for the heavy scythe was much later than Snell suggests – dating from the 1830s not the 1760s (see below, n. 91 and the quotation in my text).

73 *Northampton Mercury*, 22 August 1726, quoted in Malcolmson, *Life and Labour in England 1700–1780*, 139–40.

74 For further discussion on this subject see, M. W. Beresford, "Habitation versus Improvement: The Debate on Enclosure by Agreement", in F. J. Fisher (ed.), *Essays in the Economic and Social History of Tudor and Stuart England*, Cambridge: 1961, 40–69. Also, Appleby, *Economic Thought and Ideology*, Chapter 3. In addition, see Thompson, "The Grid of Inheritance: A Comment", 328–60.

75 Hoskins, *The Making of the English Landscape*, 153–4, 178.

76 Malcolmson, *Life and Labour in England, 1700–1780*, 34.

77 J. M. Beattie, "The Pattern of Crime in England 1660–1800", *Past and Present*, 62 (1974), 80.

78 E. P. Thompson, *Whigs and Hunters*, Harmondsworth: 1977, 241.

79 D. N. McCloskey, "The Enclosure of Open Fields", *Journal of Economic History*, 32 (1972), 35.

80 Defoe, *A Tour Through The Whole Island of Great Britain*, 349.

81 Malcolmson, *Life and Labour in England 1700–1780*, 46.

82 For a throughgoing analysis of the meaning of enclosure for cottagers see Snell, *Annals of the Labouring Poor*, 138–227. Snell demolishes the "optimistic" school of thought championed by J. D. Chambers which claimed that in exchange for common rights the poor got more regular employment ("Enclosure and Labour Supply in the Industrial Revolution", *Economic History Review*, second series, 5 (1953)).

83 John Caird, *English Agriculture in 1850–51*, London: 1852, 517–18.

84 Sidney Pollard, "Labour in Great Britain", in P. Mathias and M. M. Postan (eds.), *The Cambridge Economic History of Europe*, Cambridge: 1978, Vol. VII, Part 1, 164.

85 J. H. Clapham, "The Growth of an Agrarian Proletariat, 1688–1832", *Cambridge Historical Journal*, 1 (1923), 93–5. Clapham's method has been roundly criticized by J. D. Chambers and G. E. Mingay (*The Agricultural Revolution 1750–1880*,

London: 1966, 103, 133). See also, John Saville, "Primitive Accumulation and Early Industrialization in Britain", in John Saville and Ralph Miliband (eds.), *Socialist Register*, London: 1969, 247–71.

86 *Parliamentary Papers* (1852–3), LXXXVIII, Part 1, Table XXV.

87 For a full discussion of both the regional distribution of labourers and servants-in-husbandry and the evolution of the regional systems of labour organization in which they were employed, see Kussmaul, *Servants in Husbandry in Early Modern England*, Chapters 6 and 7. The figures on women's employment in 1841 were quoted in Snell, *Annals of the Labouring Poor*, 57, fn. 54.

88 *Parliamentary Papers* (1852–3), LXXXVIII, Part 2, Table XXXIV. There appear to be discrepancies between this tabulation and the national calculation which seems to stem from the fact that this second Table (XXXIV) appears to have been based on farmers' descriptions of their landholdings and labour supplies and apparently misses a fairly substantial number of labourers. Thus in Table XXV, 724,839 living-out, adult male labourers are counted whereas 644,056 have been included in Table XXXIV. Why is there this discrepancy? I think that it is because the farmers understood the question regarding labourers to distinguish "men" from "boys" and did not automatically consider a person's age as being, in itself, a significant characteristic of "manhood" or "boyhood". Rather, they probably included many unmarried young men (who happened to be over twenty) in the category "boys" so that they under-counted the "men" in their employ.

89 The original figures deliberately excluded both servants-in-husbandry, "boys", and female labourers.

90 Dennis R. Mills, *Lord and Peasant in Nineteenth Century Britain*, London: 1980, 73–83.

91 E. J. T. Collins, "Labour Supply and Demand in European Agriculture 1800–1880", in E. L. Jones and S. J. Woolf (Eds.), *Agrarian Change and Economic Development*, London: 1969, 86.

92 J. C. Morton, *Handbook of Farm Labour* (1876), 76, quoted by E. J. T. Collins, "Harvest Technology and Labour Supply in Britain", 464.

93 Chambers and Mingay, *The Agricultural Revolution*, 207–8.

94 Collins, "Labour Supply and Demand in European Agriculture", 62.

95 Collins, "Labour Supply and Demand in European Agriculture", 62.

96 E. L. Jones, "The Agricultural Labour Market in England, 1793–1872", *Economic History Review*, second series, 17 (1964), 322–38.

97 E. L. Jones, "The Agricultural Labour Market in England, 1793–1872", 327 ff.

98 Chambers and Mingay, *The Agricultural Revolution*, 132–3. See also, Mick Reed, "The Peasantry of Nineteenth-Century England: A Neglected Class?" *History Workshop*, 18 (1984), 53–76.

99 Hoskins, *The Making of the English Landscape*, 179.

100 Snell, *Annals of the Labouring Poor*, 166ff. For a suggestive study of the role of Parliament and parliamentarians in private members bills for enclosure, see J. M. Martin, "Members of Parliament and Enclosure: A Reconsideration", *Agricultural History Review*, 27 (1979), 101–9.

101 J. M. Neeson, "The Opponents of Enclosure in Eighteenth-Century North-amptonshire", *Past and Present*, 105 (1984), 114–39. E. J. Hobsbawm and George Rudé, *Captain Swing*, Harmondsworth: 1973, 16.

102 Marshall, *The English Poor in the Eighteenth Century*, 104–5. See also, J. R. Poynter, *Society and Pauperism*, London: 1969, 14–15.

103 Gertrude Himmelfarb, *The Idea of Poverty*, New York: 1983, 126.

104 Thomas Robert Malthus, *An Essay on the Principle of Population* (ed. Anthony Flew), Harmondsworth: 1970, 97–8. Since I am principally concerned with population dynamics and their interaction with the social organization of production, it seems just as useful to rely on this generally accessible edition of Malthus' 1798 *Essay* than to worry overmuch about the endless changes and alterations Malthus made to his own theory. He was, of course, wrong for all sorts of reasons and he did not even grasp fully the interplay between continued population growth and the mode of production but, nevertheless, he did focus our attention on the rates of growth in economy and demography and he did suggest that the two were interconnected. In some senses, I am an unregenerated Malthusian – it seems to me that his lasting intellectual contribution was to place "the principle of population" within a numerical mode of analysis.

105 Chambers, "Enclosure and Labour Supply", 337.

106 Townsend is quoted in Karl Polanyi, *The Great Transformation*, Boston: 1957, 113 (my emphasis). The full explication of this intellectual paradigm-shift is found in Chapter 10 ("Political Economy and the Discovery of Society"). Himmelfarb, *The Idea of Poverty*, note on 123. Malthus is quoted from the second edition of the *Essay* in Himmelfarb, 122–3. It might now be pointed out that among those whose minds were gripped by Malthus was Charles Darwin, another Cambridge man of a later generation. In his *Autobiography* he wrote: "In October 1838, that is, fifteen months after I had begun my systematic enquiry, I happened to read for amusement Malthus on Population, and being well prepared to appreciate the struggle for existence which everywhere goes on from long-continued observation of the habits of animals and plants, it at once struck me that under these circumstances favourable variations would tend to be preserved, and unfavourable ones to be destroyed. The result of this would be the formation of new species" (quoted in R. Keynes, "Malthus and Biological Equilibria", in J. Dupaquier, A. Fauve-Chamoux and E. Grebenik (eds.), *Malthus Past and Present*, New York: 1983, 360). It is ironic that these two devoutly Christian men were so instrumental in destroying the intellectual foundations of their faith in the popular mind. Malthus undermined the patriarchal ideal of Christian charity while Darwin exploded the notion of a providential Creation and in so doing provided an opportunity for those who argued for an historical interpretation of the Bible and the "Historical Jesus". After Malthus and Darwin had had their say, one had no choice but to accept the logic of Pascal's wager – more in blind faith than hope. It is ironic that neither Malthus nor Darwin would have been at all happy to have been seen as a champion of scientific rationalism – each thought he was justifying and explaining the ways of God.

107 Malthus, *An Essay on the Principle of Population*, 91.

108 Wrightson, *English Society 1580–1680*, 80.
109 Quoted by Homans, *English Villagers of the Thirteenth Century*, 164. Homans found this reference in G. E. Howard, *A History of Matrimonial Institutions*, London: 1904, vol. I, 349.
110 Wrightson, *English Society 1580–1680*, 88.
111 Daniel Scott Smith, "A Homeostatic Demographic Regime: Patterns in West European Family Reconstitution Studies", in R. D. Lee (ed.), *Population Patterns in the Past*, New York: 1977, 19–51.
112 Levine, *Family Formation*, Chapter 5 (Shepshed) and Chapter 8 (Terling).
113 P. G. Ohlin, "Mortality, Marriage, and Growth in Pre-Industrial Populations", *Population Studies*, 14 (1961), 190–7.
114 E. A. Wrigley, "Fertility Strategy for the Individual and the Group", in Charles Tilly (ed.), *Historical Studies of Changing Fertility*, Princeton: 1978, 135–54.
115 The classic statement of this analytical construct is by the great French demographer Louis Henry; See "Some Data on Natural Fertility", *Eugenics Quarterly*, 8 (1961), 81–91.
116 Colyton, the very first English village to have been reconstituted, provides a striking exception to this rule although subsequent work seems to underline this village's peculiarity. E. A. Wrigley, "Family Limitation in Pre-Industrial England", *Economic History Review*, second series, 19 (1966), 82–109. For a different interpretation of Colyton's demographic history see, Levine, *Family Formation*, Chapter 7.
117 On the changing ratio of illegitimate births, see Peter Laslett and Karla Oosterveen, "Long-Term Trends in Bastardy in England, 1561–1960", *Population Studies*, 27 (1973), 255–86. On the local role of proletarianization and the particularly high levels of illegitimacy in the Essex village of Terling see, Wrightson and Levine, *Poverty and Piety in an English Village, Terling, 1525–1700*, 125–34.
118 E. A. Wrigley and R. S. Schofield, *The Population History of England 1541–1871*, London: 1981, App. 10, 645–93. See also, Paul Slack, "Mortality Crises and Epidemics in England, 1485–1610", in Charles Webster (ed.), *Health, Medicine, and Mortality in the Sixteenth Century*, Cambridge: 1979, 9–59.
119 Levine, *Family Formation*, Chapter 6.
120 John Hatcher, *Plague, Population and the English Economy 1348–1530*, London: 1977.
121 Wrigley and Schofield, *The Population History of England 1541–1871*, 451.
122 E. A. Wrigley and R. S. Schofield, "Infant and Child Mortality in England in the Late Tudor and Early Stuart Period", in Webster (ed.), *Health, Medicine, and Mortality in the Sixteenth Century*, 75.
123 Wrigley and Schofield, *The Population History of England 1541–1871*, App. 5, 563–75.
124 These figures are derived from P. Corfield, "Urban Development in England and Wales in the Sixteenth and Seventeenth Centuries", in Coleman and John (eds.), *Trade, Government and Economy in Pre-Industrial England*, 214–47.
125 P. Deane and W. A. Cole, *British Economic Growth 1688–1959*, second edition, Cambridge: 1967, 127ff.
126 E. A. Wrigley, "A Simple Model of London's Importance in Changing English

Society and Economy 1650–1750", *Past and Present* 37 (1967), 44–70. R. A. P. Finlay, *Population and Metropolis*, Cambridge: 1981. For a rather different point of view, the evidence in which is largely derived from Frankfurt, Germany, see, Allan Sharlin, "National Decrease in Early Modern Cities: A Reconsideration", *Past and Present*, 79 (1978), 126–38.

127 The *net* out-migration was 544,000 between 1631 and 1700 and another 518,000 between 1701 and 1800 (Wrigley and Schofield, *The Population History of England 1541–1871*, Table 7.14, 227). It is necessary to add some unknown number to allow for the accounting error "masked in their calculations by incoming Celts who joined the native English population and made it look larger than it really was, leading to an unavoidable underestimate of the true English out-migration" (Kenneth Lockridge, "Brilliance and Whiggery", *Comparative Studies in Society and History*, 26 (1984), 301).

128 Abbot Emerson Smith, *Colonists in Bondage*, Gloucester, Massachusets: 1965, 3–4. David Galenson's study of surviving records of their indentures delineates the institution's age-and gender-specific characteristics (*White Servitude in Colonial America*, New York: 1981, 23, 26).

129 David Souden, "'Rogues, Whores and Vagabonds'? Indentured Servant Emigrants to North America, and the Case of Mid-Seventeenth-Century Bristol", *Social History*, 3 (1978), 23–78. For the phenomenon of "subsistence migration", see Slack, "Vagrants and Vagrancy in England, 1598–1664", *Economic History Review*, second series, 27 (1974), 360–78.

130 Galenson, *White Servitude in Colonial America*, 9.

131 Mildred Campbell, "Social Origins of Some Early Americans", in James Morton Smith (ed.), *Seventeenth-Century America*, Chapel Hill, 1959, 82ff. Campbell's use of the occupational designations, and in particular her belief that the un-designated people formed a random sample which conformed to the social characteristics of the others, has been severely criticized by David Galenson in "'Middling People' or 'Common Sort'?: The Social Origins of Some Early Americans Reexamined", *William and Mary Quarterly*, third series, 35 (1978), 499–524. Campbell has responded vigorously in the same issue (525–40). See also, the "Rejoinder"by Galenson and Campbell's "Reply" in the following issue, *William and Mary Quarterly*, third series, 36 (1979), 264–86.

132 Souden, "'Rogues, Whores and Vagabonds'?", 35.

133 Quoted in Galenson, *White Servitude in Colonial America*, 37.

134 A. E. Smith, *Colonists in Bondage*, Chapel Hill, North Carolina: 1946, 69–70, 77, 96, 117.

135 George Alsop, *A Character of the Province of Mary-land* (1666), quoted in Galenson, *White Servitude in Colonial America*, 24–5.

136 Souden, "'Rogues, Whores and Vagabonds'?", 33.

137 Wrigley and Schofield, *The Population History of England 1541–1871*, Table A3.3, 531–5.

138 The "back projection" statistics estimated that the *net* out-migration was 544,000 between 1631 and 1700 (i.e. about 8,000 per year) and another 518,000 between 1701 and 1800 (i.e. about 5,000 per year) (Wrigley and Schofield, *The Population History of England 1541–1871*, Table 7.14, 227).

139 Wrigley and Schofield, *The Population History of England 1541–1871*, 198.

140 See, for example, Wrigley and Schofield, *The Population History of England, 1541–1871*, 443–50. For a viewpoint more in line with the one presented in the text see, Coleman, "Labour in the English economy", 284.

141 Appleby, *Economic Thought and Ideology*, 135.

142 Mildred Campbell, "'Of People Either Too Few or Too Many'", in W. A. Aiken and B. D. Henning (eds.), *Conflict in Stuart England*, London: 1960, 191.

143 Quoted in J. H. Plumb, *Sir Robert Walpole: The Making of a Statesman*, London: 1956, 367.

144 Kussmaul, *Servants in Husbandry in Early Modern England*, 110–11.

145 This failure to distinguish between necessary and sufficient causes lies at the heart of the "revisionist" analysis of W. A. Armstrong, "The Influence of Demographic Factors on the Position of the Agricultural Labourer in England and Wales, c1750–1914", *Agricultural History Review*, 29 (1981), 71–82. A similar point of view is found in Chambers and Mingay, *The Agricultural Revolution*, 102–3.

146 Malthus, *An Essay on the Principle of Population*, 91.

147 Shepshed and Terling were part of their sample which means that there were some other villages in which the fall in the age at first marriage was neither so steep nor so complete as in our two villages. See Wrigley and Schofield, *The Population History of England 1541–1871*, 255.

148 Wrigley and Schofield, *The Population History of England 1541–1871*, 25.

149 In the Wrigley and Schofield, "back projection" analysis the highest levels of permanent celibacy were recorded in the seventeenth century when it reached almost 25 per cent of the total; at the turn of the eighteenth and nineteenth centuries the comparable figure was 8 per cent – about a third of its peak. They are themselves cautious about the peak figure and suggest that, among other reasons, later seventeenth-century migration (to stock the cities and to America) and under-registration as well as the long-term decrease in the frequency of remarriages may have made their peak rather too high. (*The Population History of England 1541–1871*, Table 7.28 and 257–65.)

150 David Levine, "Parson Malthus, Professor Huzel, and the Pelican Inn Protocol: A Comment", *Historical Methods*, 17 (1984), 21–4. Professor Huzel's response to my comment seems to miss the point of the demographic analysis. See James P. Huzel, "Parson Malthus and the Pelican Inn Protocol: A Reply to Professor Levine", *Historical Methods*, 17 (1984), 25–7.

151 Levine, *Family Formation*, Chapter 9.

152 Bolton, *Medieval English Economy*, 56.

153 Adherence to the **peasant demography model**, without the **urban counterweight** and the **colonial counterweight** would have yielded in 1851 population of about 9,500,000.

154 In contrast to the rest of Europe, English rates of urbanization during the early modern period were exceptional. Capital-intensive agricultural technologies – new methods of cropping, cultivation and breeding – and a booming demand for these products interacted to produce a specialized division of labour (E. A. Wrigley, "Urban Growth and Agricultural Change: England and the Continent in the Early Modern Period", *Journal of Interdisciplinary History*, 15 (1985), 683–728). The radically new component in this equation was the

232

cereal-producing large farm. It would have been impossible without, first, the expropriation of peasant landholders and, second, a hired labour force. Given the comparatively primitive methods of agricultural production and the subsistence imperatives of the family farm, it seems unlikely that this form of production could have provided the answer to the burgeoning demand during the period of industrialization. We shall never know the answer to that "counter-factual" proposition but I remain to be convinced that family farming could have provided the necessary surplus to accommodate both an increasing proportion of urban and industrial consumers and an absolute rise in their numbers. It did so in America in the later nineteenth century but, and it is an enormous qualification, American family farmers had extensive land and labour-saving machinery at their disposal while the early modern English capitalist farmers did not.

155 Brinley Thomas argues that before the emergence of a world-wide division of agricultural labour, England's Irish colony provided a substantial proportion of its grains, meat, butter and livestock – "as much as 13 percent" in the late 1830s: "Escaping from Constraints: The Industrial Revolution in a Malthusian Context", *Journal of Interdisciplinary History*, 15 (1985), 742.

156 Wrigley and Schofield, *The Population History of England 1541–1871*, 404.

3   The industrialization of the **cottage economy**

1 The term **proto-industrialization** was coined by Franklin Mendels ("Proto-Industrialization: The First Phase of Industrialization", *Journal of Economic History*, 32 (1972), 241–61.) Rural industries, **cottage industries** are referred to in all accounts of English economic history but the phenomenon was given a new significance with the publication of Joan Thirsk's essay "Industries in the Countryside" (in Fisher (ed.), *Essays in the Economic and Social History of Tudor and Stuart England*, 70–88; see also E. L. Jones, "The Agricultural Origins of Industry", *Past and Present*, 40 (1968), 58–71). The literature is now voluminous. Recently there have been some dissenting voices from the "theory of proto-industrialization": D. C. Coleman, "Proto-Industrialization: A Concept too Many?", *Economic History Review*, second series, 36 (1983) 435–48; also, Rab Houston and K. D. M. Snell, "Proto-Industrialization? Cottage Industry, Social Change, and Industrial Revolution", *Historical Journal*, 27 (1984), 473–92. These authors make the useful point that theorizing about **proto-industrialization** has its limits if such theories are consistently contradicted by the historical record. I share their unease with the 'theory of proto-industrialization' but am disquieted by their indiscriminate fetishism of mere facts. Having no concept of the peasant social formation of the feudal epoch, they seem to have no concept of its successor, twice-removed – the proletarian social formation in the industrial epoch. It seems to me that they are arguing for a flaccid history which excludes a conceptual approach to the political economy of social change – in this case, to the transformation of "pre-industrial" society. Once the **Industrial Revolution** occurred the rules of the game were changed in a definitive fashion. The **Industrial Revolution** occurred once in England and was then imitated elsewhere. The **Industrial Revolution** was of world-historical importance yet

the critics of the 'theory of proto-industrialization' seem to regard it as an event not as a process in which *cottage industrialization* was a necessary but not sufficient pre-condition. As I see it, it is imperative to distinguish between those instances of *cottage industry / proto-industrialization* which led to industrial capitalism and those which did not. An understanding of England's "successful" path of development does not lead us to theorizing so much as to historical knowledge.

2 Since this chapter and the next are only partly about the growth of industrial society in England – they are primarily concerned with the growth of an industrial population and only secondarily concerned with the larger framework within which that population emerged – the state and the capitalist are minor actors in the following account. Their activities will not be explained at any great length. Nevertheless, my account presumes that the state was interested in business as a means of furthering its own fiscal and military powers and that capitalists were primarily interested in profits. Both the state and the capitalist saw industry as a means to their own particular ends and it was *their* judgement of *their* situation which led them to act as they did. It should hardly need stressing that in this political economy, as in all others, there were competing demands coming from different sectors each with its own agenda. Civil society in "bourgeois" England – after the two seventeenth-century revolutions – is often likened to a limited company: the monarch was the Chief Executive Officer; the aristocracy formed the board of directors; the upper gentry and some metropolitan merchants held preferred shares; the "mere" gentry and most other members of the middle class held common shares; and the overwhelmingly proletarian majority owned nothing. Stripped bare of the quasi-mystical ideologies which buttressed medieval and Absolutist social formations, the business of England rapidly became business itself. Yet, I demur in accepting the metaphor since it has no real place for the state nor for the development process by which the revolutionary failure of the mid-seventeenth century became the success-story of the Georgian period when the *Pax Britannica* was slowly imposed over an empire, as well as over the lesser breeds without the law. In particular, it appears to conflate two phenomena: the demise of quasi-Absolutism and the emergence of "bourgeois" civil society. A profoundly telescopic vision is being employed in any argument which sees in the sufficient victory of capitalism in the necessary defeat of Absolutism. We have here no transubstantiation in which the eucharist of politics changed its very nature but rather a protracted development in which historical forces led to the emergence of specific sets of social relations and specific answers to specific problems. The specificity of these developments was English history itself.

3 Michael W. Flinn, with the assistance of David Stoker, *The History of the British Coal Industry. Volume 2: 1700–1830 The Industrial Revolution*, Oxford: 1984, 451–2.

4 Defoe, *A Tour Through the Whole Island of Great Britain*, 535.

5 John U. Nef, *The Rise of the British Coal Industry*, London: 1932, Vol. I, 220.

6 B. Faujas de Saint-Fond, *A Journey Through England and Scotland to the Hebrides in 1784* (English edn: Sir Archibald Geikie) Glasgow: 1907, 152–3. The conver-

sation reported in this text took place in Paris; among the participants was that "American Friend" Benjamin Franklin.

7 Flinn and Stoker, *The History of the British Coal Industry*, 455.
8 R. D. Baxter, *National Income*, London: 1868, 64.
9 Postan, *The Medieval Economy and Society*, 132. Hilton, *Bond Men Made Free*, 37.
10 Lindert, "English Occupations", 707.
11 Lindert's estimates are found in "English Occupations", 705; the 1851 census enumerations are quoted by J. D. Chambers, *The Workshop of the World*, London: 1961, 21–2. In order to have a strict comparision between Lindert's estimates and the 1851 census enumeration I have not revised the former to take into account its age and gender biases which are discussed in the text, above.
12 A. E. Musson, *The Growth of British Industry*, London: 1978, 149.
13 Sir John Clapham, *An Economic History of Modern Britain*, London: 1939, Vol. I, 143.
14 C. R. Harley, "British Industrialization before 1841: Evidence of Slower Growth during the Industrial Revolution", *Journal of Economic History*, 42 (1982), 267–89. N. F. R. Crafts, "British Economic Growth, 1700–1831: A Review of the Evidence", *Economic History Review*, second series, 36 (1983), 177–99.
15 Harley, "British Industrialization before 1841", 283.
16 Flinn and Stoker, *The History of the British Coal Industry*, 443.
17 Clapham, *An Economic History of Modern Britain*, Vol. I, 204.
18 Pollard, "Labour in Great Britain", 155, 128, 102.
19 Eric Richards, "Women in the British Economy since about 1700: An Interpretation", *History*, 59 (1974), 344.
20 *Parliamentary Papers* (1852–3), LXXXVIII, Part 1, Table XXXI.
21 Musson, *The Growth of British Industry*, 141.
22 E. J. Hobsbawm, *Industry and Empire*, London: 1968, 88.
23 "Class Struggle and the Industrial Revolution", *New Left Review*, 90 (1975), 66.
24 Musson, *The Growth of British Industry*, 150–1.
25 Vincent, *Bread, Knowledge and Freedom*, 69.
26 Malcolmson, *Life and Labour in England 1700–1780*, 57.
27 Joan Thirsk, "Seventeenth-Century Agriculture and Social Change", *Agricultural History Review*, 18 (1970), 171–2.
28 Quoted in Thirsk, "Seventeenth-Century Agriculture and Social Change", 167.
29 Defoe, *A Tour Through The Whole Island of Great Britain*, 491–3.
30 Defoe, *A Tour Through The Whole Island of Great Britain*, 496.
31 Jean Birrell, "Peasant Craftsmen in the Medieval Forest", *Agricultural History Review*, 17 (1969), 91–107.
32 Defoe, *A Tour Through the Whole Island of Great Britain*, 545, 408.
33 Joan Thirsk, *Economic Policy and Projects. The Development of a Consumer Society in Early Modern England*, Oxford: 1978, 125–74.
34 Quoted in D. A. Palliser, *The Staffordshire Landscape*, London: 1976, 109.
35 Pauline Frost, "Yeomen and Metalsmiths: Livestock in the Dual Economy of South Staffordshire 1560–1720", *Agricultural History Review*, 29 (1981), 38, 41.
36 Quoted in David Hey, "A Dual Economy in South Yorkshire", *Agricultural History Review*, 17 (1969), 108.
37 This reference was generously provided by Derek Gregory and is quoted from

his unpublished paper "The Dynamics of the Domestic System: Protoindustrialization and Proletarianization". A revised version is to be published in Allen Scott and Michael Storper (eds.), *Production, Work, Territory*.

38 Quoted in Thirsk, "Seventeenth-Century Agriculture and Social Change", 173.

39 See, esp., Dennis Mills' explication of this relationship in Leicestershire in *Lord and Peasant in Nineteenth Century Britain*, 73–84.

40 Thompson, *The Making of the English Working Class*, 405.

41 Pollard, "Labour in Great Britain", 118.

42 Wrigley and Schofield, *The Population History of England 1541–1871*, Table A3.1, 528–9.

43 Neil McKendrick, "Home Demand and Economic Growth: A New View of the Role of Women and Children in the Industrial Revolution", in *Historical Perspectives: Studies in English Thought and Society*, London: 1974, 158.

44 Margaret Spufford, "First Steps in Literacy: The Reading and Writing Experiences of the Humblest Seventeenth-Century Spiritual Autobiographers", *Social History*, 4 (1979), 414.

45 Vincent, *Bread, Knowledge, and Freedom*, 81.

46 Michael Anderson, *Family Structure in Nineteenth Century Lancashire*, Cambridge: 1971, 114–15.

47 Gareth Stedman-Jones, "The Mid-Century Crisis and the 1848 Revolutions", *Theory and Society*, 12 (1983), 514.

48 E. J. Hobsbawm, *The Age of Revolution*, London: 1964, 55 (emphasis in the original).

49 McKendrick, "Home Demand and Economic Growth", 184.

50 Vincent, *Bread, Knowledge and Freedom*, 80.

51 Hans Medick, "The Proto-Industrial Family Economy", in P. Kriedte, H. Medick and J. Schlumbohm, *Industrialization before Industrialization*, Cambridge: 1981, 51.

52 "Report of the Commissioners Appointed to Inquire into the Condition of the Frame-Work Knitters", *Parliamentary Papers* (1845), XV, 101.

53 J. R. Hicks, *Value and Capital*, London: 1946, 302.

54 E. A. Wrigley, "The Growth of Population in Eighteenth-Century England: A Conundrum Resolved", *Past and Present*, 98 (1983), 134. This article is a distillation of Wrigley and Schofield's enormous monograph, *The Population History of England 1541–1871*. R. S. Schofield has also written a shorter piece introducing their findings on mortality to a wider audience; see "The Impact of Scarcity and Plenty on Population Change in England, 1541–1871", *Journal of Interdisciplinary History*, 14 (1983), 265–91. In this section I have focussed my attention on Wrigley's article in *Past and Present* because it addresses directly the question of "marital strategies" which is so central to my argument. I will, however, consider their contribution together as a Wrigley/Schofield explanation. My reason for choosing to focus on Wrigley's *Past and Present* article, and not their book, is because it is more accessible and presents their point of view in no uncertain terms.

55 On this point see, esp., Wrigley, "A Conundrum Resolved", 130–2, 142–3.

56 Wrigley, "A Conundrum Resolved", 148.

57 Wrigley, "A Conundrum Resolved", 142.

58 Wrigley, "A Conundrum Resolved", 131.
59 McKendrick, "Home Demand and Economic Growth", 186.
60 Thirsk, *Economic Policy and Projects*, 173–4 (see above).
61 Medick, "The Proto-Industrial Family Economy", 56.
62 John Gillis "Peasant, Plebeian and Proletarian Marriage", in Levine (ed.), *Proletarianization and Family History*, 138, 141.
63 Gillis, "Peasant, Plebeian and Proletarian Marriage", 146–7.
64 Gillis, "Peasant, Plebeian and Proletarian Marriage", 147–8.
65 Medick, "The Proto-Industrial Family Economy", 66–7.
66 Eric Hopkins, "Working Hours and Conditions during the Industrial Revolution: A Re-Appraisal", *Economic History Review*, second series, 35 (1982), 54, 57.
67 Douglas A. Reid, "The Decline of Saint Monday", *Past and Present*, 71 (1976), 91.
68 Gillis, "Peasant, Plebeian and Proletarian Marriage", 141. It should be noted that the sexual anticipation of marriage only became a "problem" if an illegitimate birth ensued. Furthermore, in sixteenth-century communities very high levels of bridal pregnancy and low levels of illegitimacy indicate that marriage was frequently triggered by the pregnancy itself.
69 E. A. Wrigley, "Marriage, Fertility and Population Growth in Eighteenth-Century England", in R. B. Outhwaite (ed.), *Marriage and Society: Studies in the Social History of Marriage*, London: 1981, 162.
70 Levine, *Family Formation*, Chapter 9.
71 E. P. Thompson, "Time, Work Discipline and Industrial Capitalism", *Past and Present*, 38 (1967), 56–97.
72 A. V. Chayanov, *The Theory of the Peasant Economy*, ed. D. Thorner, R. E. F. Smith and B. Kerblay, Homewood, Illinois: 1966.
73 E. J. Hobsbawm, "Custom, Wages and Work-Load in Nineteenth-Century Industry", in *Labouring Men. Studies in the History of Labour*, London: 1964, 348.
74 Hobsbawm, "Custom, Wages and Work-Load", 354–6.
75 Thompson, *The Making of the English Working Class*, 424.
76 For a consideration of the spatial location of non-conformity, see Alan Everitt, *The Pattern of Rural Dissent*, Leicester University Department of Local History, Occasional Papers, second series, 4 (1972).
77 E. J. Hobsbawm, "Methodism and the Threat of Revolution in Britain", in *Labouring Men. Studies in the History of Labour*, New York: 1967, 31–2.
78 Thompson, *The Making of the English Working Class*, 379.
79 Christopher Hill, "Plebeian irreligion in 17th Century England", in M. Kossok (ed.), *Studien über die Revolution*, Berlin: 1969, 61.
80 Arnold Rattenbury, "Methodism and the Tatterdemalions", in Eileen and Stephen Yeo (eds.), *Popular Culture and Class Conflict*, London: 1981, 33.
81 Elie Halevy, "The Birth of Methodism in England", in Bernard Semmel (ed.), *The Birth of Methodism in England*, Chicago: 1971, 72.
82 Thompson, *The Making of the English Working Class*, 365.
83 Thompson, *The Making of the English Working Class*, 394.
84 On the religious motivation for the acquisition of literacy see, Spufford, "First Steps in Literacy".

85 Thomas Laqueur, "The Cultural Origins of Popular Literacy in England 1500–1850", *Oxford Review of Education*, 2 (1976), 268, 270.

86 Thomas Laqueur, *Religion and Respectability. Sunday Schools and Working-Class Culture, 1780–1850*, New Haven: 1976, 242.

87 Vincent, *Bread, Knowledge and Freedom*, 195, 131.

88 Quoted in Richard Johnson, "'Really Useful Knowledge': Radical Education and Working-Class Culture, 1790–1848", in John Clarke, Chas Chrichter and Richard Johnson (eds.), *Working-Class Culture. Studies in History and Theory*, London: 1979, 91.

89 Craig Calhoun, *The Question of Class Struggle: Social Foundations of Radicalism during the Industrial Revolution*, Chicago: 1982, 126, 137.

90 Johnson, "'Really Useful Knowledge': Radical Education and Working-Class Culture, 1790–1848", 95.

91 Michael Sanderson, "Literacy and Social Mobility in the Industrial Revolution in England", *Past and Present*, 56 (1974), 75–104. For a rather more optimistic view of literacy and industrialization, see E. G. West, "Progress in Artisan Literacy from 1790", in Gordon Roderick and Michael Stephens (eds.), *Industrial Performance, Education and the Economy in Victorian Britain*, Lewes, Sussex: 1981, 33–48.

92 David Levine, "Education and Family Life in Early Industrial England", *Journal of Family History*, 4 (1979), 368–80.

93 David Levine, "Illiteracy and Family Life During the First Industrial Revolution", *Journal of Social History*, 14 (1980), 25–44.

94 Vincent, *Bread, Knowledge and Freedom*, 194, 125–8.

95 Stone, *The Family, Sex, and Marriage in England 1500–1800*, 224.

96 This sense of paradox is neatly captured by E. A. Wrigley in his article "The Process of Modernization and the Industrial Revolution in England", *Journal of Interdisciplinary History*, 3 (1972), esp. 258.

97 Levine, *Family Formation*, 9–15, 103–15.

98 Wrigley and Schofield, *The Population History of England 1541–1871*, 451.

99 Slack, "Vagrants and Vagrancy in England", 360–79.

100 For a discussion of the shift of framework knitting from the control of the Worshipful Company of Framework Knitters in London to the East Midlands, see Levine, *Family Formation*, 16–18.

101 John Nichols, *The History and Antiquities of Leicestershire*, London: 1795, Vol. I, Part II, 620.

102 "Report of the Commissioners Appointed to Inquire into the Condition of the Frame-Work Knitters", *Parliamentary Papers* (1845), XV, 15.

103 Hoskins, *The Midland Peasant*, 228.

104 Hoskins, *The Midland Peasant, passim*. Much of the energy and sense of outrage in Hoskins' work seems to be derived from his reading – an obviously formative experience – of George Sturt's *Change in the Village* (London: 1912). The passage which I have paraphrased from Hoskins would itself appear to have been paraphrased from Sturt (77–112).

105 Tilly, "Demographic Origins of the European Proletariat", 11.

106 Pollard, "Labour in Great Britain", 128.

107 Wrigley and Schofield, *The Population History of England 1541–1871*, Table A3.2, 530.

108 Wrigley and Schofield, *The Population History of England 1541–1871*, Table 7.28, 260. I have added twenty-four years to the birth dates to derive the crude marriage dates proposed in the text.

109 Hoskins, *The Midland Peasant*, 269ff.

110 McKendrick, "Home Demand and Economic Growth", 196. The reader might remember that McKendrick's focus on the *Industrial Revolution* is rather more narrow than that which is employed in this essay. Moreover, his distinction between the *cottage economy* of the industrialized peasant household and the completely monetized family wage-economy of the proletariat is rather too stark and tends to compress an historical process into a dichotomous relationship.

111 Levine, *Family Formation*, 32–4.

112 Pollard, "Labour in Great Britain", 158. It was Karl Marx, in his concept of "absolute surplus value", who devised an explanation for it a couple of generations later.

113 Barbara Taylor, *Eve and the New Jerusalem*, London: 1983, 101–5.

114 Gillis, "Peasant, Plebeian and Proletarian Marriage", 144–5.

115 Calhoun, *The Question of Class Struggle, passim*.

116 The autobiographical view of "A Dundee Factory Boy" quoted by Vincent, *Bread, Knowledge and Freedom*, 69.

117 Anderson, *Family Structure in Nineteenth Century Lancashire*, 125.

118 Anderson, *Family Structure in Nineteenth Century Lancashire*, 47, 132.

119 Gillis, "Peasant, Plebeian and Proletarian Marriage", 141, 151.

120 Wrigley and Schofield, *The Population History of England 1541–1871*, Table A3.1, 528–9, and Table A3.2, 530.

121 Taylor, *Eve and the New Jerusalem*, 263–4.

122 Taylor, *Eve and the New Jerusalem*, 272.

123 Barbara Taylor, "Socialist Feminism: Utopian or Scientific?" in Raphael Samuel (ed.), *People's History and Socialist Theory*, London: 1981, 162. See also Jane Humphries, "Class Struggle and the Persistence of the Working-Class Family", *Cambridge Journal of Economics*, 1 (1977), 241–58.

124 Hobsbawm, *Industry and Empire*, 131.

125 Pollard, "Labour in Great Britain", 126.

126 Friedrich Engels, *The Condition of the Working Class in England*, London: 1969, 76. This version of the text was first published in Great Britain in 1892; it was originally translated into English and published in New York in 1887.

127 The 1758 description of the Oldham cottage industrialists was by a Mr Perceval, local magistrate. This quotation, and Defoe's estimate on the "independent" (i.e. non-industrial) cottages were found in John Foster, *Class Struggle in the Industrial Revolution*, London: 1974, 23 (Perceval) and 277 n. 19 (Defoe).

128 These eighteenth-century figures are found in Paul Mantoux, *The Industrial Revolution in the Eighteenth Century*, London: ref. edn, 1961, 252. The figures for the nineteenth century, after 1802, are based on three-year averages (centring on the year in question) presented in P. Deane and W. A. Cole, *British Economic Growth 1688–1959*, Cambridge: 1962, Table 43, 187.

129 Arthur Young, *Six Months Tour of Northern England*, London: 1772, Vol. III, 164.

130 The figure for Manchester's growth is found in Mantoux, *The Industrial Revolution in the Eighteenth Century*, 358. His estimate for the 1773 population of Manchester and Salford is based on a census organized by John Whitaker. It is interesting to note that 27,246 lived in 4,268 houses, an average of 6.4 per house. In most communities enumerated in early modern England the average household size was 4.75. What accounts for this difference? Could it have been a reflection of overcrowding as housing could not keep up with the industrial population's growth? Or could it have been a reflection of the character of that precocious industrial population which had had high birth rates and kept its teenaged children at home? The 1811 "census" of handloom weavers (by Lee and Ainsworth) is quoted in S. D. Chapman, *The Cotton Industry in the Industrial Revolution*, London: 1972, 60.

131 John Aiken, *A Description of the Country from 30 to 40 Miles around Manchester*, London: 1795, 203, 243. Samuel Bamford, *Early Days*, London: 1849, 98–9.

132 J. Holt, *A General View of the Agriculture of the County of Lancaster*, London: 1795, 210. William Cobbett, *Cottage Economy* (1822), Oxford: 1979, 180–1.

133 R. Guest, *A Compendious History of the Cotton Industry*, Manchester: 1823, 31.

134 The figures for the 1816 age- and sex-distribution are found in P. Gaskell, *Artisans and Machinery*, London: 1836, 142. The 1907 employment figures are from Deane and Cole, *British Economic Growth*, Table 44, 190. We shall return to the long-term implications of this peculiar age- and, especially, gender-specificity of cotton factory employment in the next chapter.

135 Edward Baines, *History of the Cotton Manufacture*, London: 1835, quoted in Peter Mathias, *The First Industrial Nation*, London: 1969, 265.

136 Later in this chapter, I will return to consider the interaction of **proto-industrial involution** and the onset of controlled fertility among the framework knitters of Shepshed, Leicestershire, another group of displaced cottage industrialists. In the next chapter the fate of the handloom weavers – in Lancashire and Ireland – will re-emerge.

137 Quoted in Steven Marcus, *Engels, Manchester and the Working Class*, New York: 1974, 91.

138 Benjamin Disraeli, *Coningsby*, Book IV, Chapter 1, quoted in Marcus, *Engels, Manchester and the Working Class*, 38.

139 Alexis de Tocqueville, *Journeys to England and Ireland*, ed. J. P. Mayer, New York: 1968, 96, quoted in Marcus, *Engels, Manchester and the Working Class*, 66.

140 Marcus, *Engels, Manchester and the Working Class*, 92, 97–9.

141 G. D. H. Cole, quoted in E. J. Hobsbawm, "History and the 'Dark Satanic Mills'", in *Labouring Men*, 137. No reference is given for Cole's statement.

142 Engels, *The Condition of the Working Class in England*, 96.

143 Engels, *The Condition of the Working Class in England*, 78.

144 Hobsbawm's criticism ("History and the 'Dark Satanic Mills'") is directed towards W. H. Chaloner and W. O. Henderson who published a new edition of Engels' work in 1958. A similar line of defence might be directed against the recent writings of Jeffrey G. Williamson. See, esp., "Was the Industrial Revolution Worth It? Disamenities and Death in 19th Century British Towns", *Explorations in Economic History*, 19 (1982), 221–45. In the course of the text I will

present my disagreements with this neo-classical approach but am not planning to deal directly with Williamson's article.

145 Thompson, *The Making of the English Working Class*, 564.
146 Marcus, *Engels, Manchester and the Working Class*, 177.
147 Engels, *The Condition of the Working Class in England*, 192.
148 Engels, *The Condition of the Working Class in England*, 188. See also Edward Shorter, *A History of Women's Bodies*, New York: 1982.
149 Engels, *The Condition of the Working Class in England*, 135.
150 *Parliamentary Papers* (1840), XXIII, 240.
151 F. A. Wells, *The British Hosiery and Knitwear Industry*, Newton Abbott: 1972, 112.
152 W. Lee, *Report to the General Board of Health on a Preliminary Inquiry into the Sewerage, Drainage and Supply of Water and the Sanitary Conditions of the Inhabitants of Loughborough*, London: 1849, 18–19.
153 Marcus, *Engels, Manchester and the Working Class*, 209–10.
154 Engels, *The Condition of the Working Class in England*, 158.
155 Engels, *The Condition of the Working Class in England*, 152–3.
156 G. W. F. Hegel, *Philosophy of Right* (trans. T. M. Knox), Oxford: 1942, 12–13, quoted in Marcus, *Engels, Manchester and the Working Class*, 248.
157 Anderson, *Family Structure in Nineteenth Century Lancashire*, 43–67.
158 The preceding discussion is drawn from Levine, *Family Formation* Ch. 5.
159 Wells, *The British Hosiery and Knitwear Industry*, 63, 80, 82, 84ff.
160 Thompson, *The Making of the English Working Class*, 12–13.

4 The decline of working-class fertility

1 It should be stated at the outset that much of the following discussion is tentative in the sense that it has been *inferred* from correlations, rather than being deduced from closely researched analyses. One of the great vacuums in our historical knowledge concerns the timing and incidence of the decline of fertility which has occurred over the past century. This chasm – no mere lacuna – has usually been papered over by a form of aggregative analysis which obscures rather more than it reveals. In this sense, my essay is meant as a polemic written *parti pris*.
2 J. A. Banks, *Prosperity and Parenthood, a Study of Family Planning among the Victorian Middle Classes*, London: 1954. See also J. A. and Olive Banks, *Feminism and Family Planning in Victorian England*, Liverpool: 1964. J. A. Banks, *Victorian Values. Secularism and the Size of Families*, London: 1981.
3 J. C. Caldwell, "A Theory of Fertility: From High Plateau to Destabilization", *Population and Development Review*, 4 (1978), 553.
4 J. C. Caldwell, "Mass Education as a Determinant of the Timing of Fertility Decline", *Population and Development Review*, 6 (1980), 225.
5 Caldwell, "Mass Education as a Determinant of the Timing of Fertility Decline", 227–8.
6 I also remain unconvinced that the ascription of causality to mass education is a particularly good guide to contemporary population problems; but that aspect of Caldwell's argument is not directly relevant to the issues before us here.

7 E. J. Hobsbawm, *The Age of Capital*, London: 1975, 31–47. H. M. Hyndman's remark concerning the new age of discovery is quoted on 34.

8 B. R. Mitchell, "The Coming of the Railway and United Kingdom Economic Growth", *Journal of Economic History*, 24 (1964), 315–36.

9 H. A. Shannon, "The Coming of General Limited Liability", in E. M. Carus-Wilson (ed.), *Essays in Economic History*, London: 1954, Vol. I, 376.

10 Hobsbawm, *Industry and Empire*, 120–4.

11 T. Tooke and W. Newmarch, *A History of Prices*, London: 1857, Vol. V, 368, 370, 387. Quoted in W. H. B. Court, *A Concise Economic History of Britain: From 1750 to Recent Times*, Cambridge: 1954, 165–71.

12 B. R. Mitchell and P. Deane, *Abstract of British Historical Statistics*, Cambridge: 1962, 146–7.

13 Patrick Joyce, *Work, Society and Politics: The Culture of the Factory in Later Victorian England*, New Brunswick, New Jersey: 1980, 91, 92, 98. Michael Huberman's recently completed Ph.D. dissertation at the University of Toronto (1985) suggests that Joyce may have over-emphasized the "turning-point" in the mid-century period and that the trade-off between job-security and secure labour supplies had its origins far earlier ("Auction or Contract: The Cotton Spinning Labour Market in Lancashire").

14 Quoted in Joyce, *Work, Society and Politics*, 90.

15 Quoted in Clapham, *An Economic History of Modern Britain*, vol. II, 33.

16 William Lazonick, "Industrial Relations and Technical Change: The Case of the Self-Acting Mule", *Cambridge Journal of Economics*, 3 (1979), 231–60. On the long-term forces dating from this historic compromise, see William Lazonick, "Competition, Specialization, and Industrial Decline", *Journal of Economic History*, 41(1981), 491–516.

17 Burnett, *Useful Toil*, 34.

18 Clapham, *An Economic History of Modern Britain*, Vol. I, 49.

19 Michael Dunford and Diane Perrons, *The Arena of Capital*, London: 1983, 300.

20 Dunford and Perrons, *The Arena of Capital*, 300.

21 Hobsbawm, "Artisan or Labour Aristocrat?", *Economic History Review*, 37 (1984), 370. The other quote comes from Patrick Joyce's superb book, *Work, Society and Politics*, 97.

22 Hobsbawm, "Artisan or Labour Aristocrat?", 370–1. Jonathan Zeitlin, "Craft Control and the Division of Labour: Engineers and Compositors in Britain 1890–1930", *Cambridge Journal of Economics*, 3 (1979), 261–72.

23 Bernard Elbaum and Frank Wilkinson, "Industrial Relations and Uneven Development: A Comparative Study of the American and British Steel Industries", *Cambridge Journal of Economics*, 3 (1979), 273–303.

24 C. K. Harley, "Skilled Labour and the Choice of Technique in Edwardian Industry", *Explorations in Economic History*, 11 (1974), 410.

25 Patrick Joyce, "Labour, Capital and Compromise: A Response to Richard Price", *Social History*, 9 (1984), 69.

26 H. J. Habakkuk, *American and British Technology*, Cambridge: 1967, 141.

27 Raphael Samuel "Workshop of the World: Steam Power and Hand Technology in Mid-Victorian Britain", *History Workshop*, 3 (1977), 8, 58.

28 Jonathan Zeitlin, "Social Theory and the History of Work", *Social History*, 8 (1983), 365.

29 Martin J. Weiner, *English Culture and the Decline of the Industrial Spirit 1850–1950*, Cambridge: 1981.

30 Joyce, *Work, Society and Politics*, 137–8.

31 Weiner, *English Culture and the Decline of the Industrial Spirit 1850–1950*, 158.

32 "The current trend is towards lifting some of the burden of guilt from the much maligned entrepreneur by interpreting his behaviour as rational in terms of the economic environment and constraints under which he operated" (Derek H. Aldcroft, "The Economy, Management and Foreign Competition", in Roderick and Stephens (eds.), *Industrial Performance, Education and the Economy in Victorian Britain*, 28).

33 Charles F. Sabel, *Work and Politics. The Division of Labor in Industry*, Cambridge: 1982, 40.

34 Angus McLaren, *Birth Control in Nineteenth-Century England*, New York: 1978, 66.

35 Angus McLaren, *Reproductive Rituals*, London: 1984, 8. J. Matras, "Social Strategies of Family Formation: Data for British Female Cohorts born 1831–1906", *Population Studies*, 19 (1965), 167–81.

36 Taylor, *Eve and the New Jerusalem*, 285, 215.

37 McLaren, *Birth Control in Nineteenth-Century England*, 222, 224.

38 Richard Price, "The Labour Process and Labour History", *Social History*, 8 (1983), 59.

39 Gillis, "Peasant, Plebeian, and Proletarian Marriage", 150.

40 Pamela Horn, "Women's Cottage Industries", in G. E. Mingay (ed.), *The Victorian Countryside*, London: 1981, 350.

41 On the inability of employers' associations to deflect the interventionism of the state, see, Andrew H. Yarmie, "British Employers' Resistance to 'Grandmotherly' Government, 1850–80", *Social History*, 9 (1984), 141–69.

42 Musson, *The Growth of British Industry*, 150.

43 R. Floud, "Measuring the Transformation of the European Economies: Income, Health and Welfare", (Centre for Economic Policy Research, Discussion Paper Series, no. 33, 1984), *passim*.

44 Geoffrey Crossick, "The Labour Aristocracy and Its Values: A Study of Mid-Victorian Kentish London", *Victorian Studies*, 19 (1975–6), 326. J. F. C. Harrison, *The Common People*, London: 1984, 276.

45 Crossick, "The Labour Aristocracy and Its Values", 307.

46 Clapham, *An Economic History of Modern Britain*, Vol. II, 468–9.

47 Foster, *Class Struggle and the Industrial Revolution*, 125–31.

48 Engels, *The Condition of the Working Class in England*, 165, 173.

49 Joyce, *Work, Society and Politics*, 55, 111–12.

50 Foster, *Class Struggle and the Industrial Revolution*, 91–9, 84–7.

51 Elizabeth Roberts, "Working Wives and Their Families", in T. Barker and M. Drake (eds.), *Population and Society in Britain 1850–1980*, London: 1982, 140–71.

52 John S. Lyons, "Family Response to Economic Decline: English Cotton Handloom Weavers in the Nineteenth Century" and "Lancashire Handloom

Weavers and the Labor Market: 1841–1851". Both of these papers are unpublished and I am grateful to Dr Lyons for permitting me to consult them.

53 The Pilgrim Trust, *Men Without Work*, London: 1938, 85, 235, quoted in Roberts, "Working Wives and Their Families", 151.

54 Hobsbawm, *Industry and Empire*, 95–6.

55 Chambers, *The Workshop of the World*, 64.

56 Robert Gray, *The Aristocracy of Labour in Nineteenth-Century Britain c. 1850–1914*, London: 1981, 39.

57 Roberts, "Working Wives and Their Families", 143, 142.

58 Hobsbawm, *Industry and Empire*, 135.

59 Hobsbawm, *Industry and Empire*, 137.

60 George Sturt, *The Wheelwright's Shop*, London: 1934, 153.

61 Plumb, "Farmers in Arms", 36, quoted in Weiner, *English Culture and the Decline of the Industrial Spirit 1850–1980*, 118. See also Martin J. Weiner, "The Changing Image of William Cobbett", *Journal of British Studies*, 13, (1974), 135–54.

62 P. J. Waller, *Town, City and Nation. England 1850–1914*, Oxford: 1983, 192.

63 Waller, *Town, City and Nation. England 1850–1914*, 190.

64 W. A. Armstrong, "The Flight from the Land", in Mingay (ed.), *The Victorian Countryside*, 130.

65 Brenda Collins, "Proto-Industrialization and Pre-Famine Emigration", *Social History*, 7 (1982), 127–46. See also Eric L. Almquist's two articles on this subject: "Pre-Famine Ireland and the Theory of European Proto-Industrialization: Evidence from the 1841 Census", *Journal of Economic History*, 39 (1979), 699–718, and "Labour Specialization and the Irish Economy in 1841: An Aggregate Occupational Analysis", *Economic History Review*, 36 (1984), 506–17.

66 K. H. Connell, *The Population of Ireland, 1750–1845*, Oxford: 1950, 29.

67 Thompson, *The Making of the English Working Class*, 434.

68 Pollard, "Labour in Great Britain", 113.

69 Quoted in Thompson, *The Making of the English Working Class*, 433.

70 Brinley Thomas, *Migration and Economic Growth*, second edition, Cambridge: 1973, 57. Of course, there was some return-migration but, in the main, most emigrants remained overseas.

71 Charlotte Erickson, "Who Were the English and Scots Emigrants to the United States in the Late Nineteenth Century?", in D. V. Glass and R. Revelle (eds.), *Population and Social Change*, London: 1972, 359–60.

72 Rowland Tappen Berthoff, *British Immigratns in Industrial America*, New York: 1953, 23, 85, (my emphasis).

73 Thomas Hardy, *Tess of the D'Urbervilles*, quoted in Raymond Williams, *The Country and the City*, London: 1973, 208.

74 John Saville, *Rural Depopulation in England and Wales 1851–1951*, London: 1957, 74.

75 "Second Report, Royal Commission on Children's Employment (Trades and Manufactures)", *Parliamentary Papers* (1843), XII, 229, quoted in Horn, "Women's Cottage Industries", 342.

76 Horn, "Women's Cottage Industries", 341–2.

77 David J. Jeremy, *Transatlantic Industrial Revolution: The Diffusion of Textile Tech-*

nologies between Britain and America, 1790–1830s Cambridge, Massachusetts: 1981, 174.

78 Richards, "Women in the British Economy", 348.

79 John R. Gillis, "Servants, Sexual Relations, and the Risks of Illegitimacy in London, 1801–1900", *Feminist Studies*, 5 (1979), 142–73.

80 Margaret Penn, *Manchester Fourteen Miles*, London: 1947, 23, quoted in Burnett, *Destiny Obscure*, 256.

81 Mitchell and Deane, *Abstract of British Historical Statistics*, 29–30.

82 Wrigley and Schofield, *The Population History of England 1541–1871*, 437, 438.

83 Gillis, "Peasant, Plebeian and Proletarian Marriage", 153.

84 Harrison, *The Common People*, 376.

85 Mary Hollinrake, quoted in Burnett, *Destiny Obscure*, 225. Frank Marling, quoted in Burnett, *Destiny Obscure*, 258. Louise Jermy, quoted in Burnett, *Useful Toil*, 52.

86 Gillis, "Peasant, Plebeian and Proletarian Marriage", 156.

87 Burnett, *Destiny Obscure*, 224–6.

88 The only example from Burnett's autobiographers of male assistance comes from the textile community of Haworth, Yorkshire. It jogs the reader's memory back to one of the most striking passages in Engels' classic in which he described family life "turned upside down" (Burnett, *Destiny Obscure*, 219–20, Engels, *The Condition of the Working Class in England*, 173).

89 Burnett, *Destiny Obscure*, 55, 218. George Orwell, *The Road to Wigan Pier*, Harmondsworth: 1962, 53. Orwell visited Wigan in 1936 and his book was published the following year.

90 Gareth Stedman-Jones, *Outcast London*, Harmondsworth: 1971, 32.

91 James Walvin, *A Child's World*, Harmondsworth: 1982, 151.

92 Stedman-Jones, *Outcast London*, 87, 125.

93 Jose Harris, *Politics and Unemployment*, Oxford: 1972, 271–2. Churchill is quoted in Briggs, "Social History 1900–1945", in Roderick Floud and Donald McCloskey (eds.), *The Economic History of Britain since 1700*, Cambridge: 1981, Vol. II, 361. A. J. P. Taylor, *English History, 1914–1945*, Oxford: 1965, 2.

94 J. W. Innes, *Class Fertility Trends in England and Wales 1876–1934*, Princeton: 1938, 19.

95 E. A. Wrigley, *Population and History*, London: 1969, 197.

96 Innes, *Class Fertility Trends*, 43.

97 Miners who had been among the best-paid workers were, of course, an exception to this statement and their special case will be considered later.

98 Horn, "Women's Cottage Industries", 343–6. See also J. S. Hurt, *Elementary Schooling and the Working Classes 1860–1918*, London: 1979, esp. Chapter VIII.

99 "Final Report", *Parliamentary Papers* (1886), XXXV, 102–11.

100 Lynn Hollen Lees, "Getting and Spending: The Family Budgets of English Industrial Workers in 1890", in John Merriman (ed.), *Consciousness and Class Experience in Nineteenth-Century Europe*, New York: 1979, 179–80.

101 Laura Oren, "The Welfare of Women in Laboring Families: England, 1860–1950", in Mary Hartman and Lois Banner (eds.), *Clio's Consciousness Raised*, New York: 1974, 238, 240.

102 "Report of the Interdepartmental Committee on Physical Deterioration", *Parliamentary Papers* (1904), XXXII, *passim*.

103 Burnett, *Destiny Obscure*, 220.

104 Vincent, *Bread, Knowledge and Freedom*, 94.

105 Burnett, *Destiny Obscure*, 220.

106 Thompson, "The Peculiarities of the English", 47.

107 Chadwick and Senior as well as Kay-Shuttleworth are quoted in Corrigan and Sayer, *The Great Arch*, 136, 137. I am in dispute with the emphasis which Corrigan and Sayer place upon the pronouncements of ideologues; they should have paid more heed to the grass-roots so as to test the real meaning of "state formation". The reality is rather more ambivalent than their quotation from these political economists would seem to suggest.

108 Quoted in David Rubinstein, *School Attendance in London, 1870–1904*, New York: 1969, 5.

109 Burnett, *Destiny Obscure*, 153.

110 Quoted in Burnett, *Destiny Obscure*, 152.

111 Frank Marling, mentioned above, seems to have been an exceptional man. Hobsbawm, "Artisan or Labour Aristocrat?", 366.

112 Burnett, *Destiny Obscure*, 170, 168, 161. The detail in the following paragraphs is drawn from this book.

113 On this point see the dialectical relationship between *declining* opportunities for child labour in London in the 1860s, and the advent of schools to mop up the ones who were loitering about the streets to the great consternation of the governing class, with the displacement of this problem to juveniles who continually "pushed many (older men) down into the ranks of casual labour", sec Stedman-Jones, *Outcast London*, 65–73.

114 Burnett, *Destiny Obscure*, 155–65.

115 On the alternatives to kin and the role of "fictive kin", see Anderson, *Family Structure in Nineteenth Century Lancashire*, 44–55, 91, 101–6, 142–3. For cockney London, see Ellen Ross, "Survival Networks: Women's Neighbourhood Sharing in London before World War I", *History Workshop*, 15 (1983), 12–13.

116 Edna Bold, *The Long and the Short of It*, in Burnett, *Destiny Obscure*, 114. On the remarkable perdurance of children's games over the centuries see Iona and Peter Opie, *Children's Games in Street and Playground*, Oxford: 1969.

117 Quoted in Burnett, *Destiny Obscure*, 229. It might be objected that there was an element of selectivity in the surviving autobiographies since it would hardly be likely that anomic children would turn their hand later in life to the extra-ordinary task of recounting their life-histories. There is probably some truth in this point but it should not be allowed to detract from the other point that in the majority of families mothers were successful in reproducing loving intimacy and a strong sense of family loyalty.

118 Ellen Ross, " 'Fierce Questions and Taunts': Married Life in Working-Class London, 1870–1914", *Feminist Studies*, 8 (1982), 576.

119 Robert Roberts, *The Classic Slum*, Harmondsworth: 1971, 44, 50.

120 The great strength of both Vincent's and Burnett's accounts is that they have used the anarchic individuality of discrete autobiographical accounts as the basic building-block for their approach to wider issues of experience and

mentalities. Methodologically, their approach does not seem very different from that of family reconstitution which analyses separate families and then looks at the whole to come up with the regularities in their behaviour.

121 F. B. Smith, *The People's Health*, London: 1979, 65–9.

122 Clapham, *An Economic History of Modern Britain*, Vol. III, 546.

123 Asa Briggs, "Social History 1900–1945", in Floud and McCloskey (eds.), *The Economic History of Britain since 1700*, 362–3.

124 Quoted in Taylor, *English History, 1914–1945*, 237.

125 Quoted in N. Von Tunzelman, "Britain 1900–1945: A Survey", in Floud and McCloskey (eds.), *The Economic History of Britain since 1760*, Vol. II, 255.

126 Clapham, *An Economic History of Modern Britain*, III, 546.

127 Rubinstein, *School Attendance in London*, 44, 36, 37, 56, 89. See also, Stedman-Jones, *Outcast London*, 83–97.

128 Flinn and Stoker, *The History of the British Coal Industry* 348–9.

129 Flinn and Stoker, *The History of the British Coal Industry*, 334.

130 "Commission for Inquiring into the Employment and Condition of Children in Mines and Manufactures", *Parliamentary Papers* (1842), XVI, Q.536.

131 Quoted in Burnett, *Destiny Obscure*, 62. Ms Foley, the autobiographer, was born in the Forest of Dean in 1914.

132 Quoted in Burnett, *Destiny Obscure*, 223.

133 Michael Haines, *Fertility and Occupation. Population Patterns in Industrialization*, New York: 1979, esp. Chapters II and III.

134 Their declining productivity seems to have been partly due to the exhaustion of the most easily worked seams and the consequent need to continue to add infrastructural costs and additional workers to get the coal out of the new seams (Robert Moore, *Pitmen, Preachers and Politics*, Cambridge: 1974, 42).

135 Orwell, *The Road to Wigan Pier*, 20–1. I have cut his text but kept its essential meaning.

136 Orwell, *The Road to Wigan Pier*, 103–4.

137 Brian Jackson and Dennis Marsden, *Education and the Working Class*, Harmondsworth: 1966, 97.

138 Michael Young and Peter Willmott, *Family and Kinship in East London*, Harmondsworth: 1962, *passim*.

139 Hobsbawm, *Industry and Empire*, 137.

140 Hoggart, *The Uses of Literacy*, 54.

141 Hoggart, *The Uses of Literacy*, 45.

142 Taylor, *English History, 1914–1945*, 165.

143 Letter of Mrs G. D. 28 February 1923. This letter is reprinted in Ruth Hall (ed.), *Dear Dr Stopes. Sex in the 1920s*, Harmondsworth: 1978, 19. For a collection of personal accounts of **respectable** motherhood and childbearing, written in 1914 by the wives of "labour aristocrats" at the onset of the widespread usage of contraception, see *Maternity, Letters from Working Women*, ed. M. L. Davies, London: 1915 (reprinted 1978), *passim*.

144 Burnett, *Useful Toil*, 18–19. The gulf between the classes and the masses was longstanding. In 1845 Henry Mosely wrote that "The fact is that the inner life of the classes below us in society is never penetrated by us. We are profoundly ignorant of the springs of public opinion, the elements of thought and the

principles of action among them" (quoted in Johnson, "Educational Policy and Social Control", 104). Similarly, the proto-typical agricultural labourer "Hodge" was considered to be beyond comprehension by their rulers. See Snell, *Annals of the Labouring Poor*, 5–9.

145 Stephen Humphries, *Hooligans or Rebels?* Oxford: 1981, 70. Orwell (*The Road to Wigan Pier*, 103–4) means "schooling" when he writes "education". For a most stimulating discussion of a most unusual and unexpected working-class use of literacy in the aid of the family economy see Ross McKibbin, "Working-Class Gambling in Britain 1880–1939", *Past and Present*, 82 (1979), esp. 170–1.

146 Paul Willis, *Learning to Labour. How Working Class Kids Get Working Class Jobs*, Farnborough, Sussex: 1978, 131.

147 Willis, *Learning to Labour*, 150.

148 Taylor, *English History, 1914–1945*, 171.

149 Jackson and Marsden, *Education and the Working Class*, 210.

150 Jackson and Marsden, *Education and the Working Class*, 210–12.

151 Hoggart, *The Uses of Literacy*, 340.

152 Orwell, *The Road to Wigan Pier*, 80.

153 Hoggart, *The Uses of Literacy*, 32.

154 *Mass Observation*, London: 1945, 74–5.

155 Beatrix Campbell, *Wigan Pier Revisited*, London: 1984, 78–9. For a similar system of entropic reproduction in the racially mixed inner London borough of Hackney, see Paul Harrison, *Inside the Inner City*, Harmondsworth: 1983, 187–8.

Index

Note: in the text several terms have been presented in bold-face italics; in this index there has not been an attempt to locate each and every instance when they appear but, rather, I have indexed the following of these terms (*cottage economy*, *Industrial Revolution*, *involutionary entropy*, *peasant demography model*, *proletarian demography model*, *proto-industrialization*, *respectability*) in such a way that the index will provide a guide to their usage. In addition, I have not indexed either people or places which occur once or even several times if they appear only in passing; thus, I have referred to people and places when they are substantively important and relevant to the argument.

249